God's Secret Armies

JOSEPH JOHNSTON

God's Secret Armies

WITHIN THE SOVIET EMPIRE

G. P. Putnam's Sons   New York

For my son, William, and my daughter, Judy, with fervent hopes and prayers that, in their time, "God's moment" may come and with it a new freedom for all men—freedom from war and the threat of war.

J. J.

Contents

Introduction

THROUGHOUT the nine million square miles of the Soviet Union, underground resistance forces, ever growing in numerical strength, are fighting anti-Communist actions and are achieving victories that inspire fear and apprehension in the men in the Kremlin.

The resistance leaders and their followers are on the farms and in the factories, in the forests and the fields. They are spread across the vast steppes, they wander the deserts of Asiatic Russia. They tend the herds, fell the timber, build the roads, run the railroads, mine the coal. In their ranks are teachers, lawyers, engineers, doctors. Many are in the Red Army. A few are in high councils of the Communist Party itself. There are even grounds for the assumption that some have penetrated the hierarchy of the government in Moscow.

Dependent upon secrecy for their safety, for their lives, the members of these hidden forces have maintained completest anonymity. When they have been apprehended by the security police—from the Cheka in the days of Lenin, through the OGPU and the NKVD, to the present MVD—the most merciful penalty has been "liquidation."

Theirs is a cause for which men and women have fanatically fought and died throughout the millenniums. That cause is religion with its appeal to something deeper than the intellect. No man can explain its power to inspire. Neither can he discount it. For in what was once called "Mother Russia," religion has always found the most mystical people on earth.

The resistance forces have been called "God's Secret Army." There are, theoretically, three separate columns: Christian, Jewish, Moslem. Their leaders are the religious of all three faiths and a score of sects.

Following the trail of the secret army was an adventure in journalism that was to consume many months of research and reporting, over a span of three years. Those years, 1950 through 1953, were to be a period of self-imposed silence, to protect the safety, the very lives, of devoted men and women, volunteers in the ranks of God's secret army.

The voluntary censorship was freely given and was scrupulously observed. Not until leaders of the resistance, both within and outside the Soviet domain, released the author from his pledge was so much as an inkling of the existence of the secret army revealed in the public prints. At that time, those who had exacted the silence almost unanimously agreed that safety and security could be served if *anonymity* of their followers was preserved.

Certain of those who have led the secret army inside the Red empire, others who have directed its activities or maintained communication with its members, via underground channels, have helped in the preparation of these pages. Wherever possible, the material has been documented. In any case where it has not been authenticated and verified, this will be noted.

All resemblance between those who are to appear in the following pages and real persons, living or dead, is purely deliberate and intentional. For they all are, or *were,* living persons. The events in which they will be the actors actually happened. For obvious reasons, real names and geographical locations cannot be used.

There can be no footnotes citing sources of information. On the score of authenticity, it is to be noted that several substantial newspaper executives knew of the existence of the secret army and shared, for all or part of the three years, the author's silence. Indeed, they authorized the more than considerable financial outlay for my expenses and salary and published the first newspaper stories about the resistance after we had been released from the promise of secrecy.

Among them were: the late Jack Lait, editor, and William N. Thomson, general manager, of the New York *Daily Mirror;* Kenneth K. McCaleb, editor of the New York *Sunday Mirror;* Bradley Kelly, general manager of King Features Syndicate; Luke McCarthy, vice president of the Hearst magazine publishing organization; and Thomas A. Brennan, of the Hearst Corporation legal staff.

The long duration of the period of silence, secrecy, and self-censorship gave an unusual opportunity to collect evidence, to piece together a document of men and women of heroic stature, bound together by the common concept and ideal of One Almighty. Far more powerful than any mere political philosophy are the common ideals for which they battle in the ranks of the secret army of resistance. Essentially, the ideas differ only slightly—how slightly can be realized when one considers that members of three great religions and a score of sects are allied in one widespread resistance to Communistic atheism.

It is no secret army to the security police. The agents and informers of the MDV know everything about its existence and activities—everything excepting *who* its members are and *where* they may be found. The soldiers of God wear no uniform. Their uniform is the faith in their hearts. Their passwords are names that have been banned in Red Russia and the captive Communist satellites. Their passwords are Jehovah—Allah—God.

In the years that I have been gathering the material which is the basis for this chronicle, I have interviewed more than sixty persons who have been engaged in direction and leadership of the religious resistance within the Soviet Union proper. (This does not include satellite territories.) Most of them have been inside and have come out of the U.S.S.R. via underground channels, since the Second World War. They are largely Christian, Jewish, and Moslem religious, although eleven are laymen who had been engaged in maintaining communications, supplying documents, identity papers, job and travel permits, expediting entries and escapes at seaports or across remote border points. Of the over-all number of those who have supplied information for these pages, twenty-one have come out of Russia since 1949. One has made three separate round trips, underground, since this book was being prepared, the last within three months of its publication. A few have returned to Soviet territory. Others are planning to go back to carry on what they all believe to be divinely inspired work.

Each of the interviewers was asked this question: "What do you consider the greatest contributing factor to the failure of the Bolshevists to eliminate religion from the secret heart of the people?"

In almost every instance, the answering opinion, stripped down to essentials, was simply "Marriage." Expanded, it provides insight into the intricacies of the human spirit, to the point where the mere mind cannot penetrate, where it fails to control or even to influence the dictates of what men, through the millenniums, have called the soul. Existence of the soul is denied by the atheist, by the Communist. It is a futile exercise in semantics to argue the point here or anywhere. It is, however, a demonstrable fact that one tenet of three great faiths has kept alive religious belief in men and women to whom public worship has been denied and to whom God has been proclaimed an enemy.

The trail of the secret army has led me to three continents, sometimes up blind alleys and dead-ends. It was a course at times tedious, more often exciting.

The personal records of the exploits of leaders of the secret army represent a great deal more than mere isolated case histories of a few outstanding individuals. Each one could be turned into a hundred biographies by the mere alteration of names, places, and minor details. For each episode, told by one who has managed to come out of the Soviet empire, a thou-

xii

sand parallels have been and are being enacted on the field of battle where God's secret army is entrenched. For every individual who has lived to tell his story, hundreds have died. For every one who has made his way from the "No-God's-Land" of Russia, five thousand have remained to carry on the fight.

The men of whom you are about to read are no professional, swashbuckling soldiers of fortune or fiction. Most of them are quiet, retiring men of God. Their accounts were told, generally, with modesty, even reticence. Not one ever mentioned that he believed he was "lucky to be alive." Unanimously, with a frightening faith that might appear naïve to one who cannot share it because he has never experienced it, they agree that "God has always been with us." Their acceptance seems almost fatalistic.

In their personal records, the locale of each is Soviet Russia proper. The satellites are omitted for reasons which will be briefly developed later.

In the presence of the men whose lives these pages relive, the author saw the incarnations of Jewish prophets and princes of old. He felt he had been in the presence of Christian martyrs and saints. He *knew* he had talked with heroes.

God's Secret Armies

1.

No More Than Hints

IT WAS SOMEWHERE in the Mediterranean, coasting the shadowed shores of North Africa between Gibraltar and the sturdy little island of Malta, that I heard the first hint of an anti-Communist resistance operating within the Soviet Union and the captive Red satellites. A black night had fallen. Clouds, heavy as iron, low-lying against the sea and the distant shore, as though weighted down by mystery, curtained the light of the mid-February moon over Africa. There was false balm overlaying the stabbing fingers of chill that soon would prod those who walked the dim decks of the liner *Atlantic* and send them bundling inside, to the light and warmth.

I could not so much as imagine any part of the picture I was to piece together, like a gigantic journalistic jigsaw puzzle, when I stood at the rail of the liner, that February night of 1950, looking shoreward over the ancient sea. Beyond the restless swells, an occasional dim light appeared, then disappeared as though a shade had stealthily been drawn. The clouds, widening splotches of spilled black ink, spread slowly across the electric-blue sky.

My being there was a matter of routine newspaper assignment. With John Wolter, art director of King Features Syndicate, and Joseph Costa, photographic chief of the New York Sunday *Mirror*, I had been sent out from New York to write a special series of daily articles about the pilgrimage of some

3

five hundred American Catholics, led by Cardinal Spellman, to Rome and the religious shrines of southern Europe. Costa was to send back photographic coverage, I was to cable daily stories, while Wolter was directing a motion picture document of the journey. Although it had been quite as unexciting as I had feared before leaving New York, it was proving vastly more interesting than I had expected.

My companion on the deck of the liner that night as we steamed for Malta was Rev. John J. Reed, of the Society of Jesus. We were alone on deck, the other passengers having gone to their cabins, for it was nearing midnight. Throughout the trip from New York, I had found the Jesuit a charming and compelling conversationalist, not only an intellectual but also an intelligent man. He was, in fact, among the most cultured men I had encountered in nearly a quarter of a century of meeting and interviewing prominent world figures.

Since I was not a communicant of the Catholic Church, Father Reed had assumed the role of my instructor in matters concerning the Church. This was most helpful in preparation of my daily stories.

A former dean of Holy Cross College, Father Reed was an extraordinary teacher, and in a comparatively limited period he had given me a thorough, if rapid, review of the history of the Church, a fair evaluation of its moral, sociologic, and philosophic concepts, and the meanings of its rituals. In the course of almost daily conversations, he had made frequent references to the Jesuits, their aims, background, training, and the many popular conceptions and misconceptions concerning the Order, the Society of Jesus.

On that particular night, off the north coast of Africa, Father Reed had chosen to discourse upon certain facts which came as a complete surprise to me. I have since learned, however, that many informed Catholic laymen have only the vaguest sort of realization, if, indeed, they are aware at all, of any such designation as the "Russian Rite" of their Church.

4

The Oriental Rite of the Roman Catholic Church antedates the schism which split Catholicism into separate divisions, the Greek and the Latin. Originally, the languages constituted the chief point of departure between the two. Differences in ritual have developed in the centuries that have intervened. So has the thesis of the Orthodox that allegiance of the clergy and the laity is due the Patriarchs of the Eastern Church, largely on a geographical basis, rather than to the Pope in Rome on the premise of spiritual universality. In the Balkans, Greece, Russia, the Slavic countries, and the Middle East, however, there are tens of thousands of Catholics who do acknowledge the Pope as a spiritual leader of all Christendom. These look to Rome, therefore, for religious guidance. Yet, the ritual of their religious services differs only in minor respects from that of the Orthodox, even though they are communicants of the Roman Catholic Church. Priests who conduct services in this branch of the Church receive special training and education and are ordained in the Eastern or Oriental Rite.

As Father Reed explained all this to me, a natural question occurred. "Is the Church still ordaining priests in the Oriental Rite?" I asked.

"Certainly," the Jesuit replied. "The Holy Father sends out calls each year for priests to train in the Russian Rite. What makes you think it would have ceased?"

"Well, in the first place," I replied, "you say that the Oriental Rite is practiced chiefly in churches in the Balkans, Russia, the Slavic countries, and the Middle East. Now, certainly, the Communists do not encourage the church and clergy. Cardinal Mindszenty is a case in point. And there must be scores of other such cases of priests of lesser stature whom nobody ever hears of in the West, because of the impenetrability of the so-called 'Iron Curtain.' "

"*Scores* of cases!" he exclaimed. "There are *hundreds* which I have heard about. And not only *priests*—but rabbis and ministers and Moslems. Not only the religious leaders but members of their congregations as well. The case of the great

5

Cardinal was designedly given world-wide publicity. Its effect was to provide an excuse for the wholesale persecutions and repressions, the seizure of religious property, the condemnation of ministers and religious teachers to imprisonment and, even, death without trial—or in the kangaroo court procedures which officially are called 'closed trials.' Under these and other circumstances, no true religious person of whatever faith could fail to take up the challenge that has been flung at God."

"How do you know these things?" I demanded.

"Information has ways of getting out, even from behind the Iron Curtain," he answered. "You cannot conceal the truth. No one can. Not even the Bolshevists, although they try mighty hard."

"Then there are channels of communication?" I asked.

"Obviously there are," Father Reed replied.

I thought about this for a moment. Then I asked, "What happens to priests ordained in the Eastern or Russian Rite? Certainly they can't find enough followers *outside* the captive countries and, let us say, Russia to absorb more than a few as parish priests. Where do they go? What do they do?"

The Jesuit looked out across the sea toward the shore.

"I cannot say, because I do not know," he replied slowly and carefully. "If I did, I am not at all sure I should tell you. Not for publication, at least. I have some ideas about it. But I have no real information. I have talked to a few priests who have been in the captive countries. A Jesuit colleague of mine in the New England Province has been inside Russia since the revolution. There is a priest I know at Georgetown University who has also been in and out of the U.S.S.R."

"If you know two priests who have been inside Soviet Russia since the revolution, then it stands to reason there could be others," I insisted.

"I did not say I knew only two. I merely mentioned two. There *are* others," he said quietly.

"Then it is a possibility that these ordained in the Eastern Rite go into the satellites, perhaps, or into Russia, let us say,

6

to lead parishioners who need spiritual confirmation in their faith? Could they go in disguise, maybe? By underground channels?"

"All things are possible, my son, to those who do God's work and His bidding. I don't like the word 'underground' in connection with God. He need not go underground. He is everywhere for men to see. They need but look up to the heavens, or into their own hearts."

Father Reed smiled and added a parting word: "You must not try to build a story out of conjecture and intuition. I should advise you to find out the facts. I am sure they are there."

"Won't you give me some help in finding out these facts?" I pleaded.

"I will if you promise not to use them—if you learn them—unless you obtain permission from the sources to which I will refer you," the priest answered.

"I promise, Father." And with that sentence began the self-imposed silence that was to last three years. "When and where do we start?"

"Possibly tomorrow in Malta," he answered. "If not, then when we get to Rome."

"Do you believe I'm on some sort of track? Or do you think I'm exaggerating what is, I must admit, purely a hunch?" I fished.

"I believe you might be exaggerating to yourself," he agreed. "I warn you, however, that you must not dramatize; you dare not romanticize the workings of God. His designs are not always evident. It is almost never possible to catalogue them neatly and set them down, one, two, three, for the purposes of explanation and exposition. Many seemingly related factors may have nothing whatever to do with His work. Yet, other remote events might well be evidence of His plan. Doing His work is never easy. But it is always rewarding. If it *is* God's work, the revealing of it will be the reward."

That first hint which came out of the darkness, almost as

though it had risen from the sea's depths, held no real promise of a story.

All night I paced the deck, prowled the salons, peered into the phosphorescence of the black waters, hunting answers to questions that flooded up out of wondering and pondering. Father Reed had dropped a hint. It takes no more to give a reporter a hunch.

God's work. It seemed a pretty large order to expect God to take a mere newspaper reporter into His confidence—especially one who could not, by the widest latitudes of semantics, qualify as particularly devout or even ordinarily religious. Chances were that any revelation of a divine design, in which the good Jesuit had so firm a faith, would be reserved for a more worthy man. I had just about reached the decision to let well enough alone and forget all about it, when the sun spilled a streak of molten bronze between the black skies and the sea, over the horizon, dead ahead of our ship's bow. Had I been a believer in the mystical, I might have seen signs and portents in the rainbows that splashed up in the spray. I didn't. They just looked blurry to my sleepless eyes.

That morning, we sailed into the light-opera setting of the harbor of Valetta where the chalk-white fortress of the Maltese Knights of the Crusades commands the hill and looks down over the centuries. To me, it was just one more stop in the coverage of a routine assignment.

There was no reason to suspect that on such a remote rock in the expanse of the sea, a British colleague was to add another hint to that of Father Reed. It was to confirm the hunch, in some slight degree, and dispel any reluctance to follow whatever clues could be found, wherever they would lead.

It was on the unbelievably lovely terrace of the luxurious Phoenicia Hotel, over delicious food, that the tantalizing second clue came. Lady Mabel Strickland, millionaire correspondent for British and American newspapers, whose dramatic reporting of the siege of Malta during the Second World War certainly earned her a place in the mythical hall of fame of our profession, had invited me to luncheon. There were three other visiting newsmen as guests: Wolter, Costa, and Charles Ridder, the editor-publisher of the *Catholic News* in New York.

Sitting over coffee, Wolter and Costa made their excuses and left to make arrangements for radio-photo transmission back to New York that evening. Ridder went to join his charming and talented wife, Elizabeth, who was doing feature columns on the activities of the pilgrims for Catholic weeklies in the States.

Left alone with the hostess, I listened to her running report of Cardinal Spellman's wartime background in Malta during the siege. While I filed away a few mental notes on the Lady herself, she filled me in on the history of the island which was her home and where her father had once been governor. A woman of enormous vitality and ability, possibly a trifle under six feet tall—she towered above the miniature Maltese whose average height is judged to be slightly over five feet—Lady Strickland was, apparently, a repository for any and all information about Malta. She knew how to sort gossip from rumor, fact from fiction, hearsay from evidence. She had none of the competitive secrecy about exclusive information which is characteristic of American newspaper people—particularly female American reporters.

Lady Strickland had a very realistic and extremely logical approach to the whys and wherefores of our profession—or trade, if you prefer. With no introductory sparring, she began to question me. It was something of a new sensation to be on the receiving end of an interview. "Why did the Hearst papers really send you all the way over here?" she quizzed.

"To cover the pilgrimage," I answered truthfully.

"I'm afraid I don't understand it," Lady Strickland went on.

"It's really very simple," I explained. "Cardinal Spellman is the best-known Roman Catholic figure in the United States.

His name is news to at least one fifth of the American population which is Catholic. In addition, he has appeared with our armed forces in Africa, Europe, and the Pacific. Millions of ex-servicemen remember him as the chief of Catholic chaplains who would go anywhere they went. As a consequence, men and women of every creed admire and respect the Cardinal. Besides, the pilgrims are from many cities, where their names are news, too. So we want to tell their relatives and friends and neighbors about them. That's about how it shapes up."

"But," insisted Lady Mabel, "aren't your editors interested in the *big* story? I didn't believe that they even had an inkling of it. But when you showed up, I assumed you had come to work on it. You couldn't have a better contact than Cardinal Spellman."

"Lady Mabel," I confessed, "I am really not quite sure what story you are talking about. Tell me what you are referring to. If I didn't know it before, I'll give it to you straight. If it's the one I have a hunch about, I'll admit it."

She laughed heartily, as she did everything else. "Frankly I was trying to pump you. I don't even know if I have so much as a hunch. I was given a clue, only yesterday in Rome. And a mighty slim clue it is, too—about a religious underground in Russia. Is that your hunch?" That last word sounded strange in her upper class British accent. She pronounced it "haunch."

"Yes, it is." I gulped and tried to smile.

"I was pretty sure of that," she said, looking over the harbor. "How I wish I had time to work on it myself. But I suspect you will have more success than I could. Men, somehow, just don't seem to trust us women with secrets."

"But what I can't fathom," I puzzled, "is why they want to keep it secret—even if I knew who 'they' were."

"Oh, I can understand that," Lady Strickland said, reasoning it out. "They are afraid of new Communist persecutions, particularly in the Iron Curtain countries."

10

"But why should they expect new persecutions?"

"Because the inference of the Communists in Russia, as well as the captive countries, would be that since one group of religious was active in an underground resistance, the way to stamp it out would be to persecute *all* religious."

"What," I fished, "is your own reaction to the story? Based upon the information you already have collected, I mean."

"I have a reaction," she explained, "but no real information. Just hints and rumors. Let us say," she amended, "that I have a clue. No lead, just a clue. You may have it for whatever you wish to make of it: the Jesuits."

It fitted. It also impelled me in a direction I didn't particularly want to follow. The Englishwoman's clue led right back to the starting point, Father Reed. It also led me one step further along a trail I had decided to abandon—a course of following new hints and clues that opened the doors to leads, all too many of which were to wind up in blind alleys of discouragement and disappointment. Yet, finally, all were to merge into a single pattern, the heroic pattern of the secret armies.

2.

Cross Above the Kremlin

A "MEMBER" of the secret army may be described as any layman who regularly attends sub rosa religious services of any denomination or sect. A Jew who, in defiance of the law, has been married in secret by a rabbi, who has had his son circumcised in the religious tradition of his faith, who has sent that son to secret instructions and *Bar Mitzvah,* is considered a member of the secret army. A Christian who attends sub rosa church—usually held in the woods or in some well-hidden and camouflaged cellar—who is married by priest or minister; who has his children christened, baptized, and confirmed; and who takes communion, is one of the secret army. All such activities are without the knowledge of the security police and in violation of the law of the Soviets.

Among the first institutions to be abolished by Lenin in the days of the revolution was religion. Churches, mosques, and temples which had escaped destruction in the wave of anti-religious hatred, whipped up by government-subsidized terrorists who called themselves the "Association of the Godless" and the "Union of Atheists," were confiscated by the state. The anti-religious terror has been kept alive ever since.

Now, Christian and Jewish leaders and, indeed, their followers in the resistance insistently emphasize that their objectives are purely religious—in general, restoration of the right to worship God in their chosen ways. Yet it would be

12

unrealistic to deny that the results achieved, so far, have had a largely political import. Re-establishment of the Greek Orthodox Church, rigidly regulated under the dictates of a state which had officially proclaimed atheism as the true faith, was undoubtedly intended as a countermeasure to relieve the pressures created by the growth of the religious resistance in the 1930's. Since this church is state controlled, the result is political. Again, during the Second World War, popular demand for public prayer for the dead became so insistent that Stalin was forced to proclaim days of national mourning in which services of all denominations could be conducted without interference by the police. After the war, the old repressive laws were put back into force, more stringently than before.

Any concessions made to religion in the Soviet Union must, of necessity, have political implications. For the basic tenet of Communism is supremacy of the state. And this premise fails if the people look to the higher authority of God.

The secret army has been, most certainly, a major deterrent to any Soviet plans for aggressive war. Although loosely organized at best, it presents the single force within the Communist world which cannot be controlled by the state. The proletarian princes of the Politburo well know how a handful, in spite of suppression and proscription, were able to overthrow the imperial government of the Czars. No more than the leaders of today's hidden anti-Communist forces did the Russian socialists of the late nineteenth and early twentieth centuries intend to overthrow the Czarist regime. Their objective, too, was reform—political reform. Today's hidden forces insist they seek only reform—religious reform. But, as the arming of the Russian populace in World War I gave radicals their chance, so the arming of the people today might well give a new counter-revolutionary element its opportunity.

Whatever hesitance at the Kremlin level may be inspired by the secret army is largely due to official ignorance of the real numerical strength of the religious resistance movement.

Estimates of the over-all membership vary widely. The most optimistic claims are based upon observations made during the national mourning periods of the war. Three religious leaders, two Christians and a Jew, all of whom were in the Soviet Union at the time, agree that as high as 70 per cent of the people participated in the religious services held outside the officially recognized Orthodox churches; another 10 per cent took part in the state-modified Orthodox rites. It would, however, be unsound to assume that so overwhelming a majority could be counted as active resisters. It would be wishful thinking to assume that they were all potentials.

More realistic is the figure arrived at by questioning more than fifty active leaders of the secret army. They assess the strength at somewhere near 20 million, all active, aggressive, and dedicated men and women. This is for the U.S.S.R. alone and represents one out of every ten in the population. It also is three times the 6,300,000 membership of the ruling Communist Party. Most conservative of all estimates runs to 15 million.

The Kremlin and the security police know—and have known for years—of the existence of the hidden columns. They have fought them with every weapon at the command of the police state: with propaganda in the controlled schools, public assemblies, press, radio, and motion pictures; with spies, informers, and betrayers; with laws, ukases, and proscription; with terror, imprisonment, and execution. Yet in spite of all measures to suppress its ideals and activities, God's secret army has continued to grow in numbers and in power.

In the years of the revolution—in this book, the revolution is considered to be the period from 1917 through 1922—the anti-religious purges succeeded in decimating the more than 250,000 Orthodox, Moslem, Protestant, Roman Catholic, and Jewish religious who were active during the Czarist regime. Of these, possibly 40,000 managed to go underground in the civil chaos that attended the revolutionary era. As many as 16,500 religious were murdered in mob violence, instigated by

14

the intellectually elite of the Union of Atheists and the Association of the Godless. Between 115,000 and 135,000 are known to have been jailed on one legal pretext or another during the five years. Of the remaining 60-odd thousand ministers, priests, and rabbis, not more than one of every ten escaped imprisonment in the years between Lenin's death in 1924 and Stalin's consolidation of power in 1936.

These figures are from Rev. Edmund J. Walsh, a Jesuit who is director of the School of Foreign Service of Georgetown University. The first priest to penetrate the borders of revolutionary Russia in 1921, Father Walsh is among the ablest authorities on recent and current Soviet history.

Vladimir V. Tchernavin, author of *I Speak For the Silent,* was imprisoned on Solovetski Island in 1932. He states that of all political prisoners in Russia in 1928-1929, no less than 15 per cent were religious. Since there were 1,500,000 "politicals" at that time, the religious must have accounted for nearly a quarter of a million.

It must be kept in mind that this figure represents largely Orthodox religious. No more than 5 per cent could have been Jewish. Possibly as high as 22 to 25 per cent were Moslem. Since Orthodoxy was the state religion under the Czars, there were few Roman Catholics or Protestants. In 1921, the Armenians, a population of roughly 3,000,000 scattered throughout Armenia, Azerbaijan, and Georgia, were taken into the Transcaucasian Federation. Among them were some 3,000 to 3,500 religious of the Armenian Church, which is neither Orthodox nor Roman but which shares many of the rites and dogma of both. Members of the first Christian state in history, the Armenians have been most tenacious of their faith. Legend traces the founding of their country to Haik, a descendant of Noah. Wave after wave of invasions by the Assyrians, the Medes, the Persians, the Parthians, the Macedonians of Alexander, the Romans, the Mongols of Jenghiz Khan and Tamerlane, and finally the Turks, have swept Armenia. In spite of efforts forcibly to convert the Armenians to Islam, they

15

have hewn as strongly as the early Christian martyrs to their faith.

A secret report on the status of the religious in Russia, which reached Rome in 1925, stated:

Among the Uniate Armenians [i.e., persons in obedience to the Pope but who practice Armenian rites] who were converted by a Dominican mission in the Middle Ages, it has been possible to establish contact with clericals who have not been apprehended by police or government officials. Priests of the old Gregorian rites [the independent Armenian Church] are able to function sub rosa and we find evidences of cooperation not only among the Uniates and Gregorians but also among both of these and certain priests of Orthodoxy. The existence of these religious, their whereabouts and their identities are being kept from the authorities by their parishioners. . . .

It is safe to assume that 20,000 to 22,000 secret parishes are active throughout Russia. They exist in defiance of the ban against God by the atheistic state . . . their parishioners are of an abiding faith which transcends the laws of men or the fear of earthly punishment.

Since we have taken vows to do the work on Earth of God and His Son, we urge that all possible steps be taken to confirm in their faith these people who, with the fervor of our saints and martyrs, look to Him for leadership and guidance.

The report ended with specific recommendations to extend spiritual aid, financial assistance, and to maintain contact and communication with the religious leadership within Russia.

It is fairly authoritatively established that the Armenian clergy were able to go underground with the apprehension of no more than a few hundred, at most. This was possible because they had been hidden inside the Turkish Empire since the inauguration of the anti-Armenian massacres a quarter of a century earlier. Of the Armenian religious, only a handful could have been Roman Catholic. The remainder bore a closer resemblance to the Anglicans. Indeed, help was to come to them from Protestants in both England and the United

16

States. Few as they were, the Armenians seemed to have had the effect of removing the narrowing restrictions of sectarianism. Their plight and their fight succeeded in giving a wider scope to the appeal of the secret armies for help from religious sources in the West.

The Moslem columns of the secret armies also are known to have extended aid to the Orthodox, as a Lebanese agent who maintains contact and communication with Moslem elements in Russia and Albania was to verify when interviewed in Tangier. This is not so contradictory as might appear on the face.

The original Russian Orthodox Church had stemmed from the Patriarchate of Constantinople. Under the Turkish Empire, the Patriarch of Constantinople held many civil rights over the Christians, which were granted by the Sultans. There was rather close liaison, therefore, between the Church government and the political government of Turkey. And, although the Russian Church was governed by a Holy Synod from the time of Peter the Great to the revolution, Russian Orthodoxy looked to Constantinople as its spiritual fountainhead. Indeed, many Russian priests escaped the revolution to sanctuary offered them by fellow-clericals in Turkey, where they became actively engaged in obtaining help for the early underground columns of the religious resistance.

The Orthodoxists were then, and always have been, by far the most numerous and most active in the ranks of the secret army. Yet, from earliest days, a loose alliance grew up among all the columns. As early as 1924, with the death of Lenin and the beginning of the ruthless struggle for power between Stalin and Trotzky, help was coming to the beleaguered religious. The Orthodoxists were finding allies in a fight that was seldom to come into the open but which was to grow in fervor and intensity through the years.

The secret army grew in strength from nothing to millions, as did Christianity in pagan Rome. And the pressures of the influence it exerted began, in the 1930's, to rise to the surface from underground.

The thirties was a period of Stalin's consolidation of power, after disposing of the opposition of his old Bolshevist comrades—Zinoviev, Trotzky, Lunacharsky, Kamenev, Bukharin, to name only those who were personally closest to him. How he "liquidated" them is history which no apologist can expunge from the biography of Joseph Dzugashvili, alias Stalin, which was written in the blood of his onetime friends. This was also the era of the elevation of Lenin to Soviet sainthood. Unquestionably, Stalin determined to succeed where his predecessor had failed, to substitute worship of the state for worship of God. With the political terror, he gave new impetus to the religious terror that had begun to die out for lack of churches to sack and religious to persecute.

Via all the media of propaganda—public assemblies, the press, the radio and motion pictures—the Ministry of Education stepped up the new campaign to repress religion. Terrorism, espionage, atrocities—largely committed by their enemies—vandalism, and political "obstructionism" were laid to the resistance by the propaganda ministry which coined the phrase "secret army." Stalin raged. "Secret" was a bad word. Stalin could not tolerate secrecy. Nothing could be secret, for that would be an admission that all was not known to the secret police! If there were one secret of the magnitude of an *army* that could be kept from the omniscient OGPU, it would encourage millions more to have secrets. It was decreed that there should be no further mention of the "secret army." But, since the phrase had already been heard nationally on official radio propaganda broadcasts, it was a bit late. The secret army gained publicity and advertising from its bitterest enemies.

Fearful of their jobs or their very lives, OGPU chiefs, headed by a lifelong Bolshevist named Tomsky, in an effort to divert Stalin's fury, put the pressure on informers, false witnesses

18

and spies to turn up scapegoats for trial. The "heat" was on them and they turned it on the secret army. In every large city, hundreds of victims were unearthed. The press went to work on them whether they knew anything of the resistance or not. The OGPU bullyboys extracted "confessions" by the usual methods. These implicated hundreds more. The 10 to 15 per cent of political prisoners, held on charges that could be traced to religious activity, rose to as high as 25 per cent in 1930 to 1932. The jails and prisons were filled literally to standing room only. The People's Courts, the Special Courts, the Closed Courts, and the Supreme Court worked overtime, railroading the accused.

The slave labor racket of the OGPU was, up to that time, never more thriving. Certain industrial "trusts" of the Soviet were assigned prison labor to attain the production quotas set in Moscow under the first Five Year Plan instituted in 1928. The OGPU was responsible for the assignment of prison labor. Now, for each prisoner's subsistence, the state allotted a certain sum, representing the cost of housing and rations. It was pitifully low, taken as an individual allotment. But multiplied by several hundred thousand it was a fortune. For a percentage of this sum, OGPU officials would assign prisoners to a particular project—a mining, timbering, or road-building operation, for example. In order to obtain the labor, operators, who were responsible to the heads of the industrial trusts in Moscow, had to bid against each other. They bargained with the health and the lives of the prisoners. The highest bidder to the OGPU would get the manpower. In some instances, the figures went as high as 70 per cent. This meant that only 30 per cent went to the maintenance of the prisoner. The operator, of course, was expected to chisel a modest additional 10 per cent.

The results were inevitable. The prisoners were undernourished, poorly clothed, housed without heat or light, and without medical attention. At Solovetski in the sub-Arctic area of

19

the White Sea, a doctor who was imprisoned there for seven years has estimated that eight out of ten prisoners contracted tuberculosis, dysentery, scurvy, or all three within two years of confinement. The crippling effects of frostbite were evident in nearly 100 per cent of the slave labor community. Many of these died of infection after crude and careless surgery. Because of undernourishment and overwork, few were strong enough to stave off attacks of virus pneumonia and influenza which were always endemic and regularly epidemic. Insanitation left the camp vulnerable at practically all times to typhoid, while rats and vermin carried the constant threat of typhus.

To such conditions were the apprehended members of the secret army sentenced if they escaped the death penalty. Surely, as "Pastor Schmitz," a Lutheran minister who supplied some of the information and verification for this book, has said, "Swift, even violent death was the more merciful."

The wholesale manhunt for real or falsely accused members of the religious resistance had much the effect of the Roman persecutions of the early Christians. New converts, stirred by the human sympathy Bolshevism had been unable to stamp out, began to swell the secret meetings. It was a danger as well as a demonstration of the power of the great religious philosophies. For spies and betrayers slipped into the anonymous ranks. Yet it was a demonstration which, to the men in the Kremlin, was to become frighteningly, disturbingly evident in public.

At a public trial in Kiev of an extremely popular Orthodox priest, a Father Radek, handbills appeared from nowhere and were circulated among the courtroom spectators. They proclaimed in bold type: "Radek's crime—love of God." Court police hurriedly confiscated the offending sheets. As they marched down the aisle, the rear of each of their uniform jackets was stamped with an Orthodox Cross. How the symbol of the resistance got onto the backs of the police was never explained, even by the all-seeing, all-knowing OGPU. Radek's trial proceeded in closed session. He was sentenced to twenty-five years at hard labor. The pastor never served a day. For the van which was to take him and a dozen other prisoners to the railroad station for transport to Chelyabinsk disappeared with driver and two armed guards.

At Kharkov, a Rabbi Kornivsky was arrested, tried for treasonous activity, and condemned to be shot. With him, seventeen alleged accomplices—whom, he stoutly maintained throughout the trial, he had never seen before—were sentenced to varying prison terms. One afternoon, after a mass interrogation by OGPU agents, they were checked back into detention cells. Next morning, all of the eighteen, together with twenty-seven of their cellmates, were missing. On the wall of each empty cell was painted a huge, rough, six-pointed Star of David in garish green. No explanation for the color was ever given, yet it was to occur again and again.

On public buildings throughout the Soviet Union, on the pavements at main street intersections, on police stations and jails, huge Orthodox Crosses and Stars of David, with sometimes a Roman Cross, began mysteriously to appear. The more vigilance the police exercised, it seems, the more the symbols appeared. When forces of police were known to be operating in the centers of town, the outskirts would be plastered and painted. When the police moved to the suburbs, the downtown area would be decorated.

One day in Tiflis, where Stalin had been educated, school children took up their books, to find the covers of every one stamped in indelible ink with the Orthodox Cross. At Krasnovodsk, during the traditional season of the Passover in 1932, windows of schools and public buildings wore huge decalcomanias of the Star, while the Roman Cross was etched in wax on the windows of stores, shops and private dwellings. The decals, traced to manufacture in Germany, were clues to outside aid and interest.

Moslem massacres of armed Soviet patrols occurred in Taskent, Murgab, Kopteky, Kyzyl, and near Irkutsk within a

21

period of twenty-three days in December of 1933 and January of 1934. The death toll in these five incidents reached nearly two hundred, of whom less than thirty were of the attacking forces. There were, undoubtedly, scores of other such attacks which were hushed up by the Information Ministry.

Stalin, who, according to his biographers, had studied for the priesthood before his conversion to Marxism, looked out of his Kremlin windows on the morning of the Russian Christmas in 1933 to see the brick walls which surrounded the ancient fortress plastered with posters of ikons, hundreds of them in color. The OGPU efficiently sprang into action and succeeded in tracing the posters to Rome. There the trail was lost.

"Never mind who printed them," Stalin is reported to have stormed. "Certainly they weren't put up by Romans. I want those who did it punished quietly so the people don't find out about it.

"How can the State be supreme," he is supposed to have continued to comrade Kamenev, the cutthroat and thief who was soon to be liquidated, "when the fools insist on putting God above it? Maybe it would be better to bring such enemies out into the open."

It took three more years for the idea of bringing them out into the open to crystallize, three years during which countless incidents not only continued to occur but increased in frequency to the point where they became almost commonplace. The plastering of ikons on walls, the painting of Stars and Crosses, became the subject of many a joke, whispered behind hands, only one of which even approaches humor in translation.

"The green star (of David) has one more point than the red star (of the Soviet Union) but you can be certain that Stalin *gets* it (the point)."

Whether two episodes that occurred close to the New Year of 1936 had the effect of persuading Stalin to pursue a new course with the religious resistance cannot, of course, ever be known. The first was one of the most daring and, at the

22

same time, most humorous that was perpetrated in all the years since the revolution when there had been almost no comedy relief at all in Russia. With *Pravda* and *Izvestia,* the news organ that acts as an official government mouthpiece is *Red Star.* Its masthead carries the name of the newspaper set off by a star at either end. One December evening of 1935, an entire edition, carrying Papa Stalin's message to his "children," was run off and delivered, and trains were speeding it to the corners of the U.S.S.R. before some genius in the lower echelons of the Information Ministry discovered that the stars on the masthead each had six points! How it happened, who was punished as a result, was never made public. Copies became items for collectors whose possession of them would bring stiff prison terms, even at this late date. Stalin didn't think it was a bit humorous. But, obviously, the growing strength, boldness and power of the secret army which it signified gave him plenty to think about.

Another event gained even more widespread publicity for the secret army. It was on the eve of the Orthodox celebration of Christmas. The official "news" broadcast—and there were no others in Russia at the time—was in progress. In the Moscow area, the commentator was reading the panegyrics of praise for Stalin that passed for hot news with the Information Ministry and particularly with Stalin. As Stalin listened in complete agreement, the smile faded from beneath his mustache. For clearly in the background he could hear a swelling chorus singing the "Ave Maria." Hastily came the announcement that the station was going off the air. There was a wail of static over the singing, a click, and the announcer could be heard no more. But voices of the choir swelled in volume and continued through one chorus, then another. When the singing had ended, a calm voice came through, "The radiance of the Cross shines over the blood red of the Kremlin. God's moment must come for Mother Russia. We shall be ready when it does. . . . The Lord Jesus Christ be praised."

It must have been eerie. It must have been frightening, at

23

least sobering, for the princes of the Politburo to know that a resistance force had achieved the power to alter the masthead of *Red Star*, and to jam the government's own radio frequency with counter-propaganda to the state doctrine of atheism!

Help and money were obviously coming from the outside. Steps had to be taken to combat the secret army more effectively than proscription and persecution. Stalin did an about-face. He decided to bring the secret army out into the open, to rob it of the obvious appeal that secrecy had given it . . . even as secrecy had given the revolutionary movement appeal in the days of Czars.

Before the year was out, Stalin proclaimed the rights, prerogatives and freedoms of the Orthodox Church restored. Since he was apparently no more a partisan of individual freedoms than the Czars or Lenin before him, the dictator hedged his restoration proclamation with restrictions, thereby nullifying what it had been designed to accomplish. Sermons were to be passed upon by the Ministry of Information. A governing body appointed by the Politburo, such as the Holy Synod that had ruled the church in Imperial Russia, took over the licensing of priests. Ancient ritual was censored and purged of "subversive content." There were regulations as to the length and composition of prayers which also had to be submitted for censorship. The prayerbook was to be rewritten, the Old Testament was forbidden as a source of sermons, and the New Testament was thoroughly revised in line with Communist doctrine. It was obvious from the beginning that the church pulpit was to be used as a sounding board for Party propaganda.

The restricted, regulated, state-controlled church accomplished, for a time, the design of Stalin. The activity of the secret army slacked off for a few months. By that time, the communicants of the new church came to the realization that they were being quietly but carefully watched by agents of the OGPU, the Atheists, and the Godless—obviously for future reference. Many whose names were on the list of churchgoers found their rations being cut, job classifications being

24

changed to less paying ones, their children not being chosen to continue their education beyond the first seven years.

Gradually, the attendance at the state houses of worship began to drop off. The secret meetings and services started to draw their followers back. Soon the outlawed resistance groups were regaining their power. If their pressure could bring about the limited restoration of the Orthodox Church, they argued, surely continued resistance could gain a great deal more. The least realistic envisioned complete restoration of religious freedom.

Although the church restoration was indeed a weapon against the secret army, an even more powerful one was the loss of leadership that had been brought about by revival of the terror which continued with increased vigor after Stalin's move to bring religion into the open. Now that there was a state-controlled church, there was even less reason for leniency than before.

But an infusion of new leadership was to come at a time and from a source least anticipated by Stalin.

In the era of the Hitler-Stalin axis, which brought on the Second World War, the U.S.S.R instituted its open policy of imperialism and expansion. Thereby, the secret army received an infusion of new blood at, it must be confessed, a tragic price. Starting in September of 1939 and continuing over the succeeding nine months, nearly ten million people were impressed into citizenship in the Soviet Union, most of them against their wills. Almost without firing a shot, the Red Army moved in on eastern Poland, "occupying" it, while the Nazi fury raged in the west, practically unopposed by the Polish Army. To Russia, in the partition which followed, went a victor's share of the spoils which Stalin was to collect, not only in territory but in the labor of an enslaved people.

By political deceit, trickery, treachery, in the Baltic states of Estonia, Latvia, and Lithuania, making use of spies and traitors, another six million souls were sold out to Stalin, and the borders of the Red empire were pushed westward to the Baltic. Since the Kremlin had previously demanded and obtained ground, air, and naval bases in these northern republics, and already had the Russian boot in the door, the denouement was clear to anyone with even the most myopic political vision.

In Poland, Estonia, Latvia, and Lithuania religious leaders had been forewarned to go underground before the blow fell. With aid from both inside and outside their countries, thousands of them had time to change their identities before the invaders, or their traitorous servants, destroyed the national independence and individual freedoms that are the implacable foes of totalitarian tyranny.

Patriots in key government posts, foreseeing the inevitable surge of the new dark age of atheism, arranged altered identity papers for ministers, priests, rabbis. Hundreds of vital statistics, records of births, family backgrounds, marriages, and deaths were changed or new ones forged. School and university reports and data were destroyed, in many cases, or falsified to give religious leaders new professions and trades. Just how many such religious were absorbed into the Soviet, disguised as farmers, tradesmen, lawyers, teachers, and workers, never will be known.

In Berlin, London, Rome, and New York, there are ecclesiastical rosters which list world-wide church assignments of the ordained religious of certain Christian sects. It is an interesting and, perhaps, a pertinent commentary on the devotion of the clergy to their calling that these record neither the transfer nor the emigration of a single minister or priest from Estonia, Latvia, or Lithuania, during the two-year period preceding the annexation, when anyone, excepting a political imbecile, could have foreseen the inevitable.

There were, conservatively, no less than 10,000 Protestant clergymen—chiefly Lutheran, Baptist, Episcopalian, and Methodist—in the three annexed Baltic nations. Estonia and Latvia were largely Protestant. In eastern Poland and the Bal-

26

tic countries, an estimated 7,000 to 7,500 Roman Catholic religious are presumed to have been forced into sub-citizenship in the Soviet. Just under 500 rabbis, spiritual leaders of the 50,000 Jews who accounted for less than 5 per cent of the entire newly captive population, brought the total up to 18,000 religious.

That all of the rabbis, ministers, and priests in the annexed territories either managed to go underground, or wanted to, is not even to be suggested. Certainly, however, according to every possible source of reliable information—and there are five which have been checked as thoroughly as circumstances permit—one-quarter of all those who were resident in the area of expansion, at the time, were able to disguise their true calling. So, surely, no less than 4,500 religious leaders, and their followers by tens of thousands, entered the ranks of God's secret army inside the Soviet Union itself.

In Finland, Soviet muscle-flexing and saber-rattling ran into unexpected opposition. The Finns made the Red Army fight. And, undoubtedly, as German Field Marshal Erwin Rommel has recorded, it was the miserable showing of Soviet arms in Finland that convinced Hitler of the military wisdom of turning on the Russians, the Nazis' partners in plunder. After six months of making the Red Army look like military amateurs and strategical blunderers, Finland was overwhelmed by the sheer exhaustion of fighting alone against manpower odds of a hundred to one.

Part of Karelia was ceded to the Soviet. With the territory went the most fiercely independent people of all Finland, with a history of rebellion, of intense, if individualistic, religious fervor, and a proud love of freedom. Their country, as wild as themselves, a land of dense forests, vast swamps, and silent lakes, ice-bound in winter, was to offer a refuge and a retreat for hunted fugitives of the secret army.

The program of repression, suppression, and proscription of the clergy in Poland and the Baltic countries was interrupted by the German invasion of Russia. In the resultant official confusion; in the wholesale transfer of peoples from one area of the Soviet Union to another; in the terrific loss of life due to bombing and shelling; in the enlistment and conscription of tens of thousands of devout and faithful religious believers into military or labor organizations; in the destruction of whole towns and villages, including their vital statistics records; in the capture of Russian territories and their populations by the Nazis, and their subsequent "liberation" by the Red Army, thousands were able to lose or to disguise their true identities. Other thousands changed their places of abode and their occupations through issuance of new identity papers. And so, the members of God's secret army entrenched themselves behind new bulwarks of secrecy and anonymity.

In the aggressive days of the Soviet's buffer state expansion, following World War II, the Balkan countries were captured as satellites through Moscow's promotion of treason, parliamentary double-dealing, and terror. Russian-schooled bullyboys, traitors, and fifth columnists, all posing as patriots and heroes of the Nazi occupation, emerged from the political chaos they themselves had deliberately created to take command of more than 60 million people and an area of 325,000 square miles on the periphery of European Russia. But this coup also placed on the border of the Soviet Union approximately 150,000 religious leaders with tens of millions of followers.

In Albania, at least 3,000 religious were Moslems with more than a million followers. It must be borne in mind that inside the Soviet Union itself, throughout southwestern European Russia and the vast expanses of Asiatic Russia, there are upward of 30 million fanatical followers of the faith of Islam. And on the borders of the Soviet lie Iraq, Iran, and Turkey, from which Moslem opponents to Communism are directing an active campaign of resistance. It is certainly obvious that Moscow has a Moslem threat of vast and vital importance.

In Hungary, Czechoslovakia, Yugoslavia, Bulgaria, Rumania, Poland, and East Germany, contrary to what might be supposed, the activity of the religious is more rigidly curtailed, more difficult to pursue than in the Soviet Union itself. This is true largely because the religious had had almost no warning of the impending domination of these countries before it had become an accomplished fact. Prior to the betrayal of the satellites by Moscow-trained fifth columnists, there was no necessity for the religious to go underground. Afterwards, there was no opportunity. Those who survived the first frantic and fanatic period of terror and "extermination of the priests" are known to the police. Those who have escaped trial on one pretext or another and the inevitable imprisonment which almost automatically follows, are under strict surveillance, and whatever freedom is allowed them is sharply curtailed.

That any movement involving so many millions inside the Soviet domain, as well as millions more in neighboring countries on its borders, could so long remain secret is, for those of us who are accustomed to free exchange of information, difficult to grasp. Perhaps "hidden" or "anonymous" might be a better term than "secret." Examine it from a number of angles, however, and it becomes quite apparent how such a vast force has been able to operate in Russia while its very existence has remained, for thirty years, the best-kept secret in history— particularly to the world outside.

By its own policy of secrecy, by its iron curtain of censorship and control of information, the government of the Soviet Union has contributed to the safety of the secret army and to its increasing strength. For secrecy has been absolutely essential to the leaders and spiritual soldiers in the ranks of God's army in Russia. Secrecy has been a bulletproof vest to protect their very lives, as the briefest review of the history of Russia since the revolution will reveal. The members of the secret army have courted anonymity as fervently as fugitives from the police in any land.

For reasons of security and safety, the secret army has sought to shroud in mystery its existence, its activities, its whereabouts, its channels of communications, both inside

29

and outside the U.S.S.R. God's secret army has had more than an unintentioned assist from the security police. Apart from occasional and unpredictable outbursts of accusations against the religious, the police have attempted to preserve two wholly false illusions which have been presented for home, as well as foreign, consumption.

The first of these is that the people of Russia, far from yearning for the spiritual to feed their appetite for the mystical, are happy with the substitution of atheism for faith.

The second is on a par, intellectually, with the single-party-system ballot. It parallels the philosophy of Voltaire's Pangloss, often used by self-proclaimed "intellectuals" to ridicule American belief in our peculiar brand of political civilization. It almost never is turned, by them, against the smug righteousness of the Soviet, in its statement of unthinking acceptance: "All is for the best in this best of all possible worlds."

Such is the false front which the Soviet has presented to the world since the defeat of the White Russian armies in 1922, marking the emergence of Bolshevism as the governing force over the bowed heads and bent backs of millions. To advertise to the outside that religious resistance existed in Russia would be to confess that one of Communism's basic policies, the establishment of the atheist state, had failed. It would, further, be an admission that all was not for the best in that vaunted best of all possible socialist worlds. It would deny the theme of "universal unity" which has always been the keynote of Communist propaganda for the domestic market, as well as for export.

3.

Alleys and an Avenue

As OUR SHIP took its leisurely course west from Malta, I found my mind reverting again and again to the guarded hints which both Father Reed and Lady Mabel Strickland had given me about a religious underground in Russia. I tried to dismiss it as an impossible assignment, yet by the time the ship docked at Naples I suddenly realized that I was committed to follow these vague leads and I was impatient to begin my investigations in Rome. Rome was almost completely unrewarding as to new clues or leads. As far as "the Russian work" was concerned, the Eternal City was a maze of blind alleys.

To begin with the Jesuits, the Very Reverend John B. Janssens, S.J., General of the Order, was away from Rome during the period of my stay. Other governing officers of this "military order of spiritual soldiers" were reluctant to give any information relating to "the Russian work." One was downright hostile.

"Were there such a movement, were spiritual leaders being sent by us into Russia and the satellites, it would hardly be conducive to secrecy to take a newspaper reporter into confidence. Particularly an *American* newspaper reporter," he scolded and accused at the same time.

Since he had been asked only generally about the rather ambiguous "Russian work," the reference to spiritual leaders

31

being sent into Russia was a gratuitous addition, duly recorded in my notes. So was the remark about "secrecy."

After a masterly exhibition of question dodging, a second Jesuit was asked a direct question. Would he deny that Jesuits had recently entered Russia or the satellites by sub rosa or irregular channels?

"Since you are asking me a generalized, rather than a specific, question," he answered, "I can only reply in kind. As a generality, I should have to deny it. In a specific instance, I should certainly be unable to confirm it."

A neat bit of Jesuitical logic, it was still no satisfactory answer to the question.

"You mean," I kept at him, "that, generally, Jesuits do *not* go on secret missions in the Communist world?"

"Precisely," he replied.

"Then, does it follow that, specifically, some might or do?" I followed up.

"Do you know of some specific instance, my son?" he asked, smiling quietly.

"No," was the reluctant reply.

"When you do, feel free to return and question me about it and I shall answer truthfully." The brief interview was over.

At the Vatican, there was only slightly more definite information. In 1926, after years of exhaustive study of the reports on the Russian revolution by his own investigators and other agencies, Pope Pius XI issued a "call" for priests to volunteer for the "Russian work." He issued it each year until his death, after which his successor, Pius XII, continued it. Exactly what the "Russian work" consisted of, how many tens, or hundreds, or thousands had answered the "call," could not then, or now, be determined.

The Jesuits in Rome had proved disappointingly uncooperative and uncommunicative. The Vatican information was, certainly, indefinite. But it confirmed my belief that I was on the track.

In the remote village of Manresa, guarded by the towering pinnacle of sacred Montserrat, a few miles distant in the Spanish Pyrenees, I encountered the first specific case, a lead of some authenticity. It pointed boldly to an anti-Communist resistance, at least partly directed by leadership supplied from outside the Soviet domain.

Some forty miles northwest of Barcelona, the ancient town had already become a shrine of the Roman Catholic faith four hundred years ago when St. Ignatius Loyola meditated in the caves beneath the cathedral that crowns an eminence commanding the sweep of the river that rushes around and through Manresa. Traveling from Barcelona by automobile, I was the first of Cardinal Spellman's party to arrive in the ancient textile milling town. I was accompanied by Rev. E. J. Broderick, of New York.

A full hour ahead of the other Americans, the young priest and I got out of our Lincoln to stretch our legs and to learn, if possible, what the people of this rather remote spot in the province of Catalonia were thinking. That didn't take long. At least, it didn't take the priest long. For he was one of those with an ear for mimicry and music who learn languages easily and speak them well. Father Broderick had, too, a way with words in any tongue. With a voice trained for singing, precise but not stilted diction, and a superb scholastic background in Latin, he was noted as a speaker. Although he was then just past thirty, he had been delivering sermons at St. Patrick's Cathedral in New York for some years.

Tall, with an infectious smile and an easy manner, he was soon circulating among the crowds of curious townsmen and country people from the surrounding hills. In its role of Holy Year host to visiting Catholics from America, Manresa was in gala and festive dress that Sunday in March, 1950. The Stars and Stripes, the flag of Spain, and the ensign of the Vatican State were displayed together in every store window and in practically every home.

33

In the square at the foot of the hill, leading five hundred yards up to Manresa Cathedral, civic and religious dignitaries stood among the crowds, waiting to welcome the Cardinal and his people. There were a bishop and a sprinkling of monsignori, an Episcopalian minister, two bearded rabbis, the mayor, and the town fathers. Although the atmosphere seemed purely religious and official, there was a detectable undercurrent of opposition. This was soon confirmed—and in print.

Our driver, in greatly exaggerative and slightly boastful mood, had soon noised it around among his admiring country kinfolk that he was chauffeuring a most important American journalist. So Father Broderick informed me, adding, "Well, you learn something new every day, even if it isn't true. . . . These good people have turned out, all in their Sunday best, to pay us homage. I detect a partly packed audience, a not unusual practice where Communism shows its red head. I rather suspect that many have journeyed from far places— my ear picks out a French intonation here and there. Undoubtedly, some had come to hiss and boo us capitalistic Americans."

Within minutes, there were a few accusatory fingers pointing my way. I could hear angry syllables, *"Jornalista . . . Capitalista . . . Excellencia."* One of the more voluble pressed forward and thrust a tabloid-sized broadside into my hand. The paper was, I suspected, being circulated through the crowds by its printers, editors, pressmen, publishers, and partisans.

The Spanish police, in their patent-leather tricorn hats, were everywhere. Yet the Leftist paper was distributed with absolutely no interference. In fact it occasioned less unfavorable attention than the same act would have in New York's Union Square.

An out-and-out Communist pamphlet, the paper carried no more real news than the *Daily Worker*. Its contents were purely editorial and slanted. On the masthead was the name *El Mundo*—The World.

34

The headline read, "Go Home, Fascist Americans." A two-column subhead proclaimed, with appalling triteness and lack of imagination, a threadbare slogan from the "Manifesto" of Marx and Engels, written a hundred and more years ago: "Religion is the opium of the people!"

Followed a typically hysterical diatribe against Cardinal Spellman, his pilgrims, the U.S. Congress and, particularly, the American press as "Fascist tools of the capitalist war-mongers of Wall Street, exploiters and despoilers of the working masses."

When the Cardinal and his pilgrims arrived, *El Mundo* was freely and openly passed out among the visitors, one copy finding its way into the hands of a Mrs. Kate O'Hara who couldn't read a word of Spanish. A cleaning woman in a downtown Manhattan office building, Mrs. O'Hara had been so exploited and despoiled by Wall Street, the Congress, the Church and its clergy, through the connivance of the American press, that she was able to afford a trip across three thousand miles of ocean and half of Europe to pay, in prayer, her tribute to the God of her faith for what she called "my blessings."

I stood in the entrance to the Cathedral and observed the service conducted by the Cardinal. As I had listened to his sermons and addresses in Portuguese, Italian, and French throughout the preceding weeks, I now heard him speak in Spanish. At conclusion of the services, I hunted up the late Msgr. Edward Murphy, then Cardinal Spellman's secretary, hoping that the contents of the sermon might, possibly, give me a lead for the day's story which I had to cable back to New York.

I walked to a spot, just outside the Cathedral, where a group of priests were standing. They were listening to a story—and this was to be my first real lead along the journalistic trail of the secret army. It was told simply and solemnly by one of them, a member of the hierarchy of the Church of Rome. Although he has authorized use of the story as I heard

35

it, and noted it down an hour or so later, he has requested that his identity should not be disclosed.

In my notes, it appears under a subheading which reads: "The tragic case of the fifteen who will never return."

4.

Tragedy of the Fifteen

THE STORY WHICH was my first real lead on the trail of the secret army was told with complete lack of detail, stressing only the salient facts that there was such a mission, that its members did prepare for it, that they embarked upon it, and that it ended in tragedy. The additional information as to the nationalities that went to make up the group, their methods of preparation, and the characterization of "Father Zabrisky" was gathered from constant inquiry of all who might be able to add to the original story as it was told at Manresa. Verification of it, from no less than ten individuals, has been possible, and documentation has come from one source not available for general publication.

The fifteen, who had been comrades for longer than a year and a half, were to part forever in the morning. There was little hope of return from such a mission as theirs. Destination: Soviet Russia and the captive countries, via secret, underground channels.

The fifteen had gathered together in Rome some time in the late fall of 1947 or early winter of 1948. They had answered a "call" that had gone out through Catholic monastic and clerical orders for "volunteers" to do "missionary work" inside Russia and its satellites.

It was difficult to fulfill the qualifications which were demanded. Candidates should, first of all, have been natives of eastern Poland, the Balkan or Slavic countries, Russia—or those lands incorporated by force into the Soviet empire, in the period of its expansion in the opening months of the Second World War. Second-generation sons of emigrants from such countries would be eligible, provided they had a grounding in Polish, Slavic, or one or more of the dialects of Russia. Next consideration was that the prospective missionaries should have a background of some trade or profession which would be a cloak to disguise their real work. Final qualifications were of a physical nature, concerned with general health, strength, stamina, and the like.

The fifteen survived months of a rigid scholastic, spiritual, and physical regimen, which was laid down by the members of the group themselves, with the cooperation, advice, and supervision of a fellow priest who, for six years, had been in the Karelo-Finnish State of the U.S.S.R. and elsewhere in European Russia as a leader of the religious resistance. They were eight Poles, two Finns, two Letts, an Estonian, a Serb, and one American.

The American—we shall call him "Father Zabrisky"—was from the soft-coal area of southern Illinois. Born of Polish-Russian parentage, he had learned the languages of both his mother and his father in childhood. At the age of fourteen, he had quit school for a job as breaker boy in the mines. Encouraged by his parish priest, young Zabrisky saved a bit of money and, by the time he was twenty-two, had enough to pay for a night school course at which he gained enough credits to earn a high school diploma. The following September, he entered a midwestern university, older and vastly more mature than his fellow freshmen who immediately dubbed him "Pops."

In his sophomore year, Pops Zabrisky ran from the fullback slot in the powerful college football team. Football fanatics began to dream of All-American honors to come in the next season. But Pops, himself, had a dream of his own—of taking priestly vows in the secular clergy.

38

After the final game of the season, Pops went home to Illinois to discuss his decision to enter the Church with his parents and with his old friend, the parish priest for whom he had served as altar boy. Pops Zabrisky never returned to the university. For December 7, 1941, intervened and Monday morning, the 8th, he became Private Zabrisky of the U.S. Army.

In the January after V-E day, Master Sergeant Zabrisky, of the 82nd Airborne Division, obtained his discharge.

After a period as a scholastic in Rome, the thirty-two-year-old Polish-American was ordained and said his first Mass in St. Peter's. Stocky, blond, powerful, athletic, the American priest was the acknowledged leader of the fifteen who had dedicated themselves as "spiritual soldiers" in the battle to win back Russia to God.

It was Father Zabrisky who realized, more than any of his fellows, the necessity for physical as well as spiritual strength in the fight for which they'd volunteered. It was the American priest who organized hikes from Rome to Naples and return. He got up soccer games and saw that they were long and rough with plenty of body contact. He insisted his friends all learn to swim. In roughest weather he took them cross-country skiing in the Italian Alps.

At linguistic studies, the others, particularly the young Finns, had a far easier time than Father Zabrisky. He attacked language as he did sports, head on, with more energy than finesse, more stamina than understanding. He hadn't used his Polish or Russian since early youth and was rusty at them.

The priests studied together, coaching and tutoring one another. They did all written work in Polish or Russian. They gave each other stiff examinations in Russian geography, history, art, literature. They memorized long excerpts from the works of Marx and Engels, Lenin and Stalin. They became experts in the devious jargon of Communist semantics.

They practiced the theory and application of their several professions and trades. Those who had none learned one. "Father Kronin," a Finn of German extraction who had

39

studied law before entering the priesthood, took up carpentry. "Father Vorkopitch," the Serb, had been ordained in the Eastern Rite of the Church of Rome and wore a bushy black beard which made him appear older than his twenty-three years. He had been a student and had never learned a trade, but now he took up the study of horticulture, farming, and animal husbandry; he put into practice what he learned in books by journeying to the farms of the Po Valley, where he worked in the fields for weeks at a time.

Among the fifteen were a bricklayer, a doctor who had studied and interned in Vienna, a civil engineer, a textile designer, an automobile and tractor mechanic, as well as the carpenter, the farmer, and Father Zabrisky, the coal miner.

For longer than a year and a half, the fifteen volunteers prepared for their mission, mentally, physically, spiritually. They had grown into close comradeship. The final weeks were given over to group councils to review the various schemes by which they would enter Russia, to determine where each would locate upon arrival, to lay plans for maintaining communication with one another, if possible, and with friends in Rome.

The day before they were to leave, in June of 1949, the day before their little group was to break up, the fifteen made a pilgrimage to the great basilicas of Rome, said Masses in St. Peter's, prayed for the success of their mission.

The next morning, armed with documents and identity papers which were by no means proof against detection, with their cassocks discarded in favor of their disguises as professionals, artisans and tradesmen, they parted. Each was to go his separate way to his separate destination—by ship, perhaps, from a German port to Murmansk, or from Greece or Turkey into the Black Sea to Sevastopol—to Finland, to steal across the forested border into Karelia, or through Berlin into the Soviet sector of East Germany—to the Balkans, the Crimea, or Poland.

It was several months before friends in Rome had word of all fifteen. Father Zabrisky was the last to be accounted for.

He had penetrated Asiatic Russia and had succeeded in becoming attached to the Mining Trust in a minor supervisory capacity. That was all to be heard of the fifteen until March 10 or 11, 1950. Then, through underground channels of communication which net the far-flung domain of the Soviet Union and reach from Moscow to Rome, Paris and New York, a grim report had filtered through—news of all fifteen, tragic news that had taken half a year to transmit. Within sixty days of Father Zabrisky's arrival at his destination, fourteen of the band of dedicated men had been arrested. Fourteen had been picked up and jailed by the secret police of L. P. Beria.

One, only one, remained free—the one who had been planted in their ranks as spy and informer, a Communist who had spent nearly two years as comrade in the ranks of the fifteen, only to repay their faith and trust with betrayal.

The tragedy of the fifteen, the probable martyrdom of the fourteen, was told freely that day in Manresa in the presence of the writer, known by all in the group to be a reporter. There could be no possible reason to doubt any detail, for the narrator was among the most conservative men I had ever met. There were, however, questions to be asked, certain gaps to be filled in. But with the very first query, a subtle change came over those who had been listening.

"The story, of course, is off the record," Monsignor Murphy warned.

Being off the record meant two things: it would be violating a confidence if the story were to appear in print and, if it were published, no corroboration could be expected. How any confidence apparently shared by so many persons could fail to become public property was beyond comprehension. In the light of later experience, it developed that the comparative few who shared the secret kept it—out of the public prints, at least.

The warning was, at the moment, an unnecessary precaution. I had, in fact, already promised Father Reed to obtain specific permission before publishing a line about the

41

secret army, of whose existence the story of the fifteen had convinced me, confirming my hunch, Father Reed's hints, and Lady Strickland's clue. Besides, by itself, as an isolated and unverified episode, the adventure of the fifteen was far outside the realm of news. As it stood, a magazine might treat it as a rather fantastic piece of highly imaginative fiction. A newspaper would want the facts, all the facts, authenticated and verified, documented where possible.

In a reporter's mind, there are always questions: Is this merely an isolated case? If so, why did they do it? Or is this part of a pattern? If so, how long has it been shaping? How many people are involved? Is it organized? How? By whom? What factors peculiar to Communism are responsible for anyone's making such elaborate preparations to disguise himself and his purpose? What has been accomplished, if anything, by those who have gone underground into the Soviet? What are the chances of their success? Who? When? What? Where? Why?

All those, and more, had to be answered before there was any real story to be told in print. In going back over the tale of the fifteen, there was one clue to the possibility that they were not the first. That was the allusion to the priest-adviser who had served six years in the Soviet before them.

Jotted down within two hours of hearing the story of the fifteen, my notes attest to the fact that all members of the group were supposed to be Jesuit novices or scholastics. That the story was told at Manresa, which is considered the birthplace of the Jesuit Order, seemed to clinch the probability that *this was true*. It was disturbing at the same time. For it led right back over old territory, to Father Reed, to Lady Strickland, and up the blind alley to the Jesuits in Rome, who refused to confirm. Whether or not this story was "specific" enough, I didn't know. From subsequent events, I reluctantly judged that, apparently, it wasn't. True, it was later confirmed, elaborated and authenticated, but it had nothing to do with Jesuits, as shall be seen.

42

Having heard the story, I could hardly wait to rush out to find Father Reed. Back in Barcelona, I was unable to locate him. Unexpectedly and unintentionally, Señor Perez-Soler came to my rescue. He was press relations manager for Ford-Lincoln in Spain, and acted as my host and guide during my stay there. With the questions which demanded answers, immediately if not sooner, I begged off going to the bullfights, scheduled for about five o'clock. I told Señor Perez-Soler it was imperative that I find my Jesuit friend. There was a reception for Cardinal Spellman at the residence of the Bishop of Barcelona. I asked to be taken there in hopes of locating Father Reed.

In the courtyard of the residence, surrounded by a high, spiked fence with massive wrought-iron gates, Señor Perez-Soler introduced me to a priest with, surprisingly, an Irish name. For reasons which will soon be obvious, it is necessary to alter his identity. Let us, then, re-christen him "Father McGrath." I had seen him among those present at Manresa. He seemed fairly well acquainted with some of his American colleagues. He was apologetic about being unable to find his fellow Jesuit, Father Reed. But as soon as I learned, accidentally but fortunately, that he was of the Society of Jesus, I lost no time backing Father McGrath into a corner.

I put him under cross-examination that bordered on a third degree in my eagerness for information. In the notes, scribbled down that evening, aboard the S.S. *Atlantic* bound for Tangier, I recorded it in question and answer form:

Q: You know the story of the fifteen who entered the Soviet, how one among them betrayed the others who were arrested, imprisoned and probably martyred?

A: I know it well. I have heard it.

Q: Just today? Did you hear it just today, as I did?

A: No, I've known of their mission since June. The particular information you heard, I came by some days ago in Rome.

Q: This particular information? Then there are other stories, other information?

A: Yes.

43

Q: As I heard the story of the fifteen, they were Jesuit novices and scholastics. Is that true?

A: I do not believe it is. That was probably a mistake in the telling—or in the hearing.

Q: I have it written down some place. Are you quite positive?

A: In this instance, yes. Quite positive.

Q: What about other instances? Would Jesuits be sent into Russia—incognito, say, or sub rosa?

A: If you will question me on specific instances, I can answer.

Q: Let's get back to the one instance I have heard about. What makes you think they were not Jesuits?

A: It is unlikely that the Father General of the Society of Jesus would send novices and scholastics on such a mission.

Q: Not even if they volunteered?

A: Not even if they volunteered.

Q: Couldn't the fifteen, or some of them, have been full-fledged members of the Jesuit Order?

A: No. You see, it takes fourteen years of preparation as novice and scholastic to attain, as you call it, flull-fledged membership. None of those mentioned was old enough to have completed his preparation.

Q: How about the American?

A: He might have been old enough but, apparently, he hadn't become a religious until after his service in the war, which would have given him four, five years at the most.

Q: Then there *was* an American? That's something. Has the Father General ever sent Jesuits to Russia or the Communist countries?

A: I suggest that you ask the Father General.

Q: I tried to in Rome. He was away but I'll have another shot at it soon. Now, just a couple more questions. Has the Pope, to your knowledge, ever sent out a call for volunteers to go underground into Russia?

A: Should you ever obtain authorization from sources which are concerned with the safety of any leaders or their followers in what you call an underground, I must insist that you quote me verbatim on this. Please write it down. Several years ago, in the lifetime of His Holiness Pope Pius XI, a call went out from the Vatican for volunteers "to prepare for the Russian work."

44

I repeat, to prepare for the "Russian work." It was in 1927 when the order also went out from the Holy Father that the prayers after every Low Mass throughout the Roman Catholic world be said for the conversion of Godless Russia. Such prayers have been offered ever since, Pope Pius XII having issued the same orders. Each year since, the Holy See has issued a call for volunteers for the "Russian work."

Q: Russian work? Meaning volunteers to go into the Soviet to lead a religious resistance?

A: I did not say that.

Q: But that is what it amounts to, isn't it?

A: Frankly, I cannot say what the Holy Father means. But if you try, you might be able to find out from the Vatican.

Q: Do you know any Jesuits who have been inside Russia since the Revolution?

A: Several. Two were Americans, one a Canadian. You shouldn't have much trouble contacting them when you get home. One, I believe, is a very close friend of Father Reed, in the New England Province—possibly all three of those whom I have mentioned.

Q: Who are they?

A: That would be up to Father Reed to tell you.

Q: Can you introduce me to others whom you know who have been in Russia or behind the Iron Curtain?

A: You haven't time left in Barcelona to meet any more. You have already talked to one—at rather great length.

Q: You!

A: Yes.

Q: In Russia?

A: No. But in three of the captive countries.

Q: May I use your true name, if ever I publish any information on the religious resistance?

A: It would be safer if you did not. I am preparing right now to return.

Q: Then I shall not. Why is it necessary to go underground, to go disguised? Why not just go as a priest?

A: I suggest, my son, that you study the history of the Russian revolution. The newspapers of the days before your country recognized the government of the U.S.S.R. will give you the answers, not only in text but also in pictures.

Q: Just one more question, Father. If the fifteen were not Jesuits, might they not have been members of other orders? Outside the secular clergy, I mean.

A: They might have been. I cannot say. Dominicans or Franciscans, possibly. You will have to follow that up yourself. I wish that I could help you. But I am afraid that the safety of priests now in the satellite states might be adversely affected by any suggestion of anti-Communist activity. Do your research into the history of Communism and you will understand why.

It was, of course, disappointing to be unable to pin the story down to the Jesuits. That would have made it easier. For the Society has a central organization in Rome where it would have been possible to get together all the details in comparatively short order.

As we sailed, only an hour after my question-answer session with the Irish Jesuit in Barcelona, I began to put things together. From the answers of "Father McGrath," I was able to deduce certain facts which lay behind them. There obviously were priests in the Communist countries who were operating sub rosa. Some, certainly, had gone inside Russia after the revolution. I could not, then, see how there could be any appreciable number.

When I posed this to Father Reed on shipboard, he answered, "You are forgetting something. That is the period of Soviet expansion in Northern and Eastern Europe. In 1939, there was eastern Poland, part of which was incorporated into the U.S.S.R. In 1940, there were Karelia—which was part of Finland—Estonia, Latvia, and Lithuania, all of which became so-called republics of the Soviet Union. Surely you can make something of that."

I thought for a moment and replied, "You mean that the religious, the Roman Catholic priests, in those countries were incorporated into Soviet citizenship along with the rest of the population?"

46

"Not only Roman Catholics," he corrected. "Lithuania, for instance, is and always has been largely Protestant, influenced by the Germans and Scandinavians. There were, then, ministers as well as, I suppose, rabbis."

"You imply," I queried, "that whatever religious resistance exists may be a coalition of Protestants, Catholics, and Jews?"

"I merely suggest it," replied Father Reed. "I imply nothing. To go even further, no resistance in the Soviet Union could be very strong without the cooperation of the Orthodox, since that has traditionally been the religion of the Russian people."

"You are trying to discourage me," I complained. "The Orthodox Church was restored to all its rights and privileges by Stalin before the war. That's history, Father."

"It is Communist history that a Russian scientist was the first to fly, that a Russian doctor discovered anaesthesia, that a Russian mechanic invented the automobile," he explained patiently. "If all those are open to doubt, I insist that their claims of freedom to worship in the Orthodox faith are certainly not acceptable without questioning."

"Then you believe the Orthodox are in on it, too?" I questioned.

"If there is a religious resistance, it is only logical to assume that Orthodox priests are in on it, as you say. It is even more logical to suppose that they play by far the greatest part."

"What about the Jews?" I pressed.

"You read that Communist paper in Manresa," he said, producing a copy from his pocket. "Here it says, 'Religion is the opium of the people.' Now that is a translation from Karl Marx. It does not say that *Christianity* is the opium. It says *religion* is the opium. And it means *all* religion, Christianity, Judaism, Mohammedanism.

"You see," Father Reed continued, "the trouble is that two generations of Americans know very little about the Russian revolution. There is our generation who were children when the revolution was news. There is a whole new generation to whom it is only history—history, I might add, which has been

47

perverted by propagandists and apologists for Socialism and Communism. Two generations have no knowledge of the proscription, the repression, the purges of the clergy of all faiths, which turned into a red river of terror in the orgy of fanaticism that was ushered in by Nikolai Lenin and the Bolshevists."

"But Lenin," I protested, "was a great man." That much defense I felt I owed to my allegedly "liberal" friends and colleagues who were legion.

"With Father McGrath," the priest added with a smile, "I can only say, my son, that you should do a bit of unbiased research on your own."

Father Reed went to take a stroll around the deck while I went to find Wolter in our cabin. My temporary boss and I briefly discussed the story of the fifteen. Although he was as thoroughly impressed as I was, Wolter claimed not to have the authority to assign me to any search and research on a story that might take weeks, at the least. Besides, in Tangier there might be orders assigning Costa and me to the Middle East.

5.

A Tip in Tangier

I SPENT THE DAY and a half of the trip to Tangier going over my notes, typing them up, and trying to draw out Father Reed further on the role which, I was convinced on the scant evidence I then had, the Jesuits were playing in whatever resistance there might be in Russia.

An assignment to the Middle East, particularly to Palestine, I believed, would lead me much farther along the road. I was sure I could contact agencies representing Jewish columns of the resistance. I had definite reservations about the Moslems, in spite of what Father Reed had surmised. These were based upon my general lack of knowledge of the Soviet Union and upon failure to realize the vast extent of Mohammedan population in Russia itself. Within two hours of my arrival in Tangier, I was to begin revamping my ideas.

Small boats took the passengers from the S.S. *Atlantic* to the quay in the shallow harbor. There I was accosted by an Arab guide who had been directed to me by other passengers whom he had questioned. He took great pride in the fact that he had acted as guide for "the great American journalist, Mr. Roy Howard" and produced a letter to prove it. He had been ordered to look me up through an American Express Company official who knew of my arrival through a cable from Quentin Warren, a personal friend in Nice and also an official of the banking agency.

At American Express, I laid my cards on the table with little hope of success. I wanted, I told the young man who had sent the guide, to get in touch with anyone who might be a known, active anti-Communist. And thereby my introduction to Hamid was arranged—which was to be the beginning of my reappraisal of the activity of the Moslems in the religious resistance.

The methods and the channels through which I met Hamal Ben Hamid in Tangier would add little to the pertinent facts which I was to learn. For a number of reasons, the chief of which has to do with violation of confidence, no details of how the meeting was arranged can be told. There is no intent to be mysterious. Every precaution to avoid any suggestion of the sensational, or cloak-and-dagger, has been and will be taken. It is merely that the contact, through whom the introduction to the Arab was effected, stipulated that neither his name, his professional designation, nationality, official connections, nor the circumstances of his participation be made public.

A memo written the afternoon I met him notes that Hamid was a Lebanese who was an agent of certain Moslem interests. My source, in whom I had supreme confidence, as he had in me, related the background of his meeting with the Arab. Three years earlier, in 1947, Hamid had gone to a British bank which had a branch in Tangier, asking to rent a safe deposit box under somewhat unusual circumstances. The box was to be rented for a period of exactly six months, at the end of which time the contents were to be turned over to an official of an Arab trading firm who would present the key as his identification. This was in the event that Hamid, in the meanwhile, did not remove the papers himself, in which case he would notify the bank officials.

Now, Tangier is an open port. It is under Spanish jurisdiction of comparative laxity and tolerance. Nationals of many countries visit the city which is a fairly regular haven and operating center for secret agents. The Spanish police, however, are quite adept at ferreting out information about even the most discreet.

Since bankers, even in North Africa, which is really not so mysterious as dirty and devious, like to know as much as possible about the customers with whom they are transacting business, the British manager went through the routine of calling upon the police for a check-up. The Spanish detectives, through their own channels, put together a brief but pointed dossier on Hamal Ben Hamid: he was, indeed, a Lebanese, agent for a Moslem society, engaged in research work, the nature of which they either could not learn or were unwilling to tell the banker. Furthermore, certain officials of Communist trading and shipping interests in Tangier suspected Hamid of being a spy. They further believed that he had, somehow, entered and left Russia, almost at will, a number of times in the years since the ending of the war. The latter fact might or might not be to his credit. Suppose Hamid had obtained entry to the U.S.S.R. with the cooperation of the Soviet government?

My contact, who by no stretch of the imagination would possibly steer me to a Communist agent without warning, assured me that he had reason to know that Hamid was trustworthy. I would have to accept that on faith—just as Hamid would have to accept the third party's assurance of my own good intentions. My contact added that he had less reason to suspect the Arab, whom he'd known for some time and with whom he had conducted certain business negotiations, than he had to doubt me, whom he had never seen until that morning, although I had come with unassailable recommendation.

We rode in a chauffeur-driven Lancia to the point at the foot of a hill near the harbor where the wide streets of the new quarter of Tangier bump into the cobbled corridors that rise steeply into the old. There my contact left me in a native shop among alleged curios, oriental rugs, camel bags, and Moroccan leather goods. I had fallen into a typical tourist trap, amid three gesticulating bargainers, all covetous of my

51

American travelers' checks. I was at their mercy for about fifteen minutes when my guide returned with a tall Arab.

Hamal Ben Hamid was in European dress of obviously superb Italian tailoring. His attire was topped off by the traditional fez. The newcomer gave me Moslem greetings, touching lips and forehead with fingertips as he bowed acknowledgment of the introduction. Our go-between disappeared with apologies that he had work to do.

Hamid and I strolled among the flea-bag donkeys which jostled each other in the flea-bag alleyways. It was difficult to communicate, although I am sure I could understand his Spanish with greater facility than he could mine. Since I had to think in English, then translate, I had at best a halting if not groping delivery, not to mention an atrocious accent.

We walked to the foot of the hill where the Kasbah ends and hailed a taxi for the European quarter. There we halted at a restaurant and took a sidewalk table. Over his coffee and my brandy, Hamid quietly asked me for my credentials. I handed him my passport, my Western Union and RCA cable identification cards, my New York City press card, my New Jersey driver's license, and my social security card, none of which he was able to read. They seemed, however, to impress him less than my travelers' checks on the Chemical Bank and Trust Company. Like all Arabs, he understood these and politely asked me to write my signature which he compared with that on the accompanying identity card. Hamid explained that one could manage to forge a passport, but travelers' checks were something else again. I didn't quite follow his reasoning but I laughed at what I presumed was a witticism.

Without my asking, he produced a number of identifying documents, mostly in Arabic, which I could read no better than he could English. I, too, was impressed by *his* evidence of financial stability. He had a letter of credit, written in English on an Anglo-Egyptian bank in Cairo, in an unlimited amount.

Hamid, however, was apparently not eager to confide whatever it was that our contact believed he might tell me. I felt

52

no compulsion to tell him anything because, frankly, I didn't have any real information—at least none that I could then verify. The conversation began to lag under language difficulties, a certain suspicion I knew he still entertained, and my own hesitance to give information, based upon such flimsy evidence. It was about to die out completely when Msgr. Edward Quinn, a handsome priest from Cincinnati, onetime classmate of Cardinal Spellman in Rome, happened past with a couple of colleagues. Monsignor Quinn hailed me heartily, as did his companions.

As my clerical friends continued along the street, Hamid smiled at me and leaned toward me across the table. His suspicions were dispelled by the priests' recognition and obvious friendliness. He said something to the effect that "no priest of Allah or God can be a friend of the Communists." Then he opened up and told me something of what I wanted to hear, yet without really telling me anything.

It was indeed true, as I had learned from our mutual acquaintance, that the Arab had been in and out of the U.S.S.R. on numerous occasions. He had gone by underground channels into the Caucasus, the Crimea, and Turkmenistan to gather certain information. Since the war, he had been in the Soviet domain—not counting two sub rosa junkets into Moslem Albania—on four separate occasions. His business was the business of the "society"—which there is no need to identify here. His job was to maintain contact with certain forces operating underground within the Communist orbit. During these years, he had collected certain documents and affidavits of a secret nature. These were to be the basis of a number of confidential reports. The first of a contemplated series of four or five had already been completed and delivered to superiors in Ankara. The second, still in the process of compilation but nearly finished, was close at hand. If I cared to hear parts of it, he would try to translate it into Spanish for me, verbally, while I made notes. So we hopped back into a taxi and dashed for a bookshop which was just around the corner from the office of the American Express Company.

My luck being better than I had any reason to hope, the book-shop proprietor turned out to be an Egyptian who spoke fairly fluent English. He was, I had learned from Hamid, some sort of unofficial agent and contact man between Moslem elements in the secret army and certain sources outside. Whether the Egyptian's authority was superior or subordinate to Hamid's, I have never been able to determine.

At first meeting, he seemed even more suspicious of me than Hamid had been. Even after the latter's assurances that our contact had vouched for me and that the Arab, himself, was convinced that I was trustworthy—meaning not a Communist —the Egyptian was most uncommunicative and counseled Hamid to go slowly. So I told him *my* story of the adventure and tragedy of the fifteen.

I told them the story as I had heard it, referring to my notes but emphasizing that I had been unable to authenticate any of it. The Egyptian and Hamid jabbered to each other in Arabic. Often they halted my narrative to ask questions I couldn't always answer. The bookman took eager interest and, ap-parently, was delighted at the probability, which he said he had long suspected, that the Christians, too, were carrying on a resistance on their own. Perhaps, he added, that wasn't quite accurate, since he had had positive information of communi-cation between . . . Hamid shut him up before he could finish.

My recital had obviously satisfied the Egyptian on the ques-tion of my sympathies. As I finished, he and Hamid talked for a few minutes in Arabic, before the Egyptian rose, went into a back room and returned with a packet of papers. Many of them were in Russian, others in Arabic, and almost all looked like newspaper clippings. A second sheaf of documents were, I was informed, the report itself. The Egyptian apologized for its being in a language I could not read. But he would help me on that score, translating the most important parts as he went along, while I feverishly scribbled notes, the contents of which are the basis of later chapters, augmented with information gathered subsequently.

The report turned out to be a number of affidavits, signed by Moslem religious leaders, attesting the activities of the underground operating among the thirty million Mohammedans in the Soviet Union. Here, I had literally fallen into a documented account of an organized anti-Communist resistance—but it turned out to be in Arabic!

It didn't help to clarify things one bit. I was more confused than I had been before. More questions were whirling around in my brain. It was too much of a coincidence and the story was breaking almost too fast for me to keep up with it. I hammered questions at Hamid and the bookshop keeper. But Arabs are not a race to be hurried. The bookman would listen to my queries in English, mull them over, put them to Hamid in Arabic. Hamid would think for a while, reply, and the bookshop proprietor would take his time framing his words to me.

The following question-and-answer session—which is a holdover habit from reporting days on city hall beats—consumed more than two and a half hours, complicated as it was by language difficulties. Sometimes, Hamid would helpfully attempt to supplement the bookseller's not too perfect English with interpolations in Spanish. This further served to confuse. But I finally clarified it to my and their satisfaction.

Q: How long have the Moslems been operating underground in Communist countries?

A: Allah has never gone underground. [This paralleled, strangely, Father Reed's reaction.]

Q: How long have Moslems in Russia been resisting Communism?

A: Since the revolution, when the Bolshevists outlawed Allah.

Q: Do the Moslems work with the Christians in the resistance?

A: Your God and our Allah are, to be profane but practical and intellectual, one and the same. Since the Bolshevists abolished both at the same time, both, therefore, are on the back of the same

55

runaway camel. The story of "Abdul" [to be told later] answers that.

Q: What of the Orthodox?

A: Moslems would, of course, work with them when it is to mutual advantage.

Q: Do the Romans send priests inside the Soviet Union as leaders of a resistance?

A: From the story you have told us, they do. That is what we want to know also. Some of our affidavits tell of cooperation with Roman priests. But we do not know how they got there. We assume they do as we sometimes must.

Q: Do you believe there is any central direction of an organized resistance, say a coalition?

A: There is an organized resistance of Moslems, directed from outside. It is also directed by Allah. And, apparently, by your Christian God. What better direction could you ask?

Q: Is there anyone else in Tangier, to your knowledge, who has been inside the Soviet domain, say within the past four years?

A: There are many Communists—from Russia and Albania. They claim to be true Moslems, but that is impossible.

Q: You mean it is impossible for a Moslem to be a Communist? Why?

A: Because there is really no distinction in the Moslem faith between religion and government. Mohammed not only was the Prophet, he was also a temporal ruler. So have all his descendants and his successors been. With us Moslems, our religion is many things—a philosophy, a way of life, and a way of government.

Q: Therefore, you are opposed to Communism as a form of government?

A: Also as a philosophy and a way of life.

Q: Have not the Communists been able to stamp our your resistance by force?

A: The Christian Crusaders could not. We Moslems are not an easy people to defeat. We are spiritually a warlike people when we are not split by sectarianism. There are many Moslem sects as there are many Christian sects. The cleavages between ours, however, are deeper and more bitter. Yet, when there is no political power at stake, we can be united, particularly in a fight. We are also what you would call "past masters" at intrigue, therefore

56

better able to cope with the Russians than you Christians are. Secret activities appeal to the Arab mind. It is our nature to have and to keep secrets. For all these reasons, and more, we have a well-organized resistance.

Q: Would you say that the Moslem arm of the resistance is weaker or stronger than that of the Christians?

A: I am, of course, inclined to be biased. But I should say that it is stronger for three reasons. First, because of the geographical concentration of the members of our religion in the U.S.S.R. as compared with the vastness of the areas over which the Christians are distributed. Second, because of the proximity of Moslem nations to the borders of Russia—particularly Iran and Turkey—we are better able to organize and direct activities from outside. We have, also, a more realistic knowledge of Soviet territorial ambitions which threaten the political and, therefore, the religious welfare of the Arab states. Third, whereas your Christian philosophy is based upon maxims and exhortations to peace and non-resistance, the Prophet inspired true believers to battle for the One God. It is written in the Koran: "O true believers, take your necessary precautions against your enemies, and either go forth to war in separate parties, or go forth together in a body."

So went the interview with Hamal Ben Hamid and the Egyptian bookseller in Tangier. I had seen written evidence. Although I could read only the few pages which were in French, compiled in Algeria—and those only with difficulty—I was convinced of their authenticity. Subsequent sessions with Moslem leaders in Iran, Iraq, and Turkey were to confirm my judgment in this respect and my confidence in Hamid.

6.

Abdul the Persian

AMONG THE MOST exciting personal records I was to hear in all the months of following the trail of the secret army was that of one who was designated by the pseudonym "Abdul the Persian." This was told me at the same sidewalk café where Hamid and I had stopped earlier and where we adjourned for luncheon with the Egyptian.

Abdul is a character who is known to every Moslem who has the slightest knowledge of the resistance in Russia. He is known by many names; "Abdul the Turk" is one. That he was, or is, many men seems obvious from the number of stories that have grown up around this name. Nor is the relating of them confined to those of the Moslem faith. For accounts that parallel the one by Hamid have recurred in the statements of Christian leaders of the secret army who have contributed their testimony toward this book. Meanwhile two chronicles of "Abdul" stand out in the notes made in Tangier, from the translation by the Egyptian of Hamal Ben Hamid's confidential report.

A number of Christians who have read both notes and finished chapters on Abdul have bitterly protested their inclusion in this chronicle of God's secret army. Their objections can be best summed up in the following quote from one most emphatic critic: "Abdul the Persian has always been a murderous cutthroat. At no time has he been motivated by other

58

than materialistic considerations or by personal vengeance. He is not a godly man. Including him in a story of saints and martyrs is a mockery."

In answer, I can only offer the opinion of one Roman Catholic priest who owes his life to Abdul: "God moves in strange and mysterious ways, my son."

Although the spoken language of the Irani, or Persians, is unquestionably the most poetic tongue to be heard anywhere on earth, given to superlatives of description and fanciful flights of narration, Abdul cannot be accounted a romantic figure, even by his own people. There is a mistaken tendency on the part of Occidentals to assume that all Arabs are tall. Abdul is squat. The hero of lady fiction writers is young. Abdul cannot be less than seventy, since he was accounted an outlaw leader to be reckoned with, in the time of the Czar before the First World War. The "sheik" of romantic literature has always been described as swarthy with gleaming white teeth and long, straight nose, a wearer of snowy-white burnoose, who rides a full-blooded Arabian steed. Not Abdul. He is black. His teeth have long since decayed to brown stubs. His nose is flattened and off-center, a reminder of a Russian rifle butt slammed into his face when he was a child. He wears the rags of a nomad goatherd, which he is and always has been. If he is mounted at all, it is on a shaggy runt of a mountain pony.

The descriptions of Abdul, from half a dozen who have seen and known him, differ only in slight details. All are agreed on the main points, which seem to be that he despises the Russian government, the Communists more thoroughly even than he did the Czarists of his youth. "The Persian," as he is sometimes called, was probably born in Russia.

The political boundaries of Persia, or Iran, have always been the subject of official dispute. Yet, they never have mattered to the tribes who roam the northern plateaus in search of grazing land for their flocks of sheep and herds of goats and horses. Wherever the grass is green, the nomad Irani

59

have always gone, along a border too vast for either Russians or Persians to patrol—more than 1,400 miles, from Maku in the extreme northwest, including 350 miles of Caspian Sea coast, to Zuhrabad on the northeast, where the political boundaries of Afghanistan, the U.S.S.R. and Iran converge. The mountain pinnacles that stand guard over the desert of the northern Iranian plateau tower two miles high. Amid these perilous crags, Abdul and his band are at home and as inaccessible to pursuers as the mountain sheep they hunt.

That Abdul is called "the Turk," as well as "the Persian," is undoubtedly due to the fact that he has always been able to find asylum in Turkey, whose northern frontier, above Iran, borders the Caucasus. More anti-Communist than any country that borders on the Soviet Union, Turkey's "politics" are the politics of Islam. Any Moslem seeking asylum is likely to find it, whether a citizen or not. Unofficially, Abdul, with the Soviet secret police and border guards in pursuit, has been sheltered by Turkish nationals on Turkish soil on half a hundred occasions, over a period of thirty-odd years.

The most fantastic single element of Abdul's depredations against the self-constituted authority of the Soviet government is that he has penetrated so deeply into Russian territory to accomplish them. Chief target, throughout the years, has been the Trans-Siberian Railroad. It extends 4,500 miles, from Chelyabinsk, just east of the Urals in Asiatic Russia, to Vladivostok. At no point is the Trans-Siberian closer to the border of Turkey or Iran than 1,200 miles. Yet, Abdul and his raiders have turned up to derail its trains, disrupt its service, loot its cars of cargo, along a stretch that parallels the northern borderlands of Iran, Afghanistan, Pakistan, and China to the territory of Mongolia, spanning half the length of the vital lifeline of rails that stretches across Asiatic Russia. Where he will appear, where he will strike, with how many followers, are problems to which an entire regiment of secret police has been assigned—fortunately in vain.

Abdul's resistance to the Russian government, as has been

60

noted earlier, dates to the time of the Czars. Imperial tax collectors of that old regime operated almost identically with those of today's Communist imperialism. They had a way of finding nomadic tribes—through tips from settlers who resented the intrusion of the wanderers, as well as through spies who were paid a portion of the tax collected—and assessing them a certain percentage of their flocks as the government's share. Then, as now, it was usually a disproportionate number of sheep, goats, or horses. For they were dealing with illiterates who could not afford to carry their grievances to the courts, where they could not obtain redress anyhow.

Abdul was not the only Moslem tribal leader from the border countries and the south of Russia to resist the levies made upon the flocks of his people. Neither was he the first, or only one, to retaliate. As a matter of fact, Abdul's father, and a hundred others of lesser fame, learned, back in the 1890's, that it was far easier to raid than to raise one's own flocks. It became a career, dangerous but exciting and adventuresome, to steal the flocks from the tax collectors. After a sizable flock or herd had been gathered by the officials, certain tribesmen would hire out as guides or shepherds to convoy the confiscated animals to shipping points for Moscow or the industrial cities of European Russia. An ambush by wild Moslem tribesmen would intercept the caravan, the animals would be stolen, and whatever guards and soldiers were not massacred were likely to be sold into slavery. They were certainly no humanitarians, those rebellious raiders and murderers of the generation before Abdul.

It would be far from truth to pretend that Abdul is a saint, motivated by humanitarian love and good will, today. He isn't. He never will be. He never was. Yet Abdul is devout, even pious in his own way. Although illiterate, he is able to quote hundreds of verses from the Koran. He knows far more of the New Testament than the average western Christian, for he has memorized it from the readings of his thirty-seven sons, many of whom have been educated in Ankara or Teheran.

61

There are those who have characterized Abdul as a greedy, ruthless, murderous, lawless anarchist who recognizes no authority but his own. There are many more who account the ugly old Persian or Turk—whichever he may really be—a man of piety and goodness who looks to his God for guidance in the things that he must do. His followers, while almost never assembled in groups of more than forty or fifty, are said to number in the tens of thousands—which probably accounts for his ability to range a thousand miles into what he, and certainly the Russian border patrols who cannot apprehend him, consider "enemy territory."

With Bolshevist emphasis on industrialization and colonization of Asiatic Russia in the middle and late 1920's, Abdul's raids began to take on new purpose. Shrewd, obviously eager to increase the wealth and welfare of his people and of himself, he soon learned that the biggest payoff in raids could come from robbing trains. His discovery of this obviously axiomatic fact came as the result of an accident.

It was in 1924. Lenin, in feeble health and feebler mentality, no longer capable of directly and personally administering the affairs of the dictatorship he had set up, was demanding of his hand-picked subordinates—Trotzky, Stalin, Zinoviev—a renewed drive for communization or nationalization of all wealth, of whatever description. Failure of this effort, three years earlier, had resulted in the institution of the New Economic Policy, a sort of compromise between Communist socialism and the opposition to nationalization, chiefly on the part of farmers, herdsmen, and small tradesmen. In the new official enthusiasm for confiscation, Abdul and his people were caught, although they did all in their power to avoid it, even to armed resistance against the military units that were sent to seize their herds.

Abdul's forces, unorganized at that time, were put to rout or were taken prisoners. When the Russians' long march out of the hill country to the plains began, half a dozen of Abdul's sons were among the captives who were forced to herd their own confiscated goats, sheep, and horses toward Merv in Turk-menistan, on the Trans-Caucasian rail line that links Samar-kand with Kradnovosk on the Caspian Sea. Their progress was reported back to Abdul, via the grapevine of communica-tion that exists among mountain people everywhere in the world.

Determined to make examples of the "obstructionists" who were blocking attainment of the Bolshevist utopia, judges of the Special Court in Bokhara, where the captives were later taken and imprisoned, sentenced forty-seven of them, Iranis as well as a few Russians, to hard labor in Siberia. They joined a prison train out of European Russia.

There were between twenty-five and thirty cattle cars, jammed with sick, half-starved, vermin-infested humanity, in the train that labored northward out of Samarkand toward the mountains and deserts of Kirghizstan, to join the main line of the Trans-Siberian Railroad. In nine days, the prison train limped no farther than Taldy-Kurgan, less than one thou-sand miles. But it was far enough for the sons of Abdul to give up hope that they might be freed. Nearly sixteen hundred miles from the mountains of Iran, they were deep in Asiatic Russian territory—Moslem territory, to be sure, but farther than Abdul or any of his people had ever traveled or expected to travel.

According to the information supplied by Hamid and the Egyptian bookseller, it was the twenty-first of July, the day of Lenin's death. It was suffocatingly hot on the desert. In the cars, the swelter of bodies was overwhelming. The diseased screamed pitiably for doctors. The starving moaned for food, for water. The Russian guards, together with those murderers, cutthroats, and thieves among the prisoners who had been armed and commissioned to enforce discipline among the po-litical exiles, were too hot, lethargic, sadistic, and inhuman to care whether their charges lived or died, as scores had, during the long haul over foreign, snow-capped mountains into the scorching plains.

At noon, the train crew halted the train for lunch. Cursing guards, under Cheka (now MVD) officers, routed each car-load of prisoners out onto the desert for a check of those who were still living. These were prodded with bayonets, women as well as men, as they hauled the lucky dead from the wooden cars and pulled the bodies into the burning sands alongside the tracks. Not all were dead as yet. Some who showed a faint flicker of life were also ordered by the guards to be carried out, to lie in the sun where they were left to blister and bloat into carrion.

The sons of Abdul had been separated and assigned to different cars; only Mohammed, the oldest, and Yassin, the youngest, then about sixteen, had managed to stay together. With the optimism of youth, Yassin had never abandoned hope of rescue, or that, somehow, they would find an opportunity to make a break for freedom. As they stood in the baking sun, deprived even of the questionable shelter of the hot-house of the cars, silence was enforced by the guards as the roll was called. Those who did not answer were checked off as dead.

At first, it was unnoticeable to any but those with the keenest eyesight. Yassin was the first to see it: a rising cloud of dust on the southwestern horizon. It swirled nearer and nearer. Long before the others, the young son of Abdul the Persian could hear—or hoped he could—the sound of galloping hooves, muffled, muted by the dry desert air. He nudged Mohammed whose black eyes squinted with puzzlement in the direction of the swirling cloud. Rising, dancing heat waves play tricks with vision on the desert. The guards, mainly recruited from the cities and the fields of European Russia, were unsure, but they undoubtedly expected the arrival of some cavalry patrol. For they lined up the prisoners with a snap and precision they hadn't shown since leaving Samarkand and prepared to welcome comrades of the Red Army.

Suddenly, a triumphant Mohammedan war cry ripped out of the parched throat of Yassin. It was taken up and echoed by his brothers, all along the line of prisoners. Like a fever,

64

in half a hundred tongues, it swept the ranks of the captives. It unnerved the guards, who turned their guns upon their prisoners and began firing. Some fell, the rest surged forward, a milling, screaming, bloodthirsty mob which in the tick of a second had been transformed from hopeless, unresisting sheep into raging, maniacal killers, lusting for vengeance.

Charging madly, with the scrawny figure of the middle-aged Abdul slouched over a shaggy pony, an army of fanatical Moslem tribesmen, whipped to the fever pitch of holy warriors, swept across the sands. On horses, on screaming camels, they came with carbines spitting death, sabers and scimitars—traditional weapons of the Turks—hot with sun and blood. Well instructed though they might have been, Abdul's warriors got out of hand that day. According to the Hamid report, they confused the mission of freeing all Moslems with their personal beliefs that this was an action in a holy war.

The wild charge of the Moslem warriors, many of whom had joined Abdul's original band of perhaps a hundred relatives and friends as it rode the back trails and desert routes to the rendezvous, carried beyond the guards, into the ranks of the manacled prisoners. It was slaughter. It was ruthless murder. It was a bedlam of pitiable, screaming pleas for mercy that went unanswered. It was a carnival of blood and fire. For they burned the cars and made pyres for bodies of the dead and dying.

That Abdul could bring any sort of order out of the blood madness is testimony to his genius of leadership. With the sons who had ridden with him and those they had freed, he bullied, threatened, punished, and beat his murderous mob into some semblance of disciplined organization. Worn out by their frenzy, his followers became docile enough and submitted to his orders. Every guard was to be put to death; every prisoner, Christian and Moslem alike, freed. Those Christians who embraced Islam were to be given mounts and taken back

65

to the mountains. Those Christians who would not renounce their faith were to be turned loose in the desert.

I have a note, made in Tangier, on Hamid's answer to my query as to whether turning men and women loose in the desert, without food, water, horses, or camels wasn't less humane than sentencing them to immediate death. Hamid shrugged.

"It is better to die free than to die a slave," the Egyptian said philosophically, adding, "No one, certainly not Abdul, really expected those Christians who recanted never to change their minds again, if they wanted to. For it is written that a man's faith lies in his heart, not on his lips." Such, in effect, was the reaction of several Moslems who were questioned subsequently and who gave added details and information on Abdul and more than fifty other Moslem resistance leaders in Russia and the satellites, chiefly Albania.

When Abdul stood on the desert in Kirghizstan amid the circle of his subdued followers, on that July day of 1924, he made a vow that was to bind him and his descendants to eternal vengeance, a private, unending war against the Russian government. For among the dead was his young son Yassin.

Mohammed silently brought his brother's bullet-ridden body before his father. No matter how he died, no matter whose bullet had brought the end, Russia was guilty of the boy's murder. Had the Bolshevists not seized their herds, the sons of Abdul would not have had to resist. Had the Bolshevists not taken, tried, and sentenced six of his sons, Abdul would have had no reason to free them. The Bolshevists, then, were responsible for Yassin's death.

With seventeen of his sons—the twelve who had come on the expedition and the five who had lived through the massacre and had been freed—Abdul took his solemn oath, to which all of his tribe were bound, and it added up to "death to the Bolshevist government." It was not strange to him that he took a religious vow against a political enemy. For, as

66

Hamid had said, Islam is not only a religion but also a political way of life.

Although his wrath almost equaled his grief at the death of the sixteen-year-old Yassin, Abdul was realistic enough to take stock of his economic situation. After dispersing those he had enlisted on the way, as well as the "converts" they had made to Islam, the leader, his sons and other relatives held a council in the desert that night. Their number was somewhere around a hundred well-armed, well-provisioned, well-mounted men. At home, there were no flocks of sheep and goats to feed them and their people, to provide wool for the markets of the cities of Persia; and few more horses than they had with them to carry them beyond the retaliation the Bolshevists were sure to seek.

The big problem, then, was how to replenish their herds and flocks. As to the best means to accomplish this, Mohammed, Abdul's twenty-five-year-old son, came forth with the wisest suggestion. Having watched the livestock being shipped by railroad to the markets of Russia, in both Europe and Asia, Mohammed reasoned that it was unrealistic to go cattle raiding, annexing a few sheep here, a small herd of goats there, a couple of camels at one place, horses at another. Why not, he argued, let the Russians collect their flocks for them? There wasn't a dissenting voice; but how, it was asked, could it be managed?

The band, Mohammed explained, should ride along the rail line until it intercepted a trainload of livestock, en route to Siberia. By the simple expedient of attacking it, the raiders could build up their herds by the carload! Besides, the longer they could prevent discovery of the raided prison train, the safer they would be in the strange country into which Abdul and his people had penetrated more than a thousand miles from the familiar sanctuary of their hills.

And so Abdul split his forces. Taking command of half himself, he headed southward. The other half, largely made up of the younger, stronger men, were put under the orders of Mohammed and headed northward, deeper into hostile country.

Abdul's contingent, it is recorded, rode no further than twenty miles, in the direction of Alma Ata, before they were rewarded. It was just before dawn. For a Russian train of that era, it was making exceptionally fast time. With no prior experience in the art of train wrecking, Abdul's men did a most efficient job. Out of the sandy track bed they simply ripped a section of rail and waited in the gathering light for results. They dug into the sand along the right-of-way, like entrenched troops, their horses lying silent before them, just in case there was to be shooting.

There was added momentum from a slight downgrade as the locomotive hit the torn-up section of track. The train lurched onto the sand, only the locomotive and the first two cars turning over, the rest piling up on the track behind with a splintering, screeching crash. There were carloads of cattle and horses, of sheep and goats, more livestock than their tribe had owned over three generations. If they were suddenly rich, they were as suddenly in double trouble—first for the prison train and then for the cattle train. No time for a victory or thanksgiving feast. They had to get out of there fast. For herding livestock on the hoof slows the progress of any band and makes mobility dependent upon the slowest animals.

Again, the genius, or perhaps the instinct, of Abdul was demonstrated. He made his decision swiftly, as any administrator and organizer often must. To herd several hundred head of animals home on the Russian side of the border was out of the question. Not only was there danger from the officials of the Russian government who would have been alerted and on the lookout for them. There also was danger from the Kirghiz, the Uzbeck, and the Turkmen tribes whose avarice and larceny were stronger than their patriotism and who would not hesitate to ambush and massacre a band of fifty for such

68

a prize. Ahead, on the Russian side, lay more than a thousand miles of territory, inhabited by those peoples.

Less than a hundred miles, directly south, lay Sinkiang. With the cattle, possibly, it was a ten-day trip into the hills of that Chinese province. Though that way was mountainous, its trails difficult and tortuous, it would remove at least one obstacle to their safety—the Russian police and border guards. It meant traversing half of Sinkiang, then 600 to 700 miles across northern Afghanistan, before they reached home. There was no help for it, but it was worth the try. If they made it, the people of Abdul would all be rich beyond dreams.

Abdul sent messengers after Mohammed to bring his band back to cover the rear of the retreat. The dark-skinned leader dispatched more messengers to Iran to recruit a body of his tribesmen who would steal or borrow horses and ponies to form a spearhead or advance guard to meet Abdul and convoy the cattle safely through the unfriendly hills of Afghanistan.

So the long trek with the purloined livestock began in late July. It was mid-November before they arrived on the Iranian northern plateau with the sheep and goats, having slaughtered, traded or sold most of the cattle on the way.

The kinsmen of Abdul almost miraculously increased with the old man's newly acquired wealth. He needed them, in fact, to keep his herds from wandering onto Russian soil, as well as to warn him of the approach of armed Communist companies who combed the hills and green valleys in search of an enemy leader for whose capture the Soviet government has, for nearly thirty years, offered a standing reward of two hundred and fifty thousand rubles, tax-and-confiscation-free!

With his newly increased importance, wealth and responsibility, Abdul gained wide renown among the Moslems of Asiatic Russia, as well as in the Caucasus, Georgia and the Crimea. His sons became the old man's lieutenants, and his influence spread across the borders into the Soviet where many hundreds of secret followers were recruited to the ranks of his company, as a result of two circumstances: the cattle train raid set the pattern of Abdul's activity against the Communist government; and his cause took on a religious flavor, as a result of his oath to Allah to take vengeance on the slayers of his son.

The religious emphasis became the stronger as his sons left their hills for schools and colleges in Ankara and Teheran and came under the influence of the great teachers of Islam. Particularly in Turkey is the attitude of Moslems strongly anti-Communist. Devout, faithful to his religion as Abdul always had been, it took little persuasion on the part of his sons to convince the old man that his opposition to Communism was an Islamic duty. It still remains a personal issue with the aging Abdul, as indeed his religion is an extremely personal relationship between him and Allah.

Through his many sons, and, it is alleged, his more than one hundred and fifty grown grandchildren, Abdul has spread his influence far and wide throughout Russia. The mere mention of his name strikes fear, as well as anger, in the men in Moscow. That Stalin's successor, Malenkov, is himself a Moslem—although as a Communist he probably professes no religion—in no way lessens the efforts to bring about the apprehension of Abdul and his secret ring of lieutenants.

In spite of the fact that every train that travels Asiatic Russia is armed, they are still raided, derailed, robbed. Prisoners are set free. Guards are killed. Of recent years, with the development of the mining areas of Siberia, the men of Abdul and half a hundred other Moslem leaders have taken to wrecking and stealing shipments of gold and silver earmarked for the Soviet treasury in Moscow. The amount of such metallic loot undoubtedly runs into several millions of rubles.

That they were engaged in undeclared holy war was not long in being brought home to all the Moslems of the Soviet and the bordering countries, if the fanatical Red anti-religious terror of the first three years of the revolution had not already convinced them. In 1926, at Ashkhabad, the capital of the Turkmen state, in the mountains bordering the Iranian country that sheltered Abdul and his people, there was the sadistic massacre of eighty-six Moslems who knelt and bowed toward Mecca at noonday prayers.

Young fanatics of the "Association of the Godless" riddled their victims with bullets in a square that was commanded by the minaret of a mosque. There, in defiance of a Moscow ukase forbidding the public or private worship of God—or Allah or Jehovah—a muezzin cried the hour and the devout fell to their knees. They were shot in as sickening an exhibition of savage inhumanity as has been recorded in the annals of modern civilization—shot in the back. The excuse, the legal excuse? Elementary to one versed in the flim-flam semantics of Bolshevist socialism; it was simply that "the law stated that unauthorized assembly by more than eleven persons constituted either a riot or a conspiracy." The Godless were merely doing the duty of any patriotic revolutionary citizens "to preserve the peace, tranquillity and security of the People's Republic."

For each man of the eighty-six who fell with prayers and blood on his lips that day in 1926, a tribe or family swore a vow of vengeance against the Godless, against the government that would countenance, even encourage, the sacrilege of shooting a man before he had finished his praise of Allah. Among those who went to his death as he knelt before his Almighty was Mohammed, the son of Abdul the Persian.

Nor was this the only incident of its type. There were, actually, hundreds. They involved public burnings of the Koran, the desecration of mosques, the official seizure of religious property. Since the Bolshevists and their demi-official arms, the Godless and the Union of Atheists, perpetrated similar atrocities upon the Christians and their churches, they brought about what thirteen centuries of preaching had failed to accomplish—a slight measure of understanding between Mos-

71

lem and Christian, and a secret, if loosely organized, alliance against the common foe of Bolshevist socialism.

The confidential report of Hamid contained more than one hundred single-spaced typed pages on the activities of Abdul and his followers. These briefed more than fifty separate incidents, only those which could be verified, over the span of the years since 1924, appearing in these pages. The final entry related the bare details of the old man's sending his son Hikmet to Albania, where he is now leading the stiffest resistance Communism is meeting in the satellites, where his secret company of followers is estimated to number one in every four among a million Moslems.

7.

A Strange Ally

ANOTHER WHOSE inclusion in this story of the religious has been contested by well-meaning critics was a man whom I shall call "Shirshov." His name, too, first turned up in the Hamid reports.

The motives of Shirshov unquestionably are personal rather than religious. In certain respects, under different conditions than exist in the resistance, he is, or could easily be considered, a criminal. That his activities have benefited hundreds in the secret army is not even open to question. That he has become an ally, no matter how deeply his methods are decried, cannot be denied.

Whether Shirshov is a Moslem or an Orthodoxist is and never has been clear. Reference to him, however, has come from a number of sources. And I am convinced of the reality of his role in the resistance because he was among those whom I have interviewed. His inclusion in these pages is a matter of the record which I have been able to compile. Under no circumstances would it be possible to omit him because of moral considerations or objections. Whether he is a criminal is not for me to decide. Whether he is a valuable ally in the activity of the secret army is not open to argument. Again, the thesis that God moves in strange ways and through strange people prevails.

I was to meet Shirshov briefly, more than two years after

my interview with Hamid and the Egyptian in Tangier. He was reticent, non-cooperative in my efforts to obtain information.

The background material on him has been gathered from three sources: from Hamid; from certain Arab agencies in New York; and from an ancient Orthodox priest, living in exile in Cannes, who had known Shirshov in the Crimea before the revolution. This was confirmed by Shirshov himself. The old priest also claimed to have had frequent contact with Shirshov in the years since both had been active in the affairs of the secret army. This, Shirshov refused either to confirm or deny.

Although the results of my personal interview with Shirshov were most unsatisfactory, to understate the case, it was impossible not to be impressed by him personally. He was in direct contrast to Abdul the Persian in almost every particular.

At the time of our meeting, Shirshov was, I judged, in his early fifties. He was tall and straight with features that romantic novelists depict for their heroes. His jaw was strong and hard-set. His lips were thin. To me they looked cruel. Although his eyes were dark and their glance, when they stopped shifting long enough to look at me, was penetrating, they were too closely set together for my personal taste. Shirshov's shoulders could not be considered broad, by American standards, but the padded shoulders of his jacket, obviously French and expensive, gave him an appearance of great strength. He walked with the assurance that marks the bearing of men of wealth and power.

What few words he had to say were in English with a strong accent. For the seventy minutes that I spent with him on a bench overlooking the stretch of beach, an attendant stood always no more than twenty to thirty feet away, but out of earshot. I suspected that this third man couldn't understand English, anyhow.

Whether Shirshov was a Moslem or not, I could not determine from looking at his unsmiling face or by trying to size up his manner of dress. I mention this because it was

74

later stated by the old priest that Shirshov was not a Moslem. Rather, he was that rare phenomenon, the product of a mixed Moslem-Christian marriage. The ancient exile was very positive of this, since he had, he said, confirmed Shirshov, whose mother was of the Orthodox faith. Shirshov's father, the priest insisted, was a Moslem.

Shirshov never cleared up the point himself, since he wasn't the sort of man who could be asked so personal a question on first meeting. He spoke only four sentences during our interview which, I must admit, was largely one-sided. They were:

"I do not know any Hamid. . . . The old priest will tell the truth, in essentials; only in details is he likely to be inaccurate. . . . I have not been in the Soviet Union for many years. . . . I would be a fool to admit anything, a bigger one to deny anything, since I trade on secrecy—or 'mystery,' if you prefer."

Shirshov walked away, down the beach. I doubt that I shall ever see him again. I will know him instantly if I do. He will not know me.

Of course, "Shirshov" is not his true name. Neither is the one by which he is known among the Kremlin bureaucracy. Shirshov is one of Russia's most mysterious men. According to all accounts—and there have been many—his name should not be confused with the Commissar of Sea Transport. Yet it often is. His signature is often mistaken for Zotov's, Molotov's —or even Malenkov's. For Shirshov is the ablest forger in Europe, perhaps in all of the world.

Without documents, no man can move far, anywhere in the Soviet Empire. There are any number of permits, cards, papers, transfers, certificates, and the like in the state where the police impose far more regulations on the lives of law-abiding citizens than on those of criminals. Without Shirshov, the secret army's leaders could not operate. All would long since have been detected, particularly those who have entered the Soviet from outside.

Just who and what Shirshov is, probably no more than two

or three men in the world know. They are unlikely to tell. For it is generally presumed that he would go to any lengths to stay out of prison. There are almost as many theories about his origin and background as there are persons who have heard the fantastic tales about him. His very existence is a subject for wide controversy.

Where legend can be distinguished from biographical reality cannot be stated with any certainty. Although there has been verification of all salient facts, there has also been complete denial of any connection between the shadowy character of Shirshov and the secret army. Yet, since Shirshov's name or reference to his activity has continuously cropped up in the course of following the trail of the story, I have concluded that no account of the secret army can omit Shirshov. The fabulous but unadorned points of his career were told me by the ancient priest in Cannes who believes that he confirmed the boy Shirshov in the Orthodox faith.

Born and raised in the Crimea, the vacationland of Russia, Shirshov was the descendant of minor nobility on his mother's side. She was a devout communicant of the Orthodox Church and raised her only son in her faith. His father, a Moslem and an ardent revolutionary, was exiled in the early years of the century for his political activities. It is believed that the older Shirshov came in contact with those who were to become Bolshevist leaders with Lenin, that he was a close and trusted comrade of Stalin and of Molotov, who saw a great deal more of him than his son did.

While young Shirshov was in the Imperial Army on Russia's Western Front in 1917, his father returned in triumph from exile and took a leading part in the Bolshevist agitation that led to the dictatorship of Lenin. As a reward for faithful service to the Party, of which he was a revered member, Shirshov Senior was appointed to an important government job as director of transport in his native Crimea. He returned to his wife but found himself unwelcome after all the years of his absence. In his enthusiasm for Marxist doctrine, the elder

76

Shirshov had passionately embraced atheism, and like all militant revolutionaries, he insisted on forcing his beliefs upon others. Among these was his wife.

Learning that Madame Shirshov was sheltering a priest who was being hunted by the local Bolshevist officials, the recently returned husband confronted his wife with the accusation. She readily admitted the truth that the priest was being hidden in a huge wine cask in the cellar. He started for the cellar and when the wife tried to bar his way, Shirshov raged at her, hit her across the mouth and pushed her down the stair. In the fall to the wine cellar, Shirshova broke her neck. She lived, however, until her son's return from the war the next day.

Young Shirshov heard his mother's story of the part his father had played in the injury that was to cause her death that same morning. As his mother lay dying, the son swore a double oath: (1) that he would kill his father and (2) he would always fight for her religion and for God.

The son had apparently inherited some of the ruthless cruelty of his father. He conceived an involved plan for carrying out the first part of his vow. There would be no poison, no knife in the heart, no shot that would end his father's life quickly. Young Shirshov wanted it to be drawn out and poetic in the justice he believed it would invoke. The state his father had so eagerly helped to establish must be the instrument of vengeance.

Then possibly in his early twenties, young Shirshov set about the task of collecting the evidence and documentary proof of treason which would be presented to the Cheka. It must be complete. It must be exhaustive, for the son foresaw that the father would base his defense upon his service to the people and the state in the revolution.

Young Shirshov carefully wove a web of falsehood and fake evidence. His father was vulnerable in small details like most officials. He had shown favoritism in one place, lack of efficiency in another, little stratagems to violate the law here, a piece of larceny there. On all of these, the youth kept a minute

77

dossier, hiring his father's subordinates to watch every move the older man made. He insisted on signed reports before he would pay them off. He got them. Since many of the informers could not write, the junior Shirshov wrote their reports himself, expanding them as he pleased, and making them sign with their marks.

His mother's family had holdings in Turkey, the income from which could not legally be sent to him in Russia. It was therefore necessary for him to go to Turkey to get the money. In order to cross the border he hired a man in Constantinople to forge the passports, visas, travel permits, and documents that were required. With the funds in hand—usually in gold, possession of which was illegal in revolutionary Russia—he would return and hire more people to get more evidence, true or false, against his father.

The most telling charge—that of treason—which was to be brought against the senior Shirshov was a complete forgery. It consisted of a sheaf of more than one hundred documents, bearing the signatures of leaders of the White Russian Army. Some were letters giving instructions for delivery of arms and munitions, allegedly slated for the Red Army, to points on the railroad lines that were under the elder Shirshov's direction. Others were false receipts for such goods. Still more were phony communications with the forged signatures of hated former Imperial generals.

It took two years to get all the material together. There was just enough truth in the charges of theft against the elder Shirshov, all of which he denied, to make the whole case look bad. His son turned the whole thing over to an ambitious young prosecutor in the Ministry of Justice. The trial of his father was a field day for the denouncers. They ranted, raved, trapped the old man in lies, got a conviction and the death sentence in the most sensational trial of a Party member up to that time.

The morning he was to be executed, the old man received a

gift by special messenger. It was the white silk-covered prayer book that was in his wife's hands when she died.

In the gathering of the documents that involved his father in practices that would be decried by the rulers in Moscow, Shirshov realized that many Party members could be implicated. By judicious editing and copying, he was able to hold certain documented evidence which, he felt, might some day be valuable to him. Also, he demanded and received detailed receipts for payments of funds to government employees of all ranks. All these he filed away in a secret place. They were the beginning of what unquestionably has grown into the biggest most carefully documented collection of ruinous evidence anywhere in the Soviet Union. Even the dossiers of the security police are held less damning to those who are high in the councils of the Party and the government. For the police are motivated usually by considerations of politics.

The receipts he demanded served a twofold purpose. First, they were evidence of the acceptance of money on private deals or for favors that could be accomplished only as a result of official influence. Both were common enough practices with all ranks of officialdom. The inexcusable thing was giving written evidence. Second, the signatures on the receipts and reports were excellent models for the art of the forger. Throughout the years, Shirshov is reputed to have obtained damaging documents and the signatures thereon of most of the hierarchy of the Party and the Kremlin. Even though he is probably suspect as the source of the greatest proportion of forged credentials in the Soviet, there are few in any position of influence and responsibility in the government who would risk accusing Shirshov.

In connection with his apparent immunity from exposure, there is another theory, probably correct, that Shirshov does not conduct his dealings from inside the U.S.S.R. One version places him in Greece, another in France, a third in Scandinavia, while the most romantic of all has him living on and operating from a luxurious yacht in the Mediterranean.

The old Orthodox priest in Cannes believes that Shirshov probably is constantly on the move between all these places, as well as the United States. He had, he alleged, talked with his former parishioner six months prior to my interview. It had been in Nice. It had been brief. Shirshov had given him American money, had asked the old man's blessing, had been picked up in front of the Negresco Hotel by a private car and had disappeared.

Obviously Shirshov is a man who would not hesitate at blackmail. There are stories that he has resorted to shakedowns in the past to protect himself or his people from arrest. It is also reported that his agents regularly collect from several highly placed officials in Moscow and elsewhere.

It is further rumored that much of the so-called evidence he holds over these victims is falsified and forged. But in the Soviet Union, no one, however influential, can face accusation or denunciation and expect unbiased justice in the courts. He has promoted fear and lived in fear himself for too long. He cannot know who or where his enemies are. Even Beria, one of the two most powerful men in the Communist world, could not face up to the denunciations that were made against him.

There has even been a suggestion that evidence by Shirshov, true and falsified, probably played a part in the conviction of L. P. Beria. Like everyone in Russia, Beria had enemies. As security commissar, he had more than most. The MVD was under his orders and direction. It is unquestionable that in his files was incriminating information against any who might accuse him, including Malenkov. But it is an odds-on bet that there was absolutely nothing against Beria in his own files. How then could his enemies produce something really incriminating, even by Soviet standards? There was always Shirshov.

Shirshov would be one to realize the most in a monetary way from whatever he had to sell. Beria's agents and friends might send an emissary to Shirshov's accomplices with an offer which would be accepted. Shirshov's agent would then go back to Beria with an offer *not* to sell for an additional sum. Beria could then do one of two things: buy, or try to escape. Meanwhile, Shirshov could do two things. He could and undoubtedly would sell to *both* sides, letting Beria and his enemies fight it out.

(This interesting connection with the Beria case was suggested by an Orthodox priest in Detroit who claims close acquaintance with Shirshov and his operation. I was referred to the Detroit religious by the old priest in Cannes.)

Shirshov, it appears, was not above a bit of artistic counterfeiting along with his other operations. During the war he is believed to have sold millions of "queer" rubles to the Nazi government which the Wehrmacht passed in occupied sectors of the Soviet Union.

For something like thirty years, Shirshov is and has been carrying out the second part of his vow to his dying mother by giving aid to the forces of God's secret army. It is in the form of spurious documents to leaders who go inside the Soviet empire or to members already there who find it necessary to alter their identities. It is assumed that his agents operate outside of Russia as well as within.

Opinion of the religious on whose behalf Shirshov is supposed to operate is practically unanimous in condemnation of him and his methods.

On behalf of accuracy, it must be stated that there is not one line of documentation to support the Shirshov story that has been told here. Of those interviewed who have aided the secret army exclusively from outside the Soviet world, few are willing to admit their belief in the existence of a Shirshov, even though I have talked with him.

"How," asked one layman who has been active for years in maintaining communication with the secret army, "could any one man possibly forge all the documents that are needed to maintain the movement and security of members of the resistance?"

To this the Orthodox priest in Detroit answers: "No one suggests that Shirshov accomplishes the forgeries by his own hand. It is obvious that he has a staff of experts in his employ."

However, Fathers Zurikov, Mueller, Maguire, Janicek, and others who have operated inside Russia *all* had heard tales of the mysterious Shirshov. "Father Markovsky, the priest of Karelia, spoke at some length about Shirshov," said Father Mueller reluctantly. He mentioned that he "had once met the man in Helsinki." Father Maguire confirmed this recollection. "Some such man unquestionably exists. But why tell about him?"

"You are telling the world about the activities of spiritual soldiers in God's fight for the restoration of decency and morality in the world," stormed one authority in Italy. "There isn't a shred of evidence, only rumor, that there is any such person as this Shirshov. Even if there were, you serve no purpose in linking up so sacred a movement with the activities of a common criminal, a blackmailer, forger, and counterfeiter. It is sacrilege."

When this was repeated to Father Zurikov, his humorous eyes snapped as he commented, "That Shirshov is certainly no *common* criminal."

Against those who have counseled that the Shirshov story be omitted from these pages, the author agrees with Father Janicek's reaction: "Was not Jesus crucified between two criminals? Why should not God work His will through a Shirshov? Who can say how or through whom His moment will come?"

82

8.

Temporary Detour

BIDDING GOODBYE to Hamid and the Egyptian bookseller a couple of hours before sailing from Tangier, I hurried around—in circles, to be sure—to locate John Wolter. Finding a friend in such an out-of-the-way place as Tangier is not so difficult as might be imagined. Until he learns his way around, any stranger will stick pretty much to the tourist spots. I found my temporary boss in the same shop where, a few hours earlier, I had met Hamid.

With Costa, our photographer, Wolter had been present when the tragedy of the fifteen had been related at Manresa. Since we had shared a stateroom and hotel rooms for several weeks, Wolter and I had discussed that particular story at some length. He had, however, been unaware that I had followed it further, that I had picked up a stronger trail in Barcelona, or that I had intended to try to get in touch with Hamid.

Costa and I had been half expecting cabled orders from New York which would send us to Israel and the Holy Land on a different assignment. They had not come at Nice, Cannes, or Barcelona. Unless they reached us there in Tangier, it would be too late. Until I had started off on the trail of the story, whose magnitude I couldn't then begin to imagine, I had not been particularly anxious to stay abroad. But in Tangier, all that had changed. I wanted to get going further along the trail of what I dimly realized was to be a real journalistic adventure. It had already started out in that direction. How, then, I asked myself, could I better pursue my story than by going to the Near East?

The chief difficulty for a reporter working on an exclusive and confidential story is selling it to the people who must authorize the expenditures of time and money to run it down. John Wolter was my temporary superior, responsible for my movements and the immediate assignment. Wolter agreed that if I were on the track of a story such as I surmised, I had something. He was certain, also, that the powers in New York would agree. He insisted, however, that it would be exceeding his own authority to grant me permission to stay in Tangier or to go to Palestine or anywhere else. It was back to New York for me—and, I gloomily imagined, the end of the trail of the story. In order to do the job right, Wolter explained, it would be better that I finish my present assignment, return to New York and then explain to our editors in person just what I had in mind. If they agreed to my expending further time and money on following up, it would be to my advantage. I couldn't help but see the logic of this artist, who had proved, over our weeks together, to be a wonderful boss and a better friend.

With a feeling that I was kissing the story goodbye, I sailed from Africa, unhappily recording the notes on the Hamid interview, which I suspected were to be the last I would ever make on the story of the resistance in Russia.

When I confided my disappointment to Father Reed, he was puzzled. "Why," he asked, "should you be discouraged? There are men in the United States far more active in the Russian work than any in the world. To begin with, you have no real background of Russian history, either recent or current, to go on. You do not even know *why* it is necessary for the religious in the Soviet and her satellites to operate sub rosa.

"You have no real realization of *why* leaders volunteer to go inside the Communist domain. You cannot just take my word for it, my son. You must *know* why. You must read. You must study, do research. You must talk to men like Father Gallagher and Father Walsh and Father Le Dit, all of whom I will try to have you meet. You must talk to the staff of the Russian Centre, soon to be in operation at Fordham University. Before you go on, you must have a background of knowledge about the *reasons* for Bolshevist proscription of religion, of God, of the Church.

"I have no doubt that you will need real knowledge of the situation with which those people under Communism are faced before you can convince any editor to send you half around the world on a story which, to you, is not based upon a really solid foundation of historic fact. You have thirty *years* to catch up on, my son. Maybe you can do it in thirty days. Even I, who know much of what you suspect, would want you to be grounded in the recent and current history of Communism so as to orient and correlate the new facts I know you will learn."

So for a few weeks, the trail I had started to follow at Malta, at Manresa, at Tangier, took a detour—back-tracking on history.

I was not long in learning that there is nothing even remotely recent about the lowering of the so-called "Iron Curtain," though it remained for Winston Churchill to dub it that after the Second World War. Actually the censorship and control of news and history through regulation of all channels of communication has existed since the Bolshevists consolidated power, as early as 1918. Nevertheless, a mass of material of facts and figures, of recent and current history have filtered through the tightest restrictions and the closest controls. *Pravda* and *Izvestia*, the official organs of the Party propaganda, often unwittingly, have given away the facts. The very words of the Red rulers of Russia have sounded keynotes to the Kremlin attitudes down the years and have supplied the highlights to history.

It is only through a study of these attitudes and of the writings of observers who have been, openly as well as sub rosa,

85

inside the Soviet domain that an understanding may be reached —an understanding of the necessity for believers in God to go underground, to join a secret army.

Any appraisal of the attitude of the Bolshevist leaders of Revolutionary Russia toward religion must, strangely enough, go back more than one hundred years. It traces to a voluminous treatise which has not been brought up to date by so much as a single phrase or comma, let alone an idea. Profanely referred to as "the Bible of Bolshevism," the work is *The Manifesto of the Communist Party*. In contrast, the Holy Bible has undergone any number of separate changes, revisions, and interpretations in the century and more since Karl Marx and Friedrich Engels issued the four-part harangue which became the basis of the philosophy of empire by world revolution.

The political, industrial, economic, and social tenets of the *Manifesto* are largely interwoven in the pattern of the treatise. The critic who would attempt to separate or segregate one tenet from the other and to treat any one as an entity would be guilty of misinterpretation and oversimplification. The same holds true for the *Manifesto's* evaluation of religion. But since Marx and Engels were permitted to resort to empirics in their treatment of the subject, one can only reconstruct their obviously prejudiced, shrewdly intolerant reasoning.

Advocating violent, terroristic, world-wide revolution, Marx suspected from his more than cursory knowledge of history that the strongest resistance would come from the religious. It had been true in the French Revolution of half a century before. It had been proved in the waves of revolt that swept over Europe in the very year of the issuance of the *Manifesto*. Today the apparent reasoning of Marx is being proved all over again by the counter-revolution of men with no political precepts, no expectation of material gain, no social or economic ambitions. These are the people of the secret army, motivated by mystical ideals that neither slavery in Egypt, nor exile into the millenniums, the swords and armies of the unbelievers, the

86

persecutions of Imperial Rome, nor the terror of Moscow have been able to erase.

Karl Marx well knew how highly individualistic were his own people. Certainly the chronicles of the Jews, since the Old Testament times of their warrior-princes, told with what tenacity the peoples of Israel had held and were likely to hold to their great civilizing commandments against every conceivable persecution and adversity.

The Christians were conditioned by their passive philosophy and beliefs to oppose violence wherever possible and actively to seek peace. They would, by some peculiar psychologic reasoning, even fight to preserve tranquillity! Therefore, they could be expected to oppose the violence of the sort Marx advocated on behalf of world-wide revolution. The early Christians, who had courted martyrdom rather than recant their faith, had conquered, paradoxically, the Roman Empire. Spiritually and temporally, Christianity, in one form or another, had extended a hold over all of Europe and the New World, had penetrated Asia and the Pacific Islands, and had contended for religious supremacy in the Middle East.

With Islam, Marx encountered a direct contrast to Christianity. Never had there been more fervent, fierce, and fanatical missionaries, in more overwhelming numbers, than the followers of Mohammed. Spreading the word and the philosophy of the Koran by the sword, they had gained political and religious dominion over the better part of North Africa, the Near East, much of Asia, and the Pacific Islands.

The power of Jehovah, God, Allah, had to be reckoned with not only in terms of ideas, ideals, and semantics, but also as a vital force of manpower which would be arrayed against revolution—on varying but obvious grounds. Jehovah was a tenacious deity; God, exacting; Allah, vengeful and warlike. The power of each over the spirit of hundreds of millions certainly stood squarely in the path to any scheme of world dominion. A mass mind, attuned to the mystical concepts of the Old and New Testaments and the Koran, could hardly be expected to entertain the bleak prospects of state-imposed materialism.

Such conclusions, which Marx apparently reached, seem perfectly obvious from even a superficial study of his writings and his exhortations to his idolators. Exterminate religion, abolish the soul, outlaw God, if you would command the mere minds of men. Destroy the seat of men's resistance, which is in the spirit, and you can then impose any and all things upon them in the name of pure reason and intellect. For no man ever found strength to resist with his mind alone.

Vladimir Iliich Ulyanov, alias Nikolai Lenin, was a fanatic disciple of Marx. But the pupil translated the wordy and sometimes obscure ideas of the maestro into blood-red actions.

It is reasonably well established that from 1914 through 1917, while his brother Russians were at war, Lenin directed sabotage against the industrial plant of his own country; that he engineered labor trouble behind the lines, with the result that his fellow countrymen were left, literally, without guns and ammunition, costing the lives of thousands of Russians who were unable even to defend themselves against enemy attack; that he conspired in Switzerland with enemy spies and agents in revealing Russian military plans which he learned through underground channels in his native land. There is a longer bill of particulars, including conspiracy to sabotage Russian food supplies, railroads, and communications so that the enemies of his country could gain victory.

With Lenin, from the haven of neutral countries which had afforded safety from military conscription, bullets, and battle for Mother Russia, came a motley mob who were to form the hard core of Bolshevist bullyboys. Among them was Comrade Zinoviev who had heroically shared Lenin's luxurious "hardships" in exile as a literary lion and revolutionary luminary in Switzerland.

There was Leon Trotzky too. He had for some years been unrelentingly defying capitalist warmongers, militaristic imperialists, bourgeois enslavers of the proletariat, President Wilson, and American entry into World War I. He "thumped the tub" for the Kaiser then, as Stalin's stooges in this country were to whack it for Hitler twenty-five years later.

Comrade Kamenev also suddenly yearned to sacrifice everything for Russia, after years of being hunted as a common sneak thief, blackmailer, and extortionist by half the police forces of Europe.

Such were the Big Four of Bolshevism. With the aid of a couple of young stooges, calling themselves Molotov and Stalin, they came to save Russia in its darkest hour.

Of the Big Four, only Lenin was to die of natural causes. Trotzky was to be assassinated in Mexico. Kamenev and Zinoviev were to be executed as "enemies of the state," even as they had signed the death warrants of thousands whose only crime had been belief in God.

It has been the "line" of the Ministry of Information and Education as well as the Ministry of Foreign Affairs of the U.S.S.R. to deny any "official" participation in anti-religious activity. As Foreign Minister under Lenin's dictatorship of the Bolshevist wing of the Communist Party and, therefore, of all Russia, Leon Trotzky piously denied accusations of "purges" of religious leaders.

"It must be admitted that great anger resides in the hearts of the people against the religious," he told a representative of the U. S. Famine Relief Commission in 1920. "The government, however, does all in its power to discourage any unlawful but spontaneous demonstration of the wrath of the people. Whatever religious leaders have been or are being prosecuted by official agencies have been engaged in politically subversive and counter-revolutionary activities."

How sincere were his words can be judged by a speech he had made, some months before, at a meeting of group leaders of the Union of Atheists: "We shall pursue Almighty God in appropriate manner. We are confident we shall subdue him. . . . We shall fight him wherever he hides himself."

Lest this be construed as a personal, rather than an official,

89

utterance, by one who has often been hailed as a kindly old martyr because he lost his ruthless battle for power to the even more ruthless Stalin, these are the words of Comrade Zinoviev, who was to become President of the Third International: "Our program is based upon scientific materialism which includes unconditionally the necessity for sponsoring and teaching atheism."

Sponsor and teach atheism they assuredly did. Even while Trotzky was telling whatever part of the civilized world that would listen that the government frowned upon anti-religious activities, the Ministry of Public Information and Education was not only sponsoring but also subsidizing the Association of the Godless, soon to vie with the Union of Atheists and the dreaded Cheka (secret police) for recognition as the most sadistic arm of the Red terror in Bolshevist Russia. Comrade Lunatcharsky, Minister of Information and Education, hailed as one of Communism's outstanding intellectuals, presided over the ceremony of the founding of the Association. It remained for this colossus to rise to the heights of inspired invective on the auspicious occasion:

"We wish the 'Godless' every success in their fight against the repugnant specter of God. We hate Christianity and we hate Christians; even the best of them must be regarded as our worst enemies. Christian love is an obstacle to the development of the revolution. What we need is hate. We must know how to hate; only thus shall we conquer universally."

In revolutionary Russia, it was applauded as the pronouncement of a gigantic genius who was to guide the education of the young.

In that connection, there was Mrs. Lenin, also known as Madam Ulyanova, and Madam Krupskaya. She was revered as a model and guide for Soviet womanhood. The welfare of little children was her most ardent concern and she was particularly interested in the influence of the home and Russian motherhood upon the development of her beloved country's

90

youth. At a meeting of the parents of school children in Moscow, she said:

"We must make our school children not only non-religious, but also actively and passionately *anti*-religious. The home influence of religious parents must be vigorously combatted."

Least moderate, most lurid, was a statement by Lenin himself. It was published on page one of Party newspapers in Moscow without so much as a single unfavorable comment. It was, of course, clothed in the catch phrases of the demi-intellectual, which made so great an appeal to the self-styled "intelligentsia" of the America of a generation ago:

God is the personification of ignorance and superstition. We must stamp him out as ruthlesly as we would any excrudescence. The cross is a symbol of the iron bars behind which the bourgeoisie have imprisoned the intellect of Man. We must tear down that cross to free men from the enslavement of the priests who are the jailers of the proletariat. . . .

Jehovah is the enemy of all except the "chosen people." He is a selfish, acquisitive deity of capitalism, the personification of greed. The Old Testament is a documentation of the struggle of the Jews to set themselves up as a class above and apart, superior to all others. Abraham was a prophet of the system which sought to exploit the labor of others. We must strip Jehovah and his chosen down to their last ill-gained ruble which they have stored up with the labor and the sweat of the exploited masses. . . .

Allah is the God of force and resistance. The Koran teaches political counter-revolution. Mohammed enslaved the bodies as well as the minds of millions. The scimitar should be the symbol of Islam. If it is necessary that we resort to the sword to strike down the scimitar, we will flex our sword arms with vengeance.

There were, of course, thousands of similar fulminations by lesser luminaries of every rank, all based upon the pronouncements by the leaders and phrased with the stultifying lack of variety which is the hallmark of Communist utterance.

Such was the atmosphere of revolutionary Russia with the

rise to power and dictatorship of Nikolai Lenin and the Bol-shevists. God was made an enemy of the State. War was de-clared against Him and His people of whatever faith. He was to be hunted with vengeance. The Cross was to be torn down. The Almighty was to be stripped of His dignity and if possible His power. He was to be fought with the sword.

But although God, Jehovah, Allah were to be denied and abolished by the masters of Moscow, were to be legislated and dictated out of existence, they have lived on, as they have through the centuries—in the hearts and souls of men and women of faith.

In the chaotic days that began with the supremacy of Lenin, anti-religious hatred and fanaticism spread like the plague of the red death across Mother Russia. Depraved minor Party members, eager for notoriety, followed with mad energy the official policy stated by Lenin, Trotzky, Zinoviev, and Luna-tcharsky, the top hierarchy of Bolshevism. From then until the blessed death of Lenin in 1924, murder of the religious, pil-lage, plunder and desecration of churches, and persecution of Jews, Christians, and Moslems turned the era of the revolution into a Dark Age of terror, violence, hatred, sadism, and ghastly bloodshed.

On Good Friday of 1919 in Kuibyshev, twelve Orthodox and Roman Catholic priests were burned at the stake. In Petrograd, now Leningrad, two Orthodox priests and a rabbi were crucified in the square, nuns having been forced to drive home the spikes before drunken soldiers hoisted the crosses. The same day in the Moscow area, twenty-two priests and three rabbis were impaled and some of them held aloft in agony in Red Square before the horrified gaze of thousands.

During the feast of Ramadan, at a mosque near Sevastopol, 133 worshipers were trapped inside. As the Moslem faithful knelt in prayer, soldiers barricaded the doors from the out-side and set the building ablaze. As those inside the flaming pyre screamed for mercy, members of the Association of the Godless herded young Moslem children and women inside to share the torture and martyrdom. Whoever tried to escape was shot down or hurled back into the inferno. Although there was no way to identify scores of charred corpses, the census of the dead totaled 147.

Ikons were stripped from shrines at which the people of Russia had worshiped for generations. Priceless art works were either wantonly destroyed in pure spiteful vandalism, appropriated for their intrinsic value by the state, or simply stolen by individual and organized looters. Altar cloths, embroidered with gold thread, painstakingly worked into magnificent patterns, were snatched as keepsakes by loutish oafs masquerading as the mental superiors of the "superstitious and ignorant religious." Chalices of gold and silver, which had been the fountainheads of hope and faith from time immemorial, were purloined by the obscene and the debased, who prided themselves on their intellect, symbolized by their godlessness.

Illiterates who were members of the Union of Atheists acted as accusers, judges, and executioners of their fellow citizens who "put their learning to no better use than reading proscribed books."

There were economic as well as ideologic designs behind the anti-religious campaign of the Bolshevists. The collectivist state had no room in it for the existence of any private property whatever. The appropriation of church lands, buildings and treasure was contemplated as a step in the breakdown of the widespread opposition to the nationalization of farms as well as industry. The Communist populace was encouraged to participate in the dismantling of thousands of churches and the demolition of thousands of others, as a conditioning agent in the public indoctrination against God. More important to the Lenin government, however, was the intrinsic worth of the property itself, as well as the historic, religious and art treasures it brought the state.

In 1919-1920, few if any of Russia's conservatively estimated one hundred and ten thousand religious establishments weathered the storm of hatred whipped up by the government leaders who uniformly set examples of intemperate hysteria. The Association of the Godless, in the first year of its official existence, took over churches and religious establishments which had escaped demolition in more than eleven hundred communities. In the succeeding five years, during which they vied with the rival Union of Atheists in a drive for membership, they extended their occupation of former church properties at a rate of six hundred a year. By the time of Lenin's death in 1924, the Atheists and the Godless rented, or received rent-free from the state, more than ten thousand places once dedicated to the worship of the Almighty. Still other thousands were in use as Party headquarters and prisons —prisons where hopeless men and women looked out through iron bars that had replaced stained glass.

If one could find a church standing, it was no crime to attend—within limiting bounds. In certain localities, petty commissars in charge of public safety had issued proclamations against public meetings. A gathering of ten or more might constitute a threat to security. Should more than ten communicants assemble at a church service, all might be arrested and accused of conspiring against the peace. In communities where such regulations had not been instituted, other ukases issued from Moscow might be invoked.

There were laws pertaining to education. It was decreed a crime to teach any religious doctrine to anyone under the age of eighteen. Reading or repeating any written passage from any book or periodical was construed as teaching. Anyone, therefore, who read or repeated any passage from the Bible, Talmud, or Koran within the hearing of a minor was, technically, teaching. It was a simple matter for a member of the Communist Youth, or a young apprentice of the Atheists or the Godless, to slip in among the congregation, listen to the sermon, the reading of the prayer book, or the singing of published hymns. He then had merely to turn informer and accuser. Not only was it easy, it also brought the informer a

94

not unflattering amount of attention, notoriety, and praise from officials.

Whether such quotation was uttered by priest, rabbi, minister, parent, or any other individual, it was construed as a "crime against the State." Indeed, today school children often innocently betray their own parents as members of the secret army, under skillful questioning of teachers and agents of the security police. A case in point was revealed in a public trial which took place in Kiev in October of 1952. It was told by a leader of the secret army, whom this reporter has interviewed and whose story has been confirmed and verified:

In a Communist indoctrination class, held one day each week in the state-directed schools, an instructor cunningly questioned pre-teen-age children on how their parents reacted to the scientific version of the origin of man.

"Do you talk over your classwork with your mother?" To an apparently innocent question one little blue-eyed girl of ten truthfully answered "Yes."

"Does she agree with what the teacher told you?" the instructor continued.

"No," the child answered, innocently and honestly.

Adroitly, the inquisitor drew out the information that the child's mother had told her the Old Testament story of the creation of the world and of man according to Genesis. The parents were arrested on the charge of perpetrating a crime against the state. While they awaited trial, they were subjected to every sort of persuasion and pressure to reveal the identity of the priest who was confirming them in the forbidden and outlawed Christian faith. In the meanwhile, their little girl was sent to a state institution for "ideological rehabilitation."

By what means the interrogators of the MVD were able to obtain a "full confession" from the parents and a complete recanting of their "heresy" cannot be imagined. The secret police have methods which are beyond the remotest comprehension of those who have never been subjected to them, says the priest who related this episode and whom we shall call

"Father Radzke," since he will have returned underground into the Caucasus by the time this is published. The parents not only confessed, they implicated a Roman Catholic priest who went on trial at an open session of the People's Court, which Father Radzke attended.

The accused priest went on trial for denying the supremacy of the government of the Soviet Union. The method of "legally" establishing what will be seen to have been an utterly ridiculous premise would have been ludicrous had not the results been so tragic. Excerpts of the trial, which later reached Paris through secret channels of communication, record part of the trial procedure as follows:

PROSECUTOR: You do not deny that you are a priest of the Roman Catholic Church whose government is located in Rome?

PRIEST: I do not deny that I am a priest of God whose presence is everywhere.

PROSECUTOR: Do you recognize what is called "the law of God?"

PRIEST: I also recognize the law of the Soviets.

PROSECUTOR: It is the law of the Soviets that the teaching of Christianity is a crime. In teaching it, you have contravened the law of the Soviets. Do you deny that?

PRIEST: I do not deny teaching the Word of God. His law is above that of men.

PROSECUTOR: No such law exists on Soviet soil. It cannot even be mentioned here.

The court arrived at a most amazing piece of sophistry. The priest had admitted that he recognized the law of God. Since no such law existed in the Soviet Union, the priest, therefore, subscribed to an "alien" law. This was, in effect, a denial of the law of the Soviets and consequently treasonable. Although born in Poland and absorbed into citizenship by the Soviet Union in 1939, his identity papers were declared void—on the grounds that he was an Italian, since he was a priest of the Roman faith!

Between 1919 and 1924, so common had the practice become of planting young informers in churches, and of using the innocent revelations of children, that between eight hundred and one thousand trials, resulting in convictions, were based upon such "evidence" every year. Upon this, students of religious history in the Soviet Union are unanimously agreed, although even police and court records of the Communist government have kept no accurate tally, since the charges are usually political.

Another "defiance of the laws of the people's Soviets" could be trumped up on the basis of monetary regulations. It was proclaimed a crime to have in one's possession silver coins or precious metal in any form which exceeded the value of three rubles. The anti-religious who wished to bring an accusation against a priest, rabbi, or minister merely waited until a collection had been taken up. He would then call the police, demand a search which would turn up the contraband coin. A charge of hoarding could then be placed against the innocently offending religious. If this failed, the informer could turn up a hidden chalice of silver or gold which, possibly, he had previously stolen or which might actually have been hidden by a priest. Altar cloths, ikons, religious books that were embossed with gold leaf, even the robes a priest wore, were seized and assayed for the criminal three rubles-worth.

In the case of coins, a more serious charge might easily be made out. That was "conspiring with foreign agents." It was based upon the remotest of possibilities, that the accused had received the coins in payment for his activities on behalf of enemy governments.

The Bolshevists were then at war with Poland, they had lost their Baltic territories with the creation of Latvia, Lithuania, and Estonia as independent nations, while there was trouble in Armenia and U. S. troops were occupying part of far northern Siberia.

The charge, "enemy of the State," was indeed a diabolical weapon forged by the Bolshevists in their open battle against

97

religion and God to force atheism upon the people of what had once been called "Holy Mother Russia."

In the year of 1921, more than six thousand religious were accused, tried . . . usually in "closed" sessions . . . imprisoned, exiled, condemned. As though in terrible vengeance of a wrathful and outraged Deity, it was then that famine struck unholy Russia.

9.

The Vanguard

THE CHRISTIANS, whom Lunatcharsky had designated "our worst enemies," showed, during the famine of 1921, "the love of their neighbor" which he had appraised as weakness. They forgave the Bolshevists their trespasses in the name of Christ Who died on the Cross. In Rome Pope Pius XI organized a mission of mercy and charity to go to the relief of the stricken people of the Soviet, which had encouraged the pillaging, burning, desecrating of churches, and the murder of priests.

Director of the Famine Relief Mission to Russia was the Rev. Edmund J. Walsh, S.J. A man of unusual versatility—administrator, author, historian, teacher—Father Walsh was later to found and direct the famed School of Foreign Service at Georgetown University in Washington, D.C., and to become, unquestionably, one of this country's leading authorities on Soviet Russia.

Father Walsh's assistant was another American, the Rev. Louis J. Gallagher, also a Jesuit. Equally distinguished as historian, teacher, and author, Father Gallagher was to become president of Boston College before retreating to St. Robert's Hall in Pomfret, Connecticut, where he was to devote all of his time to writing.

A personal reminiscence about Father Gallagher serves to

99

illustrate the sort of bizarre information which came my way in the course of tracing down the secret army.

With Kenneth McCaleb, my immediate superior at King Features, who, incidentally, shared many of the interviews and gave invaluable advice in the assaying and organizing of this material, an interview was arranged with the tall, white-maned priest. Although we had read all of the works on Russia written by Father Gallagher, we had no opportunity to meet him personally until most of our data had been collected. In attempting to check on a particular story which had already been verified but on which we still wanted additional confirmation, McCaleb queried the priest.

"Father," he asked, "have you heard the information on Father Janicek?"

"Perhaps," replied the former head of a great college. "But I don't connect the name with any particular incident."

"That's not so strange," McCaleb explained. " 'Janicek' is, of course, a pseudonym. According to reliable information, this Polish priest entered Russia with Red Army troops in the uniform of a soldier, early in 1940. He remained for some years and his career is to be the subject of a chapter in the history of the secret army."

"I did not know him." Father Gallagher replied after thinking for a moment. "But I can well credit the story."

"You mean," McCaleb insisted, "that you believe a priest actually entered Russia as a soldier, without being detected? You don't think this is, perhaps, a slightly romanticized chapter?"

"I can very well believe it," said the priest, smiling quietly. "There's nothing so very remarkable about it. From my own knowledge, I can assure you that your Father Janicek was not the only one. . . . Take my own case. I am a Jesuit and have been for thirty-five years. I claim no particular distinction for having been, when I was in Russia, not only a priest, but also a Captain of Red Army cavalry."

McCaleb looked stunned. "A *Gallagher*, a captain of Russian cavalry!"

The handsome priest, then in his mid-sixties, nodded quietly. "The Eleventh Regiment of Red Army Cavalry," he added as anti-climax.

But it was more or less openly as priests that Fathers Walsh and Gallagher and their clerical co-workers of the Vatican Famine Relief Mission went to Russia. With them went shipments of food, clothing, and medical supplies. These came from the hearts of millions whom the Bolshevists had labeled "enemies."

The Poles, their country newly reunited after one hundred and twenty-five years of oppression by Austria, Germany, and the Czars, invaded only the summer before by Trotzky's Red Army, forgot deep-seated and, certainly justifiable, national hatred. In answer to Rome's call for Christian help, the people of Poland responded more generously than they could afford. Through four years of World War I, their farms and fields had been the shell-plowed battleground for the armies of Germany and Imperial Russia, their cities pulverized to brick dust. For months their men and even their young women had borne arms in the struggle to hurl back the invading forces of revolutionary Bolshevism. With their own country on the razor's edge between economic and political chaos, facing famine and starvation, the Poles gave freely. How ironic that they gave to bolster Bolshevism, to strengthen a tyranny that had publicly declared fanatic enmity not only against the very Christian principles which were to save Communism, but also against the freedom of Poland!

The Estonians, the Letts, the Lithuanians, and the Finns responded too. Like the Poles, they also had gained independence after generations of Russian domination. Since then they had had to battle Bolshevism to keep their freedom; for how short a time, they could not know.

101

Unrevised for three quarters of a century, the Communist collectivist theories of Marx, adopted by the men in Moscow, were directly responsible, along with the wars that had been fought for two years on a dozen fronts, for the famine that threatened the Bolshevists and their subject people. When quotas were arbitrarily set for farm production, all too often by incompetent politicians, the kulaks opposed them by raising only enough for their own use. This left the government short of food for the people of the cities and towns. Hundreds of thousands of acres were neglected and went to weed. Livestock was butchered to feed only those people who lived on the land. The peasants who were opposed to nationalization refused to bring in the grain harvests and neglected to store up winter fodder for the cattle, millions of head of which starved or froze to death in the long, hard winter of the famine.

Tradesmen and storekeepers, resenting the interference of politicians, opposing low quotas and confiscation of profits—in the guise of taxation—refused to cooperate in the planned distribution of foods. Railroad equipment had deteriorated because of war, lack of attention to upkeep, and failure of government management to understand the problems of scheduling, freight movements, and efficient operation. Food that was in government warehouses and storage depots rotted because it could not be moved in the paralysis of transport, or because of careless methods of food preservation.

"Lenin's legionnaires," that mob of misfits chosen to enforce collectivization, met the problem by bullying, strong-arming, punishing, and ranting. But loud words and terror could neither harvest food nor move it to distribution centers. Russia was starving, Bolshevism tottering.

Vanguard of the Roman Catholic units of the secret army —for it was largely upon their reports that the first call for the Russian work was issued—the Vatican Mission met with tactics which since have become so typical of our own experiences with Moscow. Badly needing the supplies sent for his people, Lenin hoped to get his hands on them for distribution in the name of the government. He thereupon resorted to stalling. The food, clothing, and medical supplies, awaiting shipment, would be given clearance under government priorities. But the personnel of the mission was to be subjected to delays, red tape, frontier waits, and official hocus-pocus concerned with visas. Let the supplies in, but keep the suppliers out, particularly since they were priests. That was the scheme.

Lenin and Trotzky, however, reckoned without Father Walsh. The Jesuit's job was to see that the supplies reached the needy and he was peculiarly single-minded about doing just that. So he insisted upon placing each trainload of supplies under supervision of a clerical lieutenant with instructions that the train was not to move unless the supervisor moved with it. Meanwhile, Father Gallagher did the diplomatic work by which the governments of countries through which the shipments were to pass promised to cooperate. They pledged that no train would be allowed over the frontiers until the passports of all Vatican personnel who were to accompany it were cleared. So the first priests of Rome to enter Russia since the Bolshevists had declared war on God went on a mission of Christian mercy.

Fathers Walsh and Gallagher, with the staff of the Famine Relief Mission, arrived in Russia almost simultaneously with the advent on the scene of members of the United States Commission on European Relief, directed by Herbert Hoover. The two missions acted in cooperation; the American organization, because of its superior size, pursued its work for the most part in the larger cities, while the smaller Vatican units operated in towns and semi-rural areas. This required the members of the Papal mission to travel quite extensively. Although they were admitted into Russia by the Moscow government, their reception by officials in outlying areas set a pattern which was to become familiar in nearly all subsequent Soviet dealings with representatives of foreign nations and organizations.

Whenever they distributed supplies sent by the Vatican,

103

Fathers Walsh and Gallagher and their clerical associates insisted on appearing in cassocks. At almost every station, their experiences were the same. Arriving with wagons or sledges loaded with food and clothing, the priests would be confronted by armed and uniformed police who would demand identity papers, passes, and credentials. There would follow a long session, usually at the local jail or police headquarters, in which some officious party appointee would minutely examine them. According to Father Gallagher, many officials he encountered were unable to read. All the same, Cheka agents would question them as to the places of their birth, their method of entry into Russia, whether they kept written records, their next destination, whether they had taught, preached, conducted masses, or administered any of the Sacraments during their journeying through Russia. They seemed particularly interested in whether the priests had heard confessions or performed marriages.

Such interviews invariably consumed two or three hours and were obviously designed as delaying tactics. Meanwhile, policemen would be inspecting the contents of their boxes, bales, and cartons, with an eye to minor pilfering. Thefts by police were of a petty nature, since a hungry populace, by this time impatient at the delay, were likely to be on the verge of violence and ready to direct it against the officials whom they held responsible for their empty stomachs.

It seemed as though the Communist authorities were following the same script, day after day. In practically every locality, they put on an almost identical performance that might have grown wearisome if it hadn't been so dangerous. No sooner had the distribution been completed and the supplies exhausted than a threatening crowd would begin to gather. Certain of its leaders would loudly start demanding food. Receiving none, they would launch scathing denunciations of the foreign priests, of religion, of God. Frenzied shouting would begin, the crowd surging and pressing in around the empty wagons and the surrounded priests. Stones

104

might be thrown or clubs wielded. Fights would break out, near rioting ensue.

At this point, to the rescue would come the police. Charging in with clubs or with bayonets fixed on rifles, they would shove the crowd around breaking through it to get to the embattled priests. The police would take the members of the Vatican mission into "protective custody" to prevent "riot and bloodshed, provoked by the foreign agents," as their official reports read. The clerics would then be locked up in jail "for their own protection from a people outraged by those who had come not to help, but to spy."

The Communist press played up these carefully engineered incidents. Protective custody might last anywhere from a few hours to several days, dependent upon the time necessary to delay and disorganize the work of the mission. In such instances, every precaution was taken by jail wardens and guards to prevent the priests from coming into close contact and communication with native Russian prisoners.

Yet, in spite of every preventive measure, the Roman Catholic religious were able to talk to hundreds, whose conversations and revelations were to be the basis of the first honest report to come out of Russia after the revolution. Its authors had nothing at stake and nothing to gain, either personally or religiously. Restoration of religion and worship would mean that the Orthodox Church, not the Roman, would embrace the millions who would return to Christianity. The report was a masterpiece of reserve, undramatic, conservative understatement, considering the character of the material.

The so-called "riots" were, of course, organized and directed by well-coached instigators of the Cheka, on orders of the Ministry of Information. Father Gallagher has recalled having seen the same "secret" agents among the crowds on several different occasions, at widely separated locales.

"It has always been easier to travel by channels other than official in Sovietized Russia," Father Gallagher has recalled.

"I should not say that I had ever traveled in what is loosely called 'the underground.' Let us say I got about incognito."

In addition to bringing relief, food, clothing, and medical supplies to more than one million six hundred thousand in Russia, Fathers Walsh and Gallagher also managed to travel "incognito" across wide expanses of famine-stricken Russia. Not only did they come into personal contact with the official attitude toward the religious, but they actually witnessed the desecration of churches. The two Jesuits were responsible, too, for obtaining documentation of hundreds of other cases of desecrations, of atrocities against the religious of all denominations and sects, not only among the clergy but also among the lay members of congregations and parishes.

Varying only in individual details, unofficial and, indeed, official reports of members of the American Relief Commission bore out the findings of those first Jesuits to go inside Bolshevist Russia. It was on the basis of such facts, learned from trusted associates, that Herbert Hoover, during his term as President of the United States, steadfastly and successfully opposed all pressure and propaganda by agents, apologists, and pleaders for the Russian cause to recognize the Bolshevist government of the Soviet.

It was the report to the General of the Society of Jesus in Rome, by Fathers Walsh, Gallagher and others of the Vatican Famine Relief Mission, that made Jesuits throughout the world determined to carry on the fight for the restoration of religion in Russia. They had experienced the anti-religious hatred and warfare that Lenin had declared against God. The Association of the Godless and the Union of Atheists were not hearsay to them. Those ruthlessly powerful, demi-official arms of political and spiritual oppression were far too real to the members of the mission who had encountered the leaders and their work all too often during the months in Russia.

This first of several reports which were to find their way to Rome in the succeeding five or six years was the foundation of the decision by Pope Pius XI, taken only after years of

106

study and research, to issue a "call" for volunteers "for the Russian work," as Father McGrath had phrased it in Barcelona. Not only did it stir members of the Jesuit Order, to whose leader it was originally addressed. It inspired Dominicans, Franciscans, secular priests, friars, and brothers, members of monastic orders, and laymen of the Roman Catholic faith to enlist in the battle for the soul of Russia. It listed the articles of war for the secret army in a spiritual struggle that may end in victory, sooner than even the most optimistic dare to hope.

The signs are to be seen in the satellites as in the Soviet Union itself. They are growing daily in the clarity with which they are visible. They have been brought into the light, out of the darkness of the Soviet Empire, by men of devotion, acting in concert with what they believe to be the will of the God of their faith.

10.

The Column of Judah

THERE CAN BE no question that the Jewish column
of the secret army was in existence in Russia many years before the revolution. Their battalions date back to the Czars
and the Cossacks and the pogroms which reached their depth
of depravity and bestiality in the last twenty years of the nineteenth century.

Any attempt to trace the part played by the Jewish resistance
in connection with the secret army results in a highly involved
picture. This is true because of the complexity of the history
of the Jews in underground movements. There have been many
such movements in many parts of the world. Perhaps it might
be more accurate to say that there has been only one, that it
began with the captivity and the exodus from Egypt toward
a national homeland, and that it has existed in some form in
many parts of the world ever since. From it have stemmed a
number of columns, each of which has resisted all who would
destroy their faith.

Wherever in the world there has been a ghetto, there has
been a Jewish spiritual resistance. In eastern Poland and western Russia, it dates back a score of generations. There is
neither the space nor the need to deal here in any detail with
the history of their religious persecution in Imperial Russia.
It is too well known to bear repetition.

Neither need we further chronicle their state in the Soviet

108

or in the satellites. Two scholarly studies have been made and published, under sponsorship of the American Jewish Committee, which supply unquestionable authority for the charges of an official anti-Semitic policy on the part of the Soviet Union. These works are *The Jews in the Soviet Union,* by Solomon Schwarz, and *The Jews in the Soviet Satellites,* a compilation of exhaustive research by Peter Meyer, Bernard D. Weinryb, Eugene Duschinsky, and Nicolas Sylvain. Both studies have become standard references for scholars, journalists, and lecturers on Soviet affairs.

It has been alleged by their enemies and detractors that because Karl Marx was a Jew, the people of Judah were leaders of the revolution in Russia. So were Christians, Orthodox, and Protestant. So were Moslems.

Never in Russian history have the Jews numbered more than 5 per cent of the population. In the annals of the Bolshevist revolution, try to find 5 per cent of its leaders who were Jewish. The nearest public library with newspaper files dating back to 1917 and carrying through 1922 will supply the information. The roster of the government hierarchy of today lists not *one* Jew of any prominence. The purges of Jewish scientists, musicians, artists, and writers of the early 1930's, the more recent shocking revelations, in 1953, of the trial of physicians and surgeons because of a "Jewish plot on the lives of Stalin and members of the Politburo" give substance to the charge that the Communists of the Soviet Union have carried on an unending campaign of anti-Semitism for more than thirty years.

The earliest biography of a hero of the secret army, which I have been able to piece together out of information gathered from several sources, is of one who fought single-handed, from the outset of the revolution in Russia. He was, assuredly, in the vanguard of the columns of Judah.

The history of "Rabbi Levitzky" illustrates how the religious operated underground in the early days of the revolution, when "God's Secret Army" could muster no more than a

109

heroic corporal's guard. A pseudonym is used to designate a man who died at the age of seventy-seven, in 1951, to protect those sons who are carrying on the fight he never gave up. Sentenced, at his advanced age, to fifteen years at hard labor in a lead mine in Siberia, the old man's great Jehovah mercifully commuted his sentence by death, before he had served a month.

Whether Rabbi Levitzky was originally a chaplain, an officer, or a soldier in the ranks of the Imperial Russian Army on Germany's eastern front in 1916 has not been learned. He was taken prisoner of war, however, and sent to a detention camp. There, in the confusion of processing several hundred prisoners, the German military authorities lost his papers, along with those of hundreds of others. It is not difficult to imagine how the Germans, who prided themselves upon their efficiency, could so hopelessly compound confusion into chaos—which, incidentally, was to save the rabbi for thirty years from the arrest he ultimately was to suffer. It was the fault of the interpreters. And no wonder! Russia is and always has been made up of diverse ethnic and linguistic groups with something like one hundred and fifty separate and distinct dialects and tongues.

Perhaps he heard, with high hopes for his native land, of the return of Lenin in 1917. There was no blackout of information between the two countries, even though Germany and Russia were still, technically, at war. The Germans were banking on Lenin, Zinoviev, and Trotzky to paralyze Russia's fighting potential by political, economic, and industrial chaos and revolution. They were right. The Kaiser had Lenin's word —for whatever it was worth—that he would make separate peace as soon as he gained power. Every scrap of news, rumor, and propaganda out of Russia was fed to the prisoners. They were jubilant at the prospect of going home to peace and to the tasks of helping to build a new Russia.

What that new Russia was to be, Rabbi Levitzky was soon

110

to learn. Since 1905, the Imperial Army had harbored a hard core of revolutionaries. Many of these were members of the People's Soviets. Although they had always been vocal, they now became officially important. They received special privileges from German Socialist comrades to whom administration of the Russian prisoners of war had been given over, as a wise political move on the part of the German Army command. New Russian prisoners, obviously "plants," spies, and partisans of the new order, began to turn up. These preached to their captive comrades the doctrines of the hatred of religion and of war against God.

A reticent man, Rabbi Levitzky kept his thoughts to himself. It was to be, he concluded, no more than the old-fashioned pogrom, of which he had had first-hand experience on more than one occasion. Only this was widening the pogrom to take in all who professed belief in any religion. Levitzky did not like it.

Wise in the way of the pogrom, he was also wise in the way of the underground, as were so many Jews in Imperial Russia as well as in Soviet Russia today. Instinctively, he felt that his people must, sooner or later, be singled out as scapegoats, as they had been for fifty centuries. With never a thought of forsaking either his calling, his faith, or his duty to his people, the forty-four-year-old rabbi determined to go underground when he returned to Russia. The news which came through—of the laws that were designed to rob the churches and synagogues of their property and the religious of their influence and leadership—only strengthened his resolve.

Soon after Lenin made a separate peace with the Kaiser's government, in March of 1918, Levitzky was processed out of the camp. Political commissars from Moscow had gone to Germany to help expedite the process. Temporary papers were issued all whose army identification had gone astray. These were issued on information supplied by the individual soldier. As his occupation, Levitzky gave "artist" which was true enough. To the question "Has any of your works hung in the

111

Imperial Museum?" he answered an honest "No." The questionnaire, which accompanied his newly issued papers, developed the absolutely factual information that he had been an illustrator for popular magazines, posters, and newspapers. Not one word was a lie. It was just that the rabbi neglected to mention his real calling, adopting his avocation as his vocation instead.

The talent his newly acquired identity implied thoroughly impressed the bureaucrats from Moscow. They made opinionated notations that were to come to official notice. These gained Levitzky a reputation as an artist that was to help elevate him highly in the esteem of the demi-literates of the Party. For more than a quarter of a century, this reputation was to mask his true activity in the religious resistance movement, in which he was to become a prime leader.

For exactly what reason it has never been determined, excepting that the Bolshevists needed an artist to publicize as a favored son, but Levitzky found himself, upon his return, a celebrated citizen. He was met at the railroad station in Moscow by the Deputy Commissar of Art and Literature in the Department of Public Education. His picture, to the rabbi's personal amusement, appeared in the public prints. This was dangerous, in a sense. For some former member of his congregation, turned Communist, might recognize and denounce him. However, it was fortuitous in another direction, since it served notice on his wife, two daughters, and three sons that he had gone underground and to proceed with caution in contacting him, a procedure not unusual with Jews who had survived the pogroms of old.

Established early in 1919 in a studio for which the government supplied light and heat, as well as maid service, the rabbi in disguise was commissioned to do a series of portraits for the consumption of the "bourgeois journals of the West." These were to be deliberately romanticized studies of Lenin which would depict the leader in characters completely false to him. To enlist the adoration of the "literati"—particularly of France

112

and the United States—Lenin was to be represented as a "burning poet and philosopher." For the more prosaic and pseudo-scientific mind of the Teuton and Anglo-Saxon of Germany and Britain, Ulyanov, alias Lenin, was to be depicted as a "practical economist and political scientist." There were to be studies of Lenin "the dreamer," "the mystic," "the thinker," "the Savior of his country," "the George Washington of his people," among others equally as phony and uncharacteristic.

To carry out his assignment, Levitzky was supplied with more than one hundred and fifty photographs of the dismally dull, but ruthlessly ambitious dictator. Lenin, apparently, was as enamored by the appearance of his undistinguished face as he was by the sound of his tiresome voice. There were to be no personal sittings. But each of the artist's efforts was to be passed upon by the great man, himself, before release by the Ministry of Information.

The bureaucrats, new to their jobs, but learning with an instinct typical of their breed, were enthusiastic about the assignment for all of a week. Then they went away and left Levitzky alone. The project and the masquerading rabbi were forgotten. Apparently, he was never expected to finish. For he was never held to any sort of contract and the first mention of the assignment that ever was made officially was during his trial, more than thirty years later! In the interim, his artistic career consisted of one assignment after another, few of which were ever completed; few of which, under government supervision of art and the finer things of national life, were ever expected to be completed.

A few months after his arrival in Moscow from Germany, Rabbi Levitzky performed his first *sub rosa* religious service. Happily, it was within his own family, the marriage ceremony for his eldest daughter. Only members of the family could be trusted to attend the secret rites. Less than a year after his return, he married under civil contract, the wife he had left to go to war, then officially accounted his widow, since he

113

was carried on the sketchy records of the army as "missing in action," under his real identity! With two sons, she came to live with the celebrated artist, whose interrupted family life was thus restored.

How Rabbi Levitzky was able to pursue his secret religious duties for three decades will probably never be explained. That he escaped detection is probably due to the comparative openness with which he operated. All too many of his colleagues, of the Christian as well as the Jewish faith, were apprehended in their underground activity within days, weeks, months at most. All those in the religious movement, which at the time of which I write had not yet grown into anything like an organization, are unanimous in praise of Rabbi Levitzky as a trusted friend and ally who never hesitated to give shelter, aid, or secret haven to a fugitive, to use his position and whatever influence he had on behalf of someone accused, or to put the safety and security of others above his own.

Throughout the years, he confirmed his people in their faith, circumcising their sons, conducting *Bar Mitzvah,* instructing the children in the great commandments that are their heritage, conducting marriage services, and presiding over the last rites for the dead of his congregation. With the passing of time, his influence extended far beyond Moscow. Only once was the artist-rabbi even suspected by the secret police.

It happened that for several Saturdays in succession, an informer noted that a number of children were entering the house that had been assigned to Levitzky. On a complaint, charging violation of the laws governing assembly, Cheka agents entered in the midst of a lesson on the Exodus from Egypt. What, demanded the uniformed policeman, was going on? The rabbi smiled, led the officers to a partially completed portrait of Lenin, "the father of his people." Pulling aside a covering, the painter revealed a picture of the leader, a benign expression on his usually inscrutable countenance, the light of understanding in his usually myopic and watery eyes, surrounded by happily beaming children. That his models had been those as-

114

sembled, there could be no doubt. The Cheka man removed his hat in the presence of such moving sentiment. Then bowing to the painter of the great, he took the informer roughly by the arm and rudely ushered him to the street. Rabbi Levitzky calmly continued the lesson where he had left off.

That so many persons could be aware of the artist's true but secret calling over so many years, without his being betrayed—particularly in Communist Russia—is almost beyond comprehension. When his arrest did come, Rabbi Levitzky brought it on himself in an open People's Court procedure.

It is not healthy to rise to the defense of anyone accused in the Soviet Union. The case in which Levitzky publicly involved himself on behalf of one unjustly brought to trial was minor. It involved no more than possession of excess food ration stamps. Since the old rabbi had given them out of his own allowance to the wife of the accused, he believed it no more than his duty to come forward and clear one whom he considered was the victim of injustice. From his thirty years of experience with the state, the old man might have known better. Perhaps he really didn't care what happened to him, so long as he served truth as he had throughout an honorable lifetime.

That the season in which the so-called "crime" was committed was that of Passover was, actually, coincidental. The People's Prosecutor, Koblenoff, a notorious anti-Semite, made much of the fact, however. Seizing the opportunity to sensationalize and thereby to enhance his own reputation, Koblenoff instructed the police to obtain a "confession" from the culprit whom Levitzky had dared to defend. Within two days, Koblenoff had what he wanted, a document implicating the proud, bearded ancient in a vast black-market operation, not a word of which was truth. Other witnesses, also accused falsely or with good reason, testified to Levitzky's leadership of the "gang" as the translation approximates.

Levitzky denied it all to the end but proudly pointed to the real work of his life which had gone on, undetected and unsuspected, through the years. To protect the reputation for omniscience and super-efficiency of Beria's security police, Koblenoff and the People's Justices chose to ignore the old man's revelations and scoffed at them as an attempted treasonable reflection upon the agencies of law enforcement. Rabbi Levitzky was sentenced as the ringleader in a black-market operation which was nonexistent, so far as he was concerned. Implicated with him were fifty-four others!

According to his eldest son, who made available Russian newspaper reports of the trial, it was the subsequent treatment to which Rabbi Levitzky was subjected to obtain information about his associates in the religious resistance, about which the security police have so long known, that brought about his death in the prison labor camp in a lead mine in Siberia.

To join the column of Jewish resistance that had existed for many decades before the revolution came a new element in the mid-1930's. It came from Germany. Actually it was delayed en route to the Soviet Union. With the persecutions of Hitler and the Nazis, a stream of Jewish *religious*—not political—refugees streamed over the border of Germany to the sanctuary of Poland. They had to get there by underground channels. Their own underground organizations on both sides of the border handled the flight. It was managed with the admirable efficiency that comes only with a well-integrated organization. There were few mistakes, little confusion. That was because their underground had been long established; the people were experienced and their leaders practiced.

In Poland, the German arm of the Jewish underground column merged with the Polish contingent. Its goal was the same as that which had sent their ancestors off into the wilderness with Moses—the search for the Promised Land. Only the terminology had been changed. The modern version was "nationalism" or "Zionism." I am expressing no opinion as to the ideological or political application of Zionism. I am merely

116

stating its force as a unifying factor in what had been, and would become again, a driving resistance force.

In Poland, the Jewish community, augmented by the religious refugees from the Nazis, had set up their own schools, published their own papers in their own languages—Hebrew as well as Yiddish—and centered their social life around the home and the synagogue. For a few years they lived in harmony with their fellow citizens, contributing to the economic and cultural life of the nation.

Came September 1, 1939. The Jews again became the object of a great Nazi manhunt. The underground went into gear. Again it was flight. The Jews of Warsaw and western Poland were on the move again, under cover once more, as they had been before, as their fathers had been in Egypt.

When the Russians moved in on eastern Poland, they offered asylum to the Jews—asylum to be bought at an eventual price the Jews had never in history consented to pay. The price was acceptance of atheism, abandonment of their national culture, renunciation of their heritage of independence, disavowal of their traditional individuality.

Within six months of extending the Jews haven from the Nazis, the Soviet Union decreed the closing of their schools, the suspension of their newspapers, the confiscation of their synagogues. They struck at the sacred institution of the Jewish family by decreeing civil-contract marriages. There had been Jews who, dazzled by what appeared at first flush to be a true refuge in the Soviet Union, had embraced Communism as a great political philosophy. But their enthusiasm was short-lived. When the Nazis made their about-face and turned the fury of blitzkrieg on Russia, the plight of those German Jews who were caught between the two fires was worse than anything their people had ever endured.

If they were taken in the advance of the Wehrmacht, they were executed as Russian spies or were sent to labor battalions as fugitives from the Reich and deserters from the German army. If they succeeded in escaping to territory in possession of the Red Army, German Jews were shot as German spies; Polish Jews were sent to labor battalions as alien fugitives.

The realistic among them took the historic course. They went underground in Russia as their people had in every trial they had faced since the captivity of Old Testament times.

Thousands have migrated to Israel. Other thousands have made their way into Scandinavia or back to West Germany. But, almost to a man, those who have remained in the U.S.S.R. are steadfast in their resistance on behalf of their God.

It is my conviction that every one among the hundreds of other leaders of the Jewish columns, the contemporaries of Levitzky as well as those operating today, is quite as heroic as the old artist. I have interviewed six. None would attract any special attention in a crowd, whether in Moscow or in New York. Yet, when they speak of their work for their people, it is almost as though the listener were in the presence of the prophets of old.

If those with whom I have spoken share anything in common, it is a modesty, far from false, which seems to prompt them all to minimize the parts they have played or are playing. They prefer to speak of others, particularly, of Moses Franck.

11.

A Joshua Rises

IT IS ALMOST impossible to be completely objective about Moses Franck. No movie hero has moved more swiftly or boldly across the screen of make-believe than this leader of a Jewish corps in the secret armies whirled across the map of Asiatic Russia.

As far as it has been possible to check information, his true name was Franck. Whether or not his given name was "Moses" is debatable. A more fitting one, certainly, could not be imagined, unless it would be "Joshua."

The story of Franck was told me by a man, active in Israeli official circles, who prefers that his name not be identified with the secret army. For convenience in telling the story, we will call him "Lustig." The story was repeated in essential details by three others at widely varying times and in widely separated localities. Lustig was in the Jewish national army and a close comrade of Franck when the latter was killed in action in Israel. Franck met death as he had faced life—violently fighting the foe of his people.

"I will have to start the story of Franck in Germany," Lustig explained. "It was as he told it to me on the battlefields of Palestine. Because his German background was preparation for the climax of his utterly fantastic, yet tragic career, I have to go back to a time that was roughly fifteen years before I met Franck. However, it also bears out the thesis of the col-

119

umns, as you call them, of the Jewish resistance that converged in Poland and Russia."

Moses Franck was one of those who never really knew childhood. Born in Frankfurt-on-the-Main, in 1921 or 1922, he was the son of the editor of a Yiddish newspaper. By the time he was ten years old, young Franck was a sturdy little street fighter. A Jewish boy had to be in the Germany of those days. But if he had to be tough in 1932, he had to be unbeatable in 1934. For self-protection, young Jewish boys gathered together in bands. Indeed the famous "Stern gang" of the lusty days of Zionist resistance to the British in Palestine sprang from just such beginnings.

When Franck was about fourteen or fifteen, he was arrested in a street fight. The police had hesitated to break it up until it was seen that the Jewish boys were getting the best of the fight. Franck was locked up in a local police station with a dozen or so of his comrades. It was a week or longer before influential Christian friends of his father were able to obtain his release.

A few months after the episode of the boy's arrest, his father ran afoul of the law, because of something he published in his newspaper. When her husband was sent away, the mother could not support herself and her son. The boy was "assigned" to a school supported by the state. It was no more than a low-grade reform school. There, all Franck's young mates were Jewish boys. For ten or twelve hours each day they sat at machines turning out shoes. In whatever free moments they might steal from the watchful eyes of guards, they plotted —plotted how to murder the guards, how to escape, plotted to join the underground, how to set up their own gangs.

In 1936, after two years in the reformatory, Moses Franck was "paroled." The reformatory had taught him a harsh philosophy. Anything could be bought in Nazi Germany. If you didn't have the money, you stole it from the Nazis, who had managed to grab so much wealth, even if you had to kill them in the process.

120

Moses Franck at the age of sixteen or seventeen was not yet a killer in fact—only in theory. But that stage was not to last long. His second or third night "home," Franck and a fellow-parolee made their first attack. It was in the dark streets outside a cafe, long after curfew for Jews. A big private car was parked nearby. The two young desperados crouched on the floor behind the front seat. When the owner and his lady friend returned to the car, they felt cords flicked around their throats. Deft hands went through the man's pockets, snatched the girl's purse and the necklace from around her neck. When the victims regained the consciousness that had been choked out of them by a slight tightening of the cords, the marauders were gone without having left a trace.

The two-boy operation gradually recruited members until there were soon four or five, and finally, as many as twenty. Each night they roamed the streets. It was jail if they were caught out after curfew, for all of them had served in some school or reformatory.

Lustig here interpolated a personal observation. "Unquestionably Franck had become a hardened, merciless man by the time he was eighteen years old. But strangely, from what I was able to judge from long conversations I had with him, Franck retained a strong moral sense. Although he had murdered thirty or forty men—he wasn't quite sure how many—Franck considered it war. He looked upon his campaign, in the city of half a million population on the Main, as a sort of guerilla action. As Franck told me one night when our Israeli outfit was scouting in the desert, 'It was no different than this. They wanted to kill us. They had declared war on us Jews. I wasn't waiting around for any Nazi to get me first.' "

From robbery and mugging, Franck and his gang graduated to the more dangerous and more rewarding field of train wrecking.

In stolen possessions which might have been convertible into cash, the gang grew rich. They had millions of marks' worth of stolen goods cached away in various secret storage

121

places around Frankfurt. But they were things no Jew could risk being caught with: dozens of women's fur coats; case-lots of dress shoes for men, women and children; hundreds of radios, automobile tires, and parts; high-quality silks and woolens by the bolt; typewriters, plated and sterling silver-ware, knives, and cutlery; anything that was portable by strong young backs and alert young minds with the ingenuity to figure out methods of transport.

The difficulty lay in disposing of their loot—even in quantities that were large enough to provide money for food. What canned or preserved foods they were able to steal they used up for their own immediate needs or distributed to relatives and friends of the Jewish community, practically all of whom were undernourished, while many faced starvation.

It didn't take any genius to figure out what to do. The freight yards were too closely watched and made the risk of raiding them too great for security. They had, therefore, to loot the cars *before* they got to the yards. Obviously they had to stop them on the outskirts of the city or in the country. They were amateurs, at first. Their method was crude. They piled ties or tree trunks or stones on the tracks and lay in the neighboring fields to wait for the crash. Unfortunately, the locomotive crews could spot such blockades and could stop the train in time to clear away the obstruction. Tearing up one section of track was more effective. But after the first few wrecks, track-walkers began patrolling the lines. Too often they would find the torn-up rails in time to warn the train crews.

The best way was to dynamite. It was easy to disguise or hide an explosive charge. Should soldiers or guards or track-walkers show up at an inopportune moment, a remote operator could hold the detonation. That made for greater safety and gave the young wreckers greater control.

Having decided to use explosives, Franck took on the job of studying up on the technicalities. He read everything he could find on the subject of the manufacture and use of dynamite. He studied and experimented with detonators and small charges. He had his boys steal batteries, wire, switches. They raided a dynamite storage shed at a nearby quarry and hauled away cases of explosives and detonator caps. They were in the train-wrecking business on a wholesale scale within a few months.

Franck apparently had self-confidence to an astounding degree and a most unrealistic faith in his own personal luck. But he had, instinctively, what trained soldiers learn in textbooks on military theory, responsibility for the safety and welfare of those who served under him. So while study was difficult and unnatural for him, Franck believed it was necessary for the protection of his band. Personally, Moses Franck was impulsive. As a leader, he stopped to think of his men first.

Some time in 1938, the police had gotten onto the gang's methods of operation. Those who were left—no more than a dozen—were being systematically hunted. The homes of their friends and relatives were being watched. They mutually agreed to break up and lay low for a while. That meant getting out of Frankfurt.

Franck admitted to Lustig that this was one point where his characteristic impulsiveness almost betrayed him. He needed money and was willing to take any risk to get it. In the breakup of the gang they had divided up the cached loot. In the years that they had been accumulating it, they had learned which "fences" were the least risky. One or two of the boys handled all such negotiations, which were not the sort of thing Franck did well himself. But in this case he decided to make his own arrangements.

At nightfall he had stolen a small lighter barge and had rowed it, with a few fellow-conspirators, to an abandoned dock. While he sneaked into the city to find a dealer in stolen goods, his friends loaded up the barge with Franck's share of the loot, for convenience of transport by the dealer.

Franck found a promising dealer, but while the man went to the safe in the store which adjoined his home, Franck had a slight feeling of unease. The fellow was gone long enough to call the police, but there was nothing Franck could do about it. He had stayed to keep an eye on the dealer's wife whom he trusted even less than he did the "fence."

When the old thief returned with the money, he led Franck out to the truck they were going to drive back to the river. All the way, Franck had a feeling that they were being "tailed" by a police car. At the barge, he took the dealer aboard, showed him the furs, textiles, shoes, and the rest of the loot. The "fence" haggled for a few moments. There were automobile headlights turning into the street which paralleled the river, when the dealer finally handed a sheaf of bills to Franck.

The young gang leader stuffed the bills into his pocket and dived over the side of the barge into the blackness of the river. The "fence" screamed for help from the police who were, even then, clumping along the rickety dock and onto the barge. Then he made the mistake of going over the side after Franck.

"Franck told me," Lustig recalled, "that he never knew a man to give up the fight for life with less of a struggle. His would-be betrayer clutched at Franck's hands that were pulling him down by the hair. The 'fence' never took another breath. The water was just deep enough for Franck to stand upon the lifeless body on the bottom while keeping his own nose above water. A man can drown quickly and quietly.

"Apparently the Gestapo men had run back to their car to get lights to search the river. Afraid that the body of the dealer would rise, Franck carefully and silently worked it back to the barge, hugging the shadow and the side, with a prayer that he could escape detection by staying within a foot of the spot where he'd gone in. His prayer was answered."

How Franck escaped from Germany and arrived in Warsaw cannot be chronicled in any detail or with accuracy, since few of the facts are known. Franck never told Lustig how he managed it, beyond the mention that he had been correct in the assumption that he could bribe his way out.

He said he had stayed in the besieged Polish city as long as he could. He had sniped at the Germans as they had come into Warsaw, which the Luftwaffe had first pulverized into brick dust. He remembered retreating along blasted streets and alleyways as the Nazis had closed in.

Once more Franck's phenomenal luck held out and he was able to escape the Nazis and make the one hundred miles, roughly, to Lublin. Lublin was in territory held by the Red Army, later to be the seat of a puppet Red regime, which Moscow tried to have recognized as the legitimate and representative government of Poland.

Franck believed in the representations made by the occupation officials as to the aims of Communism, the nonexistence of racial and religious prejudice in the Soviet Union and the apparently open enmity of Red Army soldiers against the Nazis. This, he said, was understandable in view of the development and outcome of the Spanish Civil War. What he could not understand was the alliance of Hitler and Stalin which opened the way to the Second World War.

There were, after his arrival in Lublin, no immediate moves that would dispel any hopes he and thousands of other Jewish refugees might have had of new, unhampered freedom in the proletarian paradise of the People's Republics. The disillusionment came about quite gradually.

The first move came in the schools. The Jewish schools were "re-constituted" and their curricula changed, as were those of the Catholic and Lutheran parochial schools. Teaching of religious ideology was replaced by the teaching of political ideology. In similar ways were other traditional institutions of Jewish life altered. Their newspapers were first censored, then regulated and restricted, and finally made an arm of the official propaganda.

When the imperialist policy of Moscow warmed beyond the "cold war" measures the Soviet had been pursuing in Poland and attempting to pursue in Finland, Franck soon found out what the new freedom really was.

The fight with Finland certainly altered the life of Moses Franck. He had not been a citizen of that severed sector of eastern Poland which was absorbed into the U.S.S.R. But he felt he owed the Soviet something for offering him refuge from the Nazis. He applied for admission papers to Russia. Although he was a stateless Jew he was given an identity card and permitted to travel to Leningrad. Denied his request to enlist in the Red Army, the young German explosions expert was assigned to a civilian labor unit and placed in charge of certain road building operations. He blasted the beds of some of the finest roads the Red Army ever retreated over, out of Finland. He also was assigned to destroying them, at times, to keep the Finns from using them. Because of his skill at demolition with explosives, he had become quite valuable to the Red Army. A few officers and Party members in Leningrad even let down the barriers of reserve they had learned to set up against foreigners. Then, overnight his status changed.

Germany attacked. He was considered a German national. A wave of hysterical suspicion swept over the Russian people. Every German Jew in their midst was a potential spy and saboteur. As a security measure, they were rounded up and put under arrest. Special labor companies were established under armed guards. Units made up of Jews were assigned the most dangerous sectors. If they were captured, it meant almost certain death by Nazi firing squads on the grounds that they were deserters from the German army. If they were not captured, it meant only a slower death from overwork, undernourishment, and starvation at the hands of their Russian jailers.

Franck was able to understand and even tolerate the attitude of the Russians. Many of the Jews *were* Germans. He said he didn't blame the Red Army officials for the precautions they took. It was war. War was something Moses Franck understood. He was strong enough to survive. He had enough ingenuity and enterprise to take care of himself. He was accustomed to hard living, short rations. Since he was a known ex-

126

plosive expert, he was under even sharper surveillance than his fellow-prisoners among the Jews. The Red Army couldn't take chances with a potential saboteur. He was shipped to the Minusinsk area and sent to work in the coal mines. From that district, roughly two thousand miles eastward of the Urals into Asiatic Russia and about three hundred and fifty miles north of the geographic boundary of Mongolia, came the coal which supplied the Trans-Siberian, Central Asiatic, and Turkistan-Siberian railroads. The mining of all strategic metals was stepped up sharply, but production in the coal mines was pressed to the utmost to feed not only the war-vital transport system but also the blast furnaces and factories.

No one in the Soviet Union, excepting possibly the Kremlin elite in Moscow, was particularly well fed during wartime. But if the citizens were hungry, the interned Germans faced daily starvation. And nearly a hundred per cent of the German civilian prisoners were German Jews.

Even though the work was hard—sixteen to eighteen hours a day was the usual stint—and the rations scanty, even though he was poorly clothed and lived in a sub-Arctic climate in unheated quarters in winter, Franck worked with all his will and physical strength. He reasoned that things would be different after the war.

"During the months that Franck spent in the Minusinsk fields and in the Kuzbas area," Lustig recalled, "he built up a tight little nucleus of half a dozen assistants. All were Jews but one, whose name Franck told me but which I have forgotten. I always think of him as 'Schultz.' Schultz had been a German Communist who had found it expedient to flee from Hitler for political reasons.

"Franck smiled, which he did rarely, when he told me about Schultz. If there was a greater Nazi-hater than Franck, it was Schultz. He it was, too, who kept Franck convinced that the political ideologies of Communism were sound and would achieve the 'great freedoms' when the war would be over."

Since there were spies and informers among the prisoners

127

at all times, Franck suspected Schultz at first. But although Schultz lectured his fellow prisoners on the doctrines of Marx and Lenin, he was to prove his loyalty to Franck in a way that cleared him of all suspicion. It happened one noonday when Franck and his crew came upon a party of guards eating their soup and bread in a room of a mine shaft. A coal car on the temporary narrow gauge had brought food in for all the guards below ground. This was its first stop.

Franck was never one to go hungry if he could take what he wanted from anyone in authority. Seeing the unguarded car of food, Franck moved swiftly, started it coasting and jumped on. His crew members grabbed places on other cars as they went past the stunned guards. In the darkness, Schultz was the only one the soldiers recognized. He was questioned closely, given the starvation treatment, solitary confinement, browbeating, and more than a bit of physical punishment but he would not tell who his accomplices had been.

Schultz was given some form of punishment every day for six or eight weeks. It came to an end late in 1942 when the directors of the Mining Trust in Moscow sent a directive to the managers of the Minusinsk operations to send all experienced explosives handlers to the Issyq Kul fields.

Issyq Kul is a vast lake in Kirghizstan. More than 5,000 feet high, it lies near the Tien Shan mountains, barely a hundred miles from the border of Sinkiang Province, China. In the pressing need for coal, the government was conducting explorations for new fields and were developing many like Issyq Kul that had proved uneconomic before.

After a 1200-mile journey that took seventeen days by rail and boat, Franck and his blasting crew arrived under guard and in the well-recognized uniforms of prisoners, at Przhevalsk near where a new camp had been established. There were approximately eleven hundred prisoners, of which more than four hundred were of German Jewish origin.

With victory in Europe, the prisoners were as exultant and triumphant as were the Soviet civilians. At last, Franck

128

thought, prompted by Schultz, the captivity would soon be at an end. The German Jews could take part in building a nation dedicated to brotherhood and freedom. The Soviet *needed* them to help rebuild a country that had been demoralized by war, physically demolished along its western borders.

The months went by. But no freedom. Having been an observer of the Red absorption of eastern Poland, five years earlier, Franck heard of the "liberation" of the Balkan countries with mixed feelings if no emotion. He distrusted politicians. Their slogans and catch phrases left him cold. His pessimism increased when he saw hundreds of new prisoners, mostly political, herded in by the boatload to take the places of those who had died. With the war no longer occupying all their energies, the politicians and the Party turned their attention to the religious again.

Once more the purifying atmosphere of the purge hung over Russia. One didn't have to be a mathematical genius to come to the conclusion that if five per cent of the population of the Soviet were of Jewish birth or ancestry, then the percentage of prisoners should not exceed that. But Franck could count for himself more than four hundred Jews in a camp whose roster had swelled to sixteen hundred names, more than the prison had held in wartime.

When Franck expressed his misgivings to Schultz, the ideological Socialist tried to reassure his friend that they would be out of there before they knew it. But the months dragged on to a year and into a second year.

"Moses Franck was a doer, rather than a talker," Lustig told me. "He also shared with the great leaders of history a capacity to inspire others to act with him, confident in his plans and his ability to carry them out.

"The man had a love of freedom. Up to then, it had been a love of his own personal, his individual, freedom. He'd always had to fight to stay alive. He hadn't thought much about others. He hadn't read a great deal. In fact, he read with some difficulty. Zionism, to him, was just a word. His father had

129

talked theoretically about a national homeland. But Moses Franck hadn't had much time to think about it, or do anything about it.

"Now, I know what your readers are likely to say about this. But I am bound to tell it to you as Franck told it to me. You can include it in your book or pass over it. That's up to you. Anyhow, Franck insisted that among a predominance of Jews, it was Schultz, a Christian, who inspired him with the idea and ideals of Zionism."

Schultz apparently was a man of wide experience, sympathetic understanding, and quite catholic tastes in reading and study. He was probably not a well-educated man in the formal sense. Perhaps he picked up his knowledge of the Zionist movement from the official Soviet newspapers, which were exploiting and distorting news of the trouble in Palestine in order to embarrass the British.

Schultz was apparently an eloquent talker. Franck listened to him and was inspired. For the first time in his life, Moses Franck had a vision of something beyond his next meal. It was typical of the man that, having been inspired, he should do something to translate that inspiration into action. And from such beginnings grew the most fantastic adventure of our generation.

Franck took only Schultz and one other of his assistants into his early confidence. So far as these lieutenants knew, they were preparing only for their own escape. Perhaps that is all that Franck had in mind at the time. It is conceivable that the ultimate mass escape just grew, step by step, as he went along. Whichever it was, it in no way detracts from what he was able to accomplish.

Schultz was a reluctant conspirator at first, according to Franck. But once he had entered into the plot, he was an invaluable ally. Since few of their Russian overseers could speak German, they often called upon Schultz to act as interpreter of their orders to the German prisoners. They also knew him to have been a Communist in the Reich and he continued to give lectures on Marxist ideology that were a regular part of the camp's "cultural" program. So he was a comparatively trusted prisoner.

Franck needed arms and ammunition to carry out his escape plot. Both he and Schultz knew it was impossible to get them by overpowering the guards. Around the barbed wire-enclosed compounds where the prisoners spent their non-working hours, which were few enough, there were sentries with machine guns. Though he was fearless, Franck was neither foolish nor reckless enough to entertain any quixotic tactic, such as rushing the machine gun posts. Even so, the odds were ten thousand to one against the plan he worked out.

The capital of the Kirghiz state is Frunze, a city of some thirty-five thousand population. Frunze is situated on a branch of the Central Asiatic Railway, less than seventy-five miles from the western end of Issyq Kul where the branch terminates. Frunze was the administrative center for the newly developed coal fields on the shores of the lake. It was from the capital that the camp guards were assigned for tours of duty every six months.

With the change of guard personnel in October of 1946, luck played its only part in Franck's plans. M. V. Streloff, the new project manager, was out to make a reputation for himself. Soon after his arrival, he questioned Schultz as to the possible location of new, unexploited veins in the surrounding area. The German reported that the former manager had done some exploration at the southwestern extremity of the lake. This information had not been in the routine report the departing manager had left for his successor. Streloff undoubtedly reasoned that here was opportunity. Had there been *no* coal, it would have been noted in the report. Since there was no mention of the exploration, then the absent manager must have discovered something, intending to develop it and take the credit for it himself, when he returned after furlough. So worked the devious politician's mind of Streloff.

The results of Schultz' tip to Streloff were not long in

131

bringing a swift change. A special exploration party of some dozen men, including Franck and Schultz, was sent to the southwestern end of Issyq Kul, a few miles south of the terminus of the branch rail line from Frunze. There they built temporary barracks to house themselves and five guards.

The survey party was even more successful than Streloff had hoped. There was evidence of a rich vein, exceptionally close to the surface and only a few miles to the south of the end of the spur rail line. Streloff lost no time. He moved in a battalion of workmen. They cleared away the timber and, as early as January, began digging in the hard frozen earth to sink the original shaft. Men were cheaper than machines.

By the beginning of February, his new camp numbered nearly four hundred captive workers. A score or so were women. They worked alongside the men even when they were pregnant, which was almost constantly.

By February, the Jewish population of the temporary camp numbered about sixty. Besides Schultz and Franck, only one other member of the original explosives crew had been transferred. For several weeks the three stored away dynamite, a stick or two at a time. This was dangerous for a number of reasons. To begin with, it required false requisitions. Explosives were doled out for one job at a time. Any experienced explosives man can pretty well tell, to within half a stick of dynamite, how much is required for any blast. It would have been impossible for Franck to be allotted, say, ten sticks and use only five. He had to plan carefully and it took a real knowledge of his job to know when and how much could be held out and hidden.

Since there were regular inspections and searches, there was always the risk that hiding places would be discovered. Discovery would have brought swift, punitive action. Worse than any punishment they might receive, however, was the certainty that discovery of stolen dynamite would have brought an end to Franck's secret project.

It was just about March when Franck had his plans fully

132

worked out in his mind. Only then did he fully confide them to Schultz.

"Certainly it was a bold plan," Lustig recounted. "Schultz called it suicide."

The camp was situated between the spur line out of Frunze and another to the south, which led to Leninabad and which joined the main line of the Central Asiatic Railway at Samarkand. The entire distance was under two hundred miles. It was forested and snowbound for much of the year, but Franck had it all worked out. They would wait until early in May, when the guard detail would be sent relief from Frunze. Since they couldn't take the guards on duty at camp by surprise, they would have to take those who were coming to relieve them by blasting the Frunze rail line.

The camp guards would be getting ready to go home and, if they followed the tradition Franck had noted over the years he'd been there, would probably be drunk. It shouldn't be difficult for three or four prisoners to steal away in the night.

They would blast the train sky high. They also would wreck the telegraph lines to Frunze and to Przhevalsk. The boat that sailed Issyq Kul was marked for destruction, too, so that news of what had happened would be delayed long enough to give the escapers a start, possibly even as much as two days.

It was Franck's plan to blast the train so that there was little chance than anyone on it would survive. Then the blastmen would close in, take the uniforms of dead or dying guards, arm themselves and return to camp. They should be able to get up to the gates before the camp guards learned of the wreck. The guards, preparing to leave, would undoubtedly be gathered into a group, half of them drunk. It would be comparatively easy to disarm them.

With the guards out of the way, they would arm a chosen group of prisoners to keep order among the others. Then a contingent of their fellows would race back to the scene of the wreck, get all remaining uniforms, papers, guns, and ammunition, and return.

133

With perhaps fifty armed men, they would then head for the southern spur to Leninabad. Equipped with uniforms, arms, and official papers, they might be able to bluff their way, possibly even beyond Samarkand.

Franck now revealed the maddest, boldest, most insane part of his scheme. He was, he informed, Schultz, going to take all of the Jews who wanted to go. And he was going to lead them to Palestine! His route would take him to the hills that bordered Iran. They ought to be able to bluff their way that far. If not, they could fight their way.

Did Franck have any idea how far that was? Schultz asked. No? Well, it was probably no less than one thousand miles! And suppose he got into Iran. Iran was a Moslem country. It had never been hospitable to Jews at any time, let alone now when they were, theoretically if not actually, at war with the Jews in Zion. It would be a trek of eight hundred miles across an unfriendly Iran and another four hundred across Moslem Iraq before they were even close to Palestine. By the most direct route, no less than three thousand miles! Had Moses Franck gone crazy? He could count Schultz out of any such insane scheme.

Franck argued that it was worth any sort of gamble. It was better than staying there in Siberia as slaves. He was tired of waiting for the freedom Schultz had promised was coming.

Schultz stayed away from Franck for a week or ten days. He was seen in the manager's office more and more frequently. Franck confessed that he was afraid Schultz might betray him, but one day, Schultz knelt beside him at work in the mine as he placed a charge. "I have been studying geography on the globe in the director's office. I've used some pretty thin excuses to get in there," he informed Franck. "Your strategy is good. But your geography is bad. I am more convinced than ever you can't possibly be sane and try to get through all that Moslem territory with a company of armed Jews. It will be hard enough here in the Soviet Union. But at least here you have some chance, with the uniforms, of

134

getting by for three or four days. But I have worked out a travel plan I think might succeed. It might even get us all to Palestine. At least *out* of the U.S.S.R. and *not* into Moslem country."

Schultz knelt in the dark passage and drew with a stick on the dirt of the floor. For the first time in months, Franck smiled.

For the next few weeks, Franck and Schultz carefully picked out the key men around whom the escape scheme was to pivot. Schultz was designated to remain behind in the camp to lead the internal attack on the guards on E-Day, as they designated it.

Not all whom they chose for essential jobs were Jews. Two of Schultz' assistants were non-Jews who had elected to take part in the adventure and to go wherever destiny and Franck's leadership took them. So was one of the blasters upon whom the success of the whole plot hinged.

There were now ten or twelve men on the inside of the plot. The more they took in, the greater the danger of detection became.

It was the second week in April when a circumstance arose that almost wrecked all their plans. A new group of prisoners was transferred from the Przhevalsk area to the camp at the western end of the lake. With them came several new guards. Among the prisoners were some forty or fifty more Jews.

Schultz protested to Franck that the plan to escape might have to be abandoned. There were too many guards, now, for three or four armed men to handle. As for taking all the Jewish population of the camp, it was absolutely insane. The original idea of escaping with fifty to sixty was mad enough. But a hundred or more!

"Moses Franck had made up his mind," Lustig went on. "And once he'd decided on a course of action, nothing could turn him aside. He told Schultz that the more who escaped, the more could help fight their way to their destination. As for the added guards, it was no more dangerous to take thirty than it was to take twenty. He intended going through with it.

"But there was not a chance of keeping their scheme a secret if they had to let a hundred or more in on it, Schultz persisted. In answer to that, Franck now revealed that he had no intention of letting *any* of them in on the secret. He had decided that there was no reason to tell them until the moment they were faced with the accomplished fact that Franck and his lieutenants were actually in command of the camp. That would be plenty of time. At the moment, there were possibly ten or a dozen men in on the plot. There would be no others until they had either succeeded or failed. Then, if all the prisoners wanted to go with him, they could, and they would be welcome."

If Schultz' confidence ever wavered, it must have been at that moment. All possible odds were against them. Schultz was convinced there were not nearly sufficient explosives to blast the train, telegraph communications, and the lake boat, even if the four blasters were able to get beyond the barbed wire and past the guards. Schultz lived with such doubts up until the early morning hours of E-Day when swift action supplanted worry and bold decision wiped out hesitation and fear.

By the third week in April, it had become known through the grapevine that the date for the transfer of guards was set for the first day of May. This was a circumstance that definitely favored the plotters. Since May Day was celebrated as a national holiday, it pretty well assured Franck and Schultz that not only would the retiring guard garrison be celebrating, but so, also, would their relief.

Frunze, where the new guard detail was coming from, was less than a hundred miles from the Issyq Kul terminus of the northerly rail line. Ordinarily, this was a journey of six to eight hours. The train was scheduled to arrive between eight and ten o'clock in the morning. Schedules meant little on Russian railroads, particularly in Asia. Franck suspected that the train might be anywhere from two to five hours late. Every moment of delay would lessen chances of success.

136

At midnight on April 30, Franck and Schultz went over their plans for the last time. After the leader and his fellow blasters had left, it would be up to Schultz to delay discovery of their absence for as long as possible. Meanwhile, starting at two-thirty, Franck and his trio of assistants were to make their way along the mud ruts, only recently thawed of winter freeze, to their destination.

When the hour for their departure drew near, Franck and his three fellow-saboteurs stole out into the darkness of the inner compound. Lights blazed in the buildings that housed the convict-guards in the second circle of barbed wire. Beyond that, the men who stole tensely through the darkness could see an occasional silhouette against the windows of the civilian guard barracks and the residence of the director. Flickering oil lamplight slow-leaked from the portholes of the machine-gun posts.

They crouched in the compound for perhaps ten minutes until their eyes and ears became accustomed to the dark. Then, slowly, Franck began the long, painful belly-crawl across the compound toward the barbed wire.

There were four machine-gun guard posts, at intervals of about 150 to 200 feet, in a semicircle. Each post commanded the entrance to a prisoners' barrack. They were numbered from three through six. The middle posts, numbers four and five, were opposite the two barracks to which Franck and his three helpers were assigned.

Franck crawled toward post number four. One minute later, a companion started for number five. Then the third man followed Franck, while the last one crawled to post five.

Suddenly, from the barrack at the end of the semicircle, there were sounds of screaming and cursing. The door burst open and two battling figures spilled out into the compound. The gun of post three was immediately trained on the door and the rectangle of pale light that streamed from it. The gun of number four, where Franck and his companion lay close enough almost to touch it, was swung in the direction to sup-

137

plement number three with a crossfire. Franck and his partner rolled quickly and silently beneath the lower strand of wire, and crawled furiously toward the second ring of wire.

The door of the barrack, opposite post six, also swung open and curious heads thrust themselves out to determine what the disturbance was all about. For by this time, whistles were being blown and half-tipsy guards were swearing and shouting throughout the compound. Machine guns in posts five and six were turned on the second barracks. Not a sound nor a light came from the two middle barracks. So long as the guards were occupied elsewhere, there was no chance that Franck and his men would be missed.

As the guns of post five swung to give crossfire support to post six, the second pair of prisoners skinned under the wire to follow Franck.

The second ring of the compound was easier. The four converged on the northwest gate. There, they simply fell in at the rear of a guard squad that was marching toward the outer gate. The escapers were not even noticed in the light of the lantern carried by the noncommissioned officer in charge. Halfway between the northwest and main gates, all four dropped silently to the ground, lay still in the darkness for a few minutes and then rolled out into the road ruts that paralleled the fence.

Outside the compound, there was still much to be done. First, they made their way cautiously to the mine shaft where their dynamite was hidden away. Afraid to use lights, they had to grope through the darkness. As Franck and two of his crew stole into the mine, the fourth stood guard.

There were no interruptions as the explosives were loaded onto a coal handcar and hauled up in the elevator, operated manually by a hoist rope.

It was only three-fifteen when they had everything above ground. They loaded the stolen and carefully hoarded explosives into three gunny sacks and caps, batteries and wire into a fourth.

138

It was eight or ten miles from the camp to the terminus where railroad and boat joined at the western end of Issyq Kul, a place which was not even dignified by a name. In addition to the necessity for traveling without lights, the conspirators were handicapped by two added factors. They did not know more than the general direction of their goal. Neither could they risk reaching it by road, where they might encounter celebrating guards returning to the camp. So with their heavy sacks over their backs, they trudged and stumbled through the pine woods that bordered the unpaved, unlighted roadway.

No more than a mile or so from the prison camp, a Red Army command car came careening along the road from the mine with lights blazing. All that the escapees could do was to pray that their absence had not been discovered. They prayed too for the arrival of the train at a time somewhere close to the flexible schedule, give or take an hour or two.

Packing their heavy loads over difficult terrain at about five thousand feet altitude, the quartet of prisoners staggered on through the night. The eight or so miles consumed nearly three hours.

It was light, almost six-thirty, when they made out the silhouettes of the train shed, wooden coal storage shacks, and the steamer at the rickety dock. This was their first real chance to survey the job that lay ahead of them. Franck looked it over with an experienced and eager eye.

One of the little band was going to have to take a chance crossing the clearing that lay between the woods and the dock. There was no way out of it. Three of them could skirt the houses and barracks by the woods, cut around south of the tracks, and proceed a mile or so along the rail line where they would set their charge. Time was short. If the train was on schedule, they had little more than an hour to work.

It was the steamer that presented the greatest danger. How to get to it without a challenge, how to board it, set a charge, run a line back to the batteries, all without being detected, were the problems.

"A lesser leader than Franck might have assigned the complicated task to his best lieutenant," Lustig said. "Or he might have called for a volunteer, or drawn straws. The train was their more important target; the boat was the more dangerous. He assigned *himself* the boat-blasting job. It was characteristic of him that he did. The others he sent hurrying through the woods bordering the rail line."

Already, a uniformed man was moving about the deck of the boat. No one had yet appeared on shore. Franck judged that all of the free civilians, guards, officials, and sailors had celebrated the eve of May Day aboard the boat. If they had made a big night of it, he assumed that most of them would be sleeping it off. He decided to approach boldly, and, if challenged, to try to bluff it through—a rather difficult job for one with almost no Russian, obviously a prisoner, and a German.

Franck filled his shirt with sticks of dynamite, his pockets with caps, and hung a reel of about one hundred and fifty feet of wire over his shoulder. He carried his batteries boldly up to a coal shed, which he judged was about the length of his wire from the boat. He managed to hide them in the shed and to stride out onto the dock before he was detected.

The deck watch commanded him to halt. Franck looked into the barrel of what he well recognized as a German army luger. He made a great show of searching his pockets for his green prisoner's ticket which he finally produced with an explanation in heavily accented Russian and about three-quarters German that he was to be transferred back to Przhevalsk and had come aboard to wait for sailing time.

The watchman snatched the wire from Franck's shoulder and moved in for a routine search. It was here, said Franck, that his usual luck held out.

A woman saved Moses Franck that May Day morning. As the deck officer started to search him, a frowzy brunette in a dirty cotton nightgown staggered out of the deck cabin

140

in bare feet. She tottered to the rail, leaned over the side and was violently, retchingly ill. The deck watch turned, tucking his pistol into his belt, marched to her side and gallantly stood holding her head.

Things began to happen even more swiftly than Franck had hoped—or feared. The officer shouted instructions to him to get below. A second officer appeared from the cabin and shoved Franck in the direction of the engine room. The lieutenant of the camp guards was aboard, the prisoner was informed. When the officer woke up, they'd check on the story of the transfer.

In the crew's quarters, Franck found everyone soddenly sleeping off the effects of the night before. He explored the engine room without challenge. With swift decision, he picked a spot just aft of the steam boilers to set his charge. He worked swiftly, his deft hands stringing together a charge that was heavy enough to blow a fleet sky high. It was Franck's plan to wait, if he had the opportunity, until he heard the blast which would mean that his companions had disposed of the train.

With his wire gone, he'd have to use a live fuse. It was dangerous but there was no help for it. All he could hope was that he could get away before the boat went up.

There was no interruption of his work. He had the dynamite neatly concealed under a pile of coal and was laying out the fuse when the deck watch came down the ladder with the lieutenant of camp guards.

"Franck decided it was no time to be waiting around," Lustig went on. "He wasn't the sort of man to weigh the pros and cons before he went into action.

"Franck took the initiative away from the officers, not with talk or explanations but by deeds. He instinctively knew the moment to move.

"He swooped down and lighted the length of fuse. From his crouch he charged into the lieutenant who fell back onto

141

the deck officer. Franck said that he heard shouts and commands but he never knew what they were.

"He bolted out of the engine room, up the ladder onto the deck. He ran to the stern which was away from the dock. He remembered seeing the woman who had been sick. She was sprawled on the deck, passed out. Franck sped past her, cleared the rail in a running dive and hit the water.

"He swam as far as he could under water and came up, possibly twenty-five or thirty yards away. He figured he had half a minute or so to put distance between himself and the doomed boat. He watched over his shoulder as he swam furiously.

"It was fascinating to him to watch for the destruction he expected any second.

" 'It was curiously peaceful,' he told me. 'Nobody came on deck. I don't know what the lieutenant and the deck officer were doing down there. Whatever it was, they failed to kill the fuse. Suddenly the old hulk lifted out of the water. It seemed to hang in air before the explosion burst it apart.

" 'The deck cabin blew forty or fifty feet straight up. Then it broke into a thousand pieces of flying siding that flew and fell like the arms of a wooden fountain. A heavy plank fell and hit me in the shoulder. Just then, a second blast split the sinking hull. It was probably the boilers. The force of it in the water carried me under. It knocked me out for a moment. When I came to, my shoulder was paining more than anything I had ever known. But somehow I was still swimming toward the shore to the south of where the coal sheds stood.'

"There was panic on shore," Lustig continued from notes he had made after Franck's death, intending that his friend's story should one day be published, as it is here for the first time.

"Perhaps a dozen or so guards and soldiers, completely at a loss without officers to command them, were running madly about or were just standing and staring uncomprehendingly

142

at the wreckage. The concussion had knocked some of the rickety coal sheds down. Oil lamps had been overturned, apparently, and their flames had set the old wooden shacks ablaze.

"Franck made the shore below the spur rail line and dashed into the pine woods undetected. The growing pain in his shoulder began to numb his mind as well as his muscles. He ran along in a daze, trusting to his luck that he would find his three partners."

He staggered and stumbled through the woods for possibly a mile and a half beyond the lake. More afraid of losing his way in the unfamiliar woods than of being overtaken by pursuers, he cut to the rail line. Only half-sensible, he ran along the ties.

Dimly he was aware that the train was later than they had feared it might be. Where his men were or where they had placed the blast, he couldn't know. Suddenly, around a bend in the tracks he heard the train coming. He instinctively dived for the woods and ran for cover. It was only a matter of seconds. On a slight downgrade, the train was rolling at an unusual clip.

Franck was no more than fifty feet from the track when it happened. The engine was exploded right off the tracks. Franck ducked his head into his arms as he waited the shock of the concussion he knew would follow. It beat against his ears. He could feel tremors run through the earth he was hugging. He heard the grinding, screeching crunch of steel and wood, the hiss of steam and the crashing of cars that piled up on those in front.

He waited a minute or so for survivors of the train to appear. When they didn't, he got up and carefully stole back to the tracks. It was too soon.

There was a second explosion, followed by a third and a fourth. A pole, supporting telegraph wires beside him, cracked. Franck hit the ground and blacked out.

143

Back at camp, after Franck and the three blasters had succeeded in getting out of the compound, the guards had rushed into the inner circle of barbed wire to quell the fighting which had broken out in the two end barracks. When order had been restored, a check of prisoners in the two barracks was made, while Schultz watched silently in one of the others.

Somewhere between four o'clock and four-thirty, one of Schultz' barrack-mates, a known informer, slipped out the side door of the building. One of the conspirators who were in on the plot followed him.

In a couple of minutes the man was back with a report that the informer had been let out of the inner compound by the guard at the lower machine-gun post. Schultz knew what that meant. There would be a check within minutes, unless he did something to forestall it. Franck's absence would be discovered. Someone who was in on the plot would crack under threats of punishment and would confess the details. The only chance now lay in a scheme Schultz had had in mind for weeks. He hadn't revealed it even to Franck.

Speedily, Schultz ordered every man out of his bunk and into a line at the center door. Working swiftly, he ordered a fellow-conspirator to help him pile bunks and straw mattresses into the center of the building. Then, he stood looking out through a crack in the boards of the wooden wall.

Five minutes, ten, fifteen ticked away. Schultz grinned to himself in the darkness. Every minute's delay was in their favor. Then, he saw light from the guard barrack, as the door opened and half a dozen uniformed men tumbled and staggered out.

They lined up in lantern light and started marching raggedly toward the machine-gun post opposite the central barracks. Schultz threw two oil lamps that provided illumination onto the pile of straw. The pile of beds and plank tables, dry as tinder, were in roaring flame in a matter of seconds. He sent the line of prisoners out into the night. Thoroughly frightened

144

and surprised, they added to the confusion of the fire by shouting and screaming.

Schultz was the last one out. By this time, the entire barrack was in flames. From the other three buildings of the inner compound, prisoners ran out and joined the milling mob. The guards rushed in shouting orders, trying to organize the prisoners into fire-fighting units. It was confusion compounded by chaos and pandemonium.

The wind helped their cause. Sparks from the pineboard building were carried to a nearby outhouse, which was soon blazing dangerously.

Because of improper care, the fire hoses had rotted and cracked, and water leaked from holes in a hundred places. There wasn't enough pressure to force more than a trickle through the nozzles.

Suddenly, the roof of the guard barrack was ablaze. The prisoners were turned into the second ring of wire to fight this fire that threatened the administration center.

For more than two and a half hours the excitement of the fire absorbed the attention of both guards and prisoners, giving Franck and his blasters precious time and preventing discovery of their absence. When the guards had restored enough order to line the prisoners up for a roll call, the absence of the quartet was discovered. Schultz told a sad story of their heroic death, trying to fight the fire—a story well supported by evidence supplied by his fellow-conspirators. They prepared affidavits to this effect to be turned over to the relieving guard captain.

It was more than an hour before Franck regained consciousness. His lieutenants had found him under the pole and had pulled him out. They told him how, when they reached the train, they had found half a dozen guards alive but too stunned or injured to offer any resistance. The trio of escapees had spent half an hour at the scene, ripping uniforms from the dead and wounded, loading guns and ammunition into a small coal car which had been not too badly damaged in the blast,

145

and which they had gotten back onto the track ahead of the wrecked engine.

The few guards and soldiers who had lived through the train wreck wouldn't give them any trouble. They'd been finished off with their own guns.

Only a few hundred yards from the docks, the escapees saw a dozen guards, thoroughly frightened by the blasting of the boat as well as by the sounds of the explosions from up the track and demoralized by the absence of commissioned officers, starting to get a handcar under way.

The prisoner who was disguised as the relieving guard officer took command of the situation. He issued orders for a weapons carrier, a command car, and a jeep. He briefed the frightened guards on what had happened on the railway line, officiously adding that he was holding them responsible in the report he was sending to Moscow. Right now the important thing was for him to get to the camp without losing a moment. He had captured the prisoner—pointing to Franck—and wasn't letting him out of sight. He wanted all guards ready to receive orders immediately.

Within five minutes, the twelve or fifteen remaining guards were rounded up. The masquerading commander mounted a machine-gun carrier. The guards presented arms—and he mowed them down with no more mercy than he had seen their kind show for prisoners on many an occasion before. The prisoners stripped the uniforms from their victims and loaded the cars with arms and ammunition.

On the road back to camp, Franck fully regained consciousness which had come and gone fleetingly since the train blast. It was nearly noon. Smoke hung heavily over the woods, increasing in density, the closer they got to camp. As they drove up to the gate, they were appalled at the destruction they saw. The camp guards were lined up along the barbed wire that separated the inner compound from the second. Each had a rifle in his hands. The machine guns were turned toward the lineup of prisoners in the inner compound. There

146

was only one guard at the main gate. On the shouted order from the false commander he opened the gate, snapped to salute as the three cars rolled inside.

Before the real guards knew what had hit them, the gun carrier had gone to the end of the outer compound, had turned and sped along the line of barbed wire. With its mounted gun spurting lead, the carrier, now driven by Franck, plowed through the secondary street between the two lanes of wire.

Unable to fathom where the attack was coming from, the gunners in the posts, which were open in the rear, didn't know where to direct their fire. Within seconds, they were dead.

A handful of guards who had been inside their barracks began screaming for mercy while their commander waved a white flag out the windows of the administration building.

The ten or twelve other prisoners who had been let in on the plot by Franck and Schultz were soon armed and restoring order among their fellow-prisoners inside the compound. In Polish, German, and Russian, Franck and his co-plotters explained the plan to deliver the Jews in a body, but inviting all who wanted to go, whether Jew, Christian or Moslem.

There were approximately one hundred and twenty uniforms, which were given out to those who the leaders believed would be dependable in a fight. Those who did not have uniforms and guns were to give strength to the story agreed upon, that the guards were transferring a community of prisoners back to European Russia to work in the timberlands of Karelia. The leaders took over the administration center and its small armory. In addition to the three cars they already had, they took over five coal trucks, seven Red Army jeeps that had been obtained via American lend-lease, three Dodge touring cars, and two more command cars. The trucks they loaded down with everything that would hold gasoline. They rifled the guard commissary of bread, cheese, liquor, and canned goods which none of the prisoners had even seen for months.

"That they took time to prepare as carefully as possible," Lustig volunteered, "was certainly to the credit of Franck and

147

Schultz as leaders. That they took no longer and were able to organize a mob of more than four hundred into some semblance of an ordered group was also on the credit side. By four o'clock in the afternoon they were ready for their flight.

"Yes, I know I said it earlier that Franck delivered about one hundred Jews out of Asia," Lustig explained in answer to a question. "But there were also Christians and Moslems. Leaders came forward for the two latter groups.

"There was strength in numbers, they all agreed, particularly so long as they were still inside the U.S.S.R. They would join forces until they reached the borders of the Soviet Union. Once within reach of safety, when military strength would not further their cause, they would split up.

"So, just before sunset, one of the strangest cavalcades that could be imagined started south and westward away from Issyq Kul.

"For one of the few times in his life, Moses Franck thought about God. He decided that God was with them and offered a silent prayer of thanksgiving as he marched at the head of the column of his people, leading them, possibly, to death— but out of slavery."

12.

The Exodus

UP TO THIS POINT in the chronicle of Moses Franck and his activities, those from whom I have obtained information, in addition to or in verification of Lustig's, are generally agreed on the important facts as they have been set down. They are at variance only as to details. From here on, there are also certain minor points of departure. One lies in the estimates of the numerical strength of the strangely assorted army of escapees.

Franck himself was vague on the subject of numbers. This is unusual since he was accustomed to thinking in terms of military strength, according to Lustig who soldiered with him. Furthermore, Franck was to lead them for the succeeding thirty-two days. It is strange that he could not name them all from memory.

Lustig says he never pressed his friend on such details. "I assume, from what Franck told me, that there was a group numbering about one hundred. He was quite definite that fourteen died or were killed on the way."

A series of three letters from a member of the escape party mentions that the Jewish group, augmented by four or five Christians, totaled "between one hundred and fifty and one hundred and seventy five." The letters were written from Madrid, in January and February of 1950, by the escapee to an uncle in Berlin. The latter, who operates in the Jewish col-

149

umn of the religious underground in East Germany, is a rabbi and one of three who supplied information, not only on Moses Franck but also on other and more routine activities of the resistance.

Since we have, so far, relied upon Lustig's notes, we will accept his figures which apply only to the Jewish contingent. Franck had already put the census of the camp at between four hundred and fifty and five hundred prisoners. The non-convict guard detail (civilian) numbered twenty five to thirty, it is assumed. Lustig also stated the Jewish escapees appropriated about forty uniforms. The remainder later went to the Christians and Moslems when their paths parted.

Franck's injured shoulder pained him badly. He also had caught cold from the exposure in his soaked clothing, and he was in semi-delirium for days, with alternate chills and fever.

Schultz had warned the leader against too free distribution of their arms and ammunition. In the arsenal they had appropriated were possibly fifty rifles and half a dozen machine-guns. As a precaution, they armed another twenty men besides themselves. The remaining weapons they distributed among the trucks. Each truck was supplied with a guard.

Franck's success at every point in planning and executing the mass escape was certainly an endorsement of his qualities of leadership. But before the liberation was an hour old, his authority was challenged—by a woman!

In a separate small compound, removed from the barracks by perhaps fifty yards, were the quarters of the fourteen or fifteen female prisoners who were assigned to clerical, kitchen, and other tasks in the camp. With between four hundred or five hundred sex-starved men released from all discipline and rules—so they believed—the liberation of the women threatened to turn into an orgy. Screaming and laughing hysterically, half a hundred men stormed for the women's quarters. Schultz halted them with orders and threats backed up by a machine-gun.

There were angry curses at the newly appointed leadership.

Franck went to reinforce his friend. One of his young lieutenants, who had been armed among the first, fired at the leader. Franck turned in cold fury, and shot his would-be murderer in the chest.

The men, who had so long lived in subservience and fear, fell back in disorder. This was the moment Franck seized to issue orders and a warning. He would lock them all up in the compound and leave them there to await the arrival of the avenging authorities, unless there were obedience and discipline. They reacted with docility, the habit of months, of years, reasserting itself.

For hours, throughout all the excitement and activity, the women had been in a frenzy. Some had torn off their clothing and were dancing and posturing in a madness of exhibitionism and hysteria. They were singing and shouting obscenities. One among them who was a known informer had been stripped and hurled repeatedly against the barbed wire and, finally, had been tied to the topmost strand by her hair. There she dangled, a pitifully sobbing, tortured thing, crying for mercy. A group of perhaps three or four knelt in prayer.

Schultz commanded order before he would open the gates. They only howled and wailed the louder, sang and danced the more wildly. Franck went to cut the informer from the wire. He was still on the outside. As he hacked at the poor woman's hair with a knife, one of the naked dancers came at him with a club, beating at his head and hands, screeching foul names at him.

Quietly, calmly, Franck went to the gate. Schultz warned him against going in before order had been restored. But Moses Franck had his own ideas about establishing order. Covered by Schultz with an automatic rifle, Franck entered the women's compound. He realized that if he failed here, he could never lead these people.

Except for the one screaming woman, there was a strange silence over the camp for a moment. As though drawn by a telepathic magnet, the crowd of milling men surged toward the barbed wire surrounding the women's compound. Franck walked slowly toward the woman who was mocking him and making obscene gestures in her nakedness. For a moment, she stood, exaggeratedly grinding her hips in front of him. As he reached to take her arm, she moved suddenly and snatched the pistol he had in the holster which had belonged to a guard officer on the train. She backed away with the gun aimed at Franck's stomach. He followed her three or four steps.

Suddenly, from outside the barbed wire, a deep voice was raised, calmly singing a hymn in Polish. The voices of other men took it up. All the women joined in half a dozen different tongues. Those who didn't know the words just sang the melody or hummed.

Franck followed the woman with the pistol for a half a dozen more steps. She sobbed once, dropped to her knees with both hands pressing the trigger. There was a shot. Blood spread in a spurt against the leg of Franck's uniform at the thigh.

The sound of the shot cut off the singing as suddenly as it had started. There was a hush. Franck leaned over and took the pistol from the limp hands from which it now sagged. He turned to one of the women who had earlier been praying. "Take care of her," he said quietly.

As the nude woman was led away, Franck turned to face the men he had freed. "Will someone please show us how to pray?" he asked in a quiet tone.

Heads were bowed, some men and women sank to their knees. A former Orthodox priest raised his voice in a prayer of thanksgiving for their liberation.

"In that moment, I think," Lustig said, "Moses Franck showed the rare quality of truly great leadership. Had he ever been able to live in a world at peace, I am convinced that he would somehow have made a great mark."

Franck's wound was in the flesh of the thigh, burning but not painful enough to keep him out of action. Added to the developing cold and the injured shoulder, however, it con-

152

tributed to the fever that made him only half aware of what was happening.

Probably with the able assistance of Schultz, he kept the early organization of the party moving at a brisk clip. The trucks were loaded. Just an hour or so before sunset, the column got under way. A handful elected to stay behind and take their chances with the authorities, rather than to set out on the uncertainties of flight. These were chiefly the old and the infirm—and the craven.

There were five women, three with small children, among Franck's party. They rode on the trucks and cars. There was no further mention ever made by Franck about the woman who had shot him. Presumably she was left behind.

The Jewish contingent under Franck's leadership led the way. Schultz and an Estonian priest of the Roman faith led the group of Christians which was the largest. The Moslems, under a young Georgian, brought up the rear. The marchers of each column set the pace. The trucks followed. Up ahead of the whole motley army, acting as outriders or scouts, went the command car and the jeeps.

In the matter of the drivers, Franck and Schultz took realistic measures to insure their transport. Traveling in an official car, a uniformed man might easily get the understandable urge to take off and leave the slow-moving hikers. To remove such temptation, it was ruled that each driver must wear prison clothes. That way he was safe only as long as he stayed with the escapees where he had a fighting chance for freedom.

At the pace they were traveling, there was no need for lights when darkness fell. The mountain roads were little more than trails through the woods. Although it was May, the night turned bitterly cold as they headed eastward.

They were going in the direction of Naryn, a village some twenty-five miles from Issyq Kul. By midnight, the shivering columns had covered well over half the distance. About six miles from Naryn, they halted behind a hill which shielded

153

the light of the one small fire which Franck permitted them to build.

No soldier likes to be without intelligence as to the enemy. Franck was no exception. Had the alarm gone out? Had their flight yet been discovered? Were the authorities everywhere on the alert for them?

Schultz volunteered to enter the town to scout out the situation. He took the Orthodox priest who had led them in prayer, for Schultz' accent might give him away. Dressed as officers, they climbed into the command car and whirled down the bumpy road toward Naryn.

It was just after dawn when Schultz and the priest returned. The escape had been discovered late the night before. When the telegraph lines to Alma Ata, 50 miles north of Issyq Kul, had gone dead, no undue suspicion had been aroused, for breakdown of communication in that part of Siberia was not unusual. But when there had been no restoration of service by noon, and it was learned that Frunze also had had no word for several hours from Issyq Kul, nor had Przhevalsk, administration center for the mining area at the western extremity of the lake, it began to dawn on the official minds that all might not be well.

It was fortunate for the escapees that it was May Day, and the official celebrations were on. The parades and oratory delayed investigation until evening. From Alma Ata went an automobile load of police. A boat was sent across the 50-odd miles of the lake to investigate the delay in the arrival of the guard relief at Przhevalsk. The railroad administration in Frunze sent a couple of handcars full of men along the spur line to Issyq Kul.

Not until sometime after midnight were they able to rig temporary tie-in lines to the telegraph wires to Frunze to relay information about what had happened.

Schultz and the priest learned that all rail points and roads were to be watched, particularly those leading east. Reinforcements of police were being sent to all accessible border points.

Red Air Force scout planes would converge on the area to scan all possible routes of escape and to hunt the fugitives from the sky. Moscow was expected to offer a huge reward to any police, army unit, or individual aiding in apprehension and capture of the escapees. News of the escape, broadcast on the official police wavelengths only, was not to be made public—a decision of the Information Ministry for reasons of "public security policy."

Franck, Schultz, and the priest decided also on the basis of "security policy" not to reveal to their people the news that the escape had been discovered so early. All hope for using the railroad had to be abandoned. The nearest spur point to Naryn was 100 miles west. Even if they made it, the railroad would lead them to Samarkand. This was away from the border. From Naryn, Schultz estimated, they were probably less than 100 miles, possibly little more than 50, from the border of Sinkiang Province, China.

While his original decision had been to rely upon numbers for safety, Franck now saw the dangers inherent in so large a group as that which he commanded. There were conflicting elements. Certain of the Moslems and Christians, only a few hours after their liberation, had already begun to show signs of anti-Semitism. He realized that soon they would be questioning his leadership. Already friction had begun to generate a heat dangerously near to flaring into rebellion. Franck called his lieutenants into a council.

The young Moslem leader, a native of Turkmenistan, had been formulating a plan for his own followers. The best chance for the Moslem people lay in dispersal, rather than in maintaining a group. They were in friendly country. Their own people would take them in. The Moslem leader quite frankly told the Christians and Jews that there was little hope they would find either refuge or welcome in that part of the country. Particularly was this true if the government were to offer rewards.

Even more frankly he pointed out the dangers and difficul-

155

ties of turning south to the Sinkiang border. There, the peaks rose 16,000 to 20,000 feet. To travel in them was a challenge to mountain people, and certainly no place to take an unorganized army of undernourished, ill-clothed, and ill-shod men —not to mention the women and children.

Nor were there any roads fit for motor transport, the Moslem pointed out. Whatever provisions they were able to take they would have to carry. In Sinkiang, too, whomever they might encounter would likely be unfriendly Mohammedan tribesmen. They would, therefore, need arms and ammunition. Even in midsummer, the temperature in the Tien Shan dropped below freezing and the fugitives were certainly physically unfit to withstand the hardships of both hunger and exposure, in addition to the tortuous travel.

Schultz and the Orthodox priest surveyed the situation as it applied to the Christian contingent. Schultz rebelled at the idea of leaving Franck. He had been concerned from the beginning of the plot only with the escape of Franck and himself. He saw no reason why they should part now, simply because Franck and the priest thought the Christians would profit by his leadership.

It was then that the priest came forward with the first inkling that either Schultz or Franck had ever had of the existence of a religious underground movement. All the while he had been at Issyq Kul, the priest had kept contact with the Orthodox column of the secret army!

At Talass, to the north, they could get help. With as many as 250, however, chances of success seemed very slim. The sturdy priest proposed splitting the group in half, on the basis of the physical and health conditions of the individuals. Those who were stronger would turn south with Franck and him, while Schultz would take the weaker to Talass.

Talass, the priest judged, was 150 to 200 miles north, through fairly passable mountain terrain. Anticipating that the fugitives would head for the border, the authorities would likely not be looking for them in the opposite direction. With

God's help and the trucks, they might make it in, say, twelve hours, when it would be dark. At Talass, maybe his friends in the underground could take care of possibly one hundred fugitives a week, obtaining false papers, credentials, and orders.

Although the council took no longer than an hour, the people were growing restive and fearful. There were grumblings and complaints of hunger. Somehow, the Moslems had learned that they were to go it on their own. Many of them were impatient, demanding a split of the food, supplies, cars, and particularly the arms and ammunition.

Schultz, Franck, the young Moslem, and the priest went back among the ranks to restore order.

Franck called his people together apart from the Christians and the Moslems. He explained the necessity for breaking up. When he told them the decision of the Mohammedans among them, there was noticeable relief. When he explained the priest's plan to divide the remaining group, regardless of religion, into two groups, there were protests. Franck had expected them. He knew the age-old instinct of his race to face their trials together. He knew the urge of his people for concerted action in spite of their characteristic personal individuality.

They had, Franck explained, to make a choice: To go south into the mountains with him, or to subscribe to the priest's plan to be divided. He would let them make the choice, although it could not be an individual choice. They must decide as a group. They had ten minutes to talk it over, not argue, and to choose.

Franck left them to supervise the division of supplies and arms. The Christians already were complaining about the probability that some of them would have to go south with Franck, against their wills. Like some men about to be drafted, several were already developing symptoms of incurable physical disability. Others were contesting the amount of rations and arms that was going to the Moslems. Schultz and the young

157

Mohammedan leader were handling the quarrelsome ones with their fists and the butts of their pistols.

When Franck returned to his people, he found them bickering and arguing. Ordering silence, he demanded a vote. It was unanimous. Every hand rose on the proposition not to divide the group. The same held for the proposition of heading south with him—their goal, India! Eventually, perhaps, Palestine if their mighty God were with them as He was with their fathers in Egypt.

No more than an hour and a half after sunrise, Moses Franck marched into the mountains and the unknown to the south. He had neither map nor compass. He had only an insatiable desire to be free, and a people with varying degrees of faith in their God.

With Frank went the command car and one truck. The jeep had gone to the Moslems and the remaining trucks to the Christians. Schultz and Franck had had to enforce the division of transport with the threat of their guns. Even the young Mohammedan leader had complained at awarding the priest's people the four trucks.

They set their course by the sun. Two who had gone on the train- and boat-wrecking expedition with him assumed the responsibility of acting as lieutenants. The first day, eager to put as much distance as possible between themselves and the scene of their unhappy imprisonment and escape, they traveled at a fairly respectable rate. The terrain, although constantly rising in altitude as they progressed southward, aided them. For it was pine forested, but growing more sparsely so as they ascended.

It is possible that, before nightfall, they covered a dozen miles. If anything, the vehicles slowed their pace, since they were following nothing more than a path. They were safe enough from contact with any sort of a force at night. It was unlikely that even troops would travel the increasingly precipitous trails after dark. Night-flying airplanes could be heard

158

when they were miles away, time enough to let them put out the one fire that Franck permitted them to cook their food. Possibly 40 miles lay between them and the boundary of Sinkiang.

The second day, the trails became steeper, the atmosphere more rarified, the trees sparser. Those in poor health found more difficulty going on. At noon, the sound of an airplane, which Franck had been expecting, was heard. Every member of the column threw himself to the ground and lay there motionless while the plane cruised in seemingly endless circles for perhaps half an hour. Although it was the third of May, it was bitterly cold and they were chilled through in the ragged prison clothing. Even those with guard uniforms were stiff with cold.

Soon after noon, they abandoned the command car. The truck had been left behind several hours before. Franck who had been riding, in a state of semiconsciousness, took to the trail again, carrying an extra heavy part of the added burden of food, in spite of his injured shoulder and lame leg. Late in the afternoon, they were climbing above the scrub timberline. They could see the cruel snowline stretching above and beyond.

The third day they had what the superstitious among them considered an omen. One of Franck's young assistants had gone ahead, as he did whenever the group approached the top of a rise or peak, to scout what lay on the other side. It was craggy, snow covered, and treacherous. Franck watched from a few hundred yards away. Several minutes later, when the lieutenant did not reappear to signal the column forward, Franck sensed trouble. Quickly he scrambled up the icy slopes in the footsteps of his scout.

At the top, there was vast silence. The lieutenant had disappeared. Instinctively, without seeing the evidence, Franck knew what had happened. He found a wide crevice that opened a dark icy void to the east of the trail. Against a protruding boulder lay a rifle. The marks where it had skidded over the

159

snow told the story. The young scout had slipped and fallen to his death.

Next morning Franck began to experience trouble with stragglers. Many, to ease the pain of their travel, were abandoning their food and supplies. Only threats that they would be left behind to die unless they kept up the pace could move them to make an effort.

Their fourth day on the trail was given over to resting and taking stock of the situation. Ahead lay towering peaks of discouragement and despair.

Hardly one among the fugitives had a shoe that was whole. Poor stuff at best when they had been issued at the prison camp, most of the shoes had been well worn before they started. Those with boots, which they had stolen or had taken from the guards, cut the tops from them to repair others which were farthest gone. Many cut rags from their clothing and wrapped them around their feet.

It is strange what unsuspected talents come to the fore in the stress of common danger. Among the younger members was a former student of medicine. He had never before seen fit to reveal that part of his past. He had hesitated to give medical aid at the camp since he had, as he now stressed, never been licensed to practice. The Communist grab of the Baltic Republics and his arrest had interrupted his education in Riga. Lack of confidence had prevented him from asserting himself as a practitioner. But he now came forward to aid an elderly doctor who was treating Franck's leg and shoulder.

Between the two medically trained members and a woman who had once been a nurse in Germany, they were able to look after the health of their comrades. They were limited in what they could accomplish by the lack of more than the bare necessities of rudimentary first aid which was all that had been available in the quarters of the camp guards. The three were busy the whole day of rest, ministering to the needs of their fellows.

A former cobbler took over direction of shoe repairing.

160

Franck found this artisan a very useful subordinate who had a bantering way and inexhaustible good humor. He was most successful at bringing up the rear of the column and keeping stragglers moving. According to this man's own story, he had been not only a cobbler but also a sailor, a gambler, a convicted robber in Poland, a printer's helper, carpenter, and circus acrobat.

Although this jack of all trades wore an outward air of humorous optimism, he had few illusions concerning the ultimate success of their flight. Like Franck, he believed in luck and in his own ability to take care of himself. As for the group, he thought it foolhardy to attempt their adventure with more than a handful of the most able and resourceful. But he was willing to go as far as he could without jeopardizing his own chances. Every minute, he told Franck, lessened those chances. He doubted, for example, that they had progressed as much as 20 miles beyond Naryn. He further felt that it was disaster to spend a day resting, but realized that it was a necessity for the old, the weak, and the ailing as well as for Franck who needed the time to pull together some sort of an organization.

They took a chance with a fire. A hot meal from the canned stores of the guard commissary was a must for morale. But whatever morale the day and night of rest built up was dissipated the next morning. After the frigid night and just before dawn, a mountain blizzard swirled in on them. In the wind-whipped snow it was impossible to continue their flight over the dangerous unknown trails.

The uncertainty of the few grew into doubt and fear of the many. There were whining and grumbling, complaints and accusations against Franck. He had taken them from the comparative security of the camp into the greater discomfort and danger of the mountains. God had forsaken them. Ahead could lie only pain and death. If they would only turn back, they would take their chances with the prison authorities.

The loudest and least talented of the rebellious faction

161

boasted that he would lead all who elected to return. The cobbler counseled Franck to let them go. They should be free to choose to go back to slavery, if they preferred the security which the prison represented, to the gamble which the road to freedom symbolized.

Schultz was no fool, the brash, mouthy spokesman for the dissidents taunted Franck. He had seen where safety lay. Schultz hadn't entrusted his safety to Franck's hands. Schultz had had the good sense to get out while he could. It was probable that Franck's best friend was, at that very moment, safe and warm and well fed and sheltered a couple of hundred miles nearer to freedom than any of the poor Jews would ever be.

Weary with all the words, sicker with the defeat he foresaw than with the pain and fever in his body, Franck turned into the blizzard and limped half a mile or so back along the trail that they had come.

Coincidence plays a far stronger role in the dramas of real life than in fiction.

"What happened then," Lustig commented, "could hardly be called 'coincidence.' For it just didn't happen without plan. To Franck it certainly was a surprise. Perhaps 'unexpected' is the best term.

"For out of the storm, with the wind at his back, came the wearily trudging figure of Schultz!"

Since Schultz had planned to overtake and rejoin his friend, it was no coincidence that they met. It was the timing of his arrival that was in the realm of the coincidental.

Franck did not exult over those who had opposed him. He merely returned to his people with his friend and co-leader.

Their mood changed in an instant. They crowded around Schultz who told them how he had seen both the Christians and the Moslems safely on their ways and then had followed to overtake his friend. Their trail had not been hard to follow, once he had reached the snowline. The abandoned truck, the

162

jeep, the empty cans, and the ashes of their fires had all been signposts along the way they had come.

Behind them lay danger of pursuit from Naryn. For the evidences of the gathering of some five hundred people in the hills before the city were clear to anyone who happened upon the place. They would have to move fast. At the abandoned truck, the resourceful Schultz had paused long enough to magnetize a needle with the current from the battery. They would no longer be groping blindly, since he had constructed a makeshift compass to guide them.

Almost with his arrival, as though it were an omen, the storm had died down. Now, just before noon, they were able to travel once again. After all the dissension, not one chose to return.

The boost in morale which the return of Schultz had brought carried them through the next two days. Progress, however, was slower. For now they were traveling at an altitude that averaged nearly 15,000 feet, where exertion of any sort is painful. There was no ordered formation. They straggled and struggled rather than marched. At times, Franck estimated, they were strung out more than two miles from the front to the rear of the column.

For the completely unprepared fugitives who had lived on prison fare for years, whose health had been ignored, whose spirits had been broken by imprisonment, this trek across the pitiless peaks was a triumph of leadership, shared by Franck, Schultz, the cobbler, and half a dozen others who had risen under the stress of danger and the demands of necessity. Their only climbing aids were improvised out of a few short lengths of rope and several hundred feet of electrical wire. By boosting, pushing, pulling, hauling with the rope and wire, they managed to scale the unavoidable faces, although they scouted for passes or traversed the peaks wherever it was possible.

By the end of the first week, Schultz estimated they had progressed possibly 35 to 40 miles. They had altered their course to south-southeast. Schultz and Franck figured they

163

should cross the boundary into Sinkiang by the ninth day. They congratulated themselves on the single casualty to date —the lieutenant who had fallen into the crevasse.

Their seventh night in the mountains was the worst from the standpoint of weather. The skies were clear but the wind was high and piercing. The temperature was well below freezing. The caution about fires had to be relaxed. A dozen fires blazed like beacons and were reflected by the snows. Around them gathered the shivering refugees, most of them in tattered prison uniforms, hatless, and with boots and shoes now beyond repair.

Their feet were torn and swollen. They were weak with exposure and fatigue, since only the youngest and healthiest could sleep for more than a few minutes at a time in the sharp cold. They were beginning to feel the results of the daily hunger that was largely their own fault. Because in spite of warnings and threats, many had abandoned their burdens of supplies, while others had disregarded the rations and had eaten more than the allowance set by Franck.

The morning of the eighth day brought new but not unforeseen trouble. An epidemic, probably influenza, struck down more than twenty of the party. All that could be done for the fever-stricken was to wrap them in the woolen coats of those who had guard uniforms, move them close to the huge fire that had to be built, and administer what the young medical student called "the water treatment." This consisted of melting snow and dosing each patient with all the water it was possible for him to hold.

The theory was that this would flush him out and with it, possibly, the infecting germ or virus. The result in all too many cases was wracking vomiting and retching that soon had their campsite a vile, evil-smelling, germ-infected surface cesspool, in which the two doctors, and twenty volunteers worked to ease the suffering and the agony of the stricken.

Unable to move his pitiable little army, Franck organized two scout parties. The first, under his leadership, would recon-

164

noiter ahead. The second, under Schultz, would scout back along the route they had come, to learn, if possible, whether they were being pursued.

Both parties were gone all day. Franck's was the first to return. They brought good news: Ahead to the southeast, maybe six hours' journey for the entire column, lay a vast plateau. It stretched to the farthest horizon that could be seen from surrounding peaks. The plateau was sparsely forested with scrub pine, which would offer some shelter after the open exposure of the denuded peaks around and over which they had been struggling. The flatness of its surface would make for greater speed of travel—as much, perhaps, as ten or twelve miles a day.

Franck became concerned when Schultz did not return by nightfall. Posting lookouts on surrounding heights, he took ten of the youngest men, armed them, and went to find his aide.

Fast and mobile, in comparison to the cumbersome column, with its old, its sick, its weak, and its four women, the small detachment retraced the trail of a whole day's march in three hours. Near nine o'clock Franck, in the lead, slowed cautiously and then halted his men with a hushed command. He had seen a pinpoint of light flicker on the trail before him and then black out.

The group waited tensely in the darkness for the stealthy footsteps they could hear coming up the path that had been left in the snow by the trampling bloody feet of the fugitive army. Then a form Franck recognized even in the blackness loomed up and halted—Schultz. He signalled silence and whispered a command to follow him.

Half a mile farther along the back trail, Franck saw the cause for all the caution. There at the distance of about a mile, flamed four campfires. Looking down, he could distinguish the silhouettes of a dozen soldiers moving about among four or five tents. Quickly, in a whisper, for sounds

165

carry and are magnified by the echo in the mountains, Schultz briefed Franck:

His party had been about to turn back in late afternoon when they had spotted the column of soldiers coming up the trail. He had counted twenty-five armed men. Knowing that Franck would come to find him when he did not return, Schultz had staked out his men in ambush, against the possibility that the Russians might continue their pursuit after sunset.

Franck smiled at the suggestion of an ambush. With the prospect of "real action," as he phrased it to Lustig, after the idleness of the day and the snail's pace of his column, the leader was happy again. This was more to his liking than herding his people along in their tiresome march.

Swiftly, Franck figured all the elements in the plan that flashed into his mind. It would take a couple of men possibly four hours to get back to the main body. Two fresh men could return in another four hours, allowing for the night travel, making it roughly five o'clock in the morning. That would give him an hour and a half, two hours with luck. It should be enough.

A couple of volunteers started out. Franck and Schultz explored the trail in the dark, the captain explaining his tactic to the lieutenant. Schultz grinned in the dark, relishing the anticipation of the action to come.

It was nearly six o'clock and there were stirrings in the Russian camp before the two new men from the main column returned. They joined the others on watch over the pursuing enemy, while Franck and Schultz went feverishly to work a quarter of a mile or so up the trail. Every few minutes, one of the fifteen men on watch would carry a bulletin to his leaders. The Russians were gathered about the fires at breakfast. Now they were striking their tents, dousing the fires. They were packing up, forming for inspection. Now they are marching out. No more than half an hour left.

Schultz hurried back to his men, ordered them to withdraw. They scrambled back up the trail, past where Franck was

166

making a final checkup. The men deployed and waited on their bellies for the coming of the Russians, taking shelter behind rocks and mounds of snow.

Schultz was grinning, Franck was steely-eyed with a snarl on his lips as they watched the approaching soldiers. On they came. Franck's men were nervous, tense, uncertain. Fingers trembled dangerously around triggers. Schultz turned and made a ludicrous face at his men. They grinned in return and relaxed.

The Russians came on, puffing, grunting, cursing, perspiring in their heavy woolen overcoats in spite of the chill.

Not fifty feet from where Franck lay, the young lieutenant in command of the soldiers halted, brusquely barked an order at the stragglers, re-formed his detachment in closer formation. When all was in military order again, he turned and shouted the order to march. Excepting for his death cries a moment later, that was the last sound he ever uttered.

A detonation that sounded like a thousand explosions roared and reverberated among the peaks. The side of the mountain to the right of the soldiers bulged out crazily, then hung as if suspended in air for a split instant. The thunder of tons of rock and snow, falling from a hundred feet above their heads, echoed through the peaks and crags, drowning out the screams of death and terror. Grotesquely tumbling arms and legs were whirled up in the madly flooding avalanche of rock that careened and rumbled down the mountain, gathering momentum as it rolled.

Franck's men watched in fascinated horror. To the leader it was just one more necessary, nasty job in the war for freedom and survival that he'd had to fight all his life.

"Franck said he had no feelings whatever about it, excepting satisfaction that he had gotten them before they had a chance to get him," Lustig elaborated. "In many ways he was a very primitive sort of person, as you probably have gathered long before this.

"It was completely in character for Franck to blast the

167

avalanche down onto the Russians without bothering to tell any of his men excepting Schultz. I doubt that he would have told Schultz, excepting that Franck needed help and only his lieutenant was qualified to give it to him. Otherwise, he unquestionably would have let Schultz figure it out for himself, as he did the men, even the two who had returned with the dynamite, batteries, and wire.

"Once having made up his mind to a course of action, Franck went ahead with it. He hated debates and had little faith in talkers."

Although the influenza was at its worst when Franck and his men returned to camp by noon that day, he insisted that those who were capable of moving go on to the plateau. He had reasons for this, too, yet he didn't think it was necessary to tell even Schultz. To begin with, he felt it was bad for morale to allow his followers to sit about and listen to the grumblers. The sight of the plateau, after the mountains, might hearten them. And, finally, he figured that nomads undoubtedly inhabited the plateau, not in sufficient numbers to be a threat, and that his people might find a couple of stray goats or sheep which would serve as much-needed food.

Twenty-four stricken members were left behind with a dozen more, including the nurse and doctors, to look after them. The other seventy-odd pressed onward. They reached the plateau near midnight, finding a cheery fire awaiting them and in a circle around the fire, patches of green grass between piles of rock.

The morning of the tenth day, Franck ordered scrub pine cut to make stretchers to carry the sick. Twenty young men started back for the sick camp to bring the epidemic victims to the plateau. By late afternoon, they were back with ten of the least ailing who were lodged in a rough pine lean-to which had been set up to shelter them.

Again the next day, the stretcher-bearers went over the trail. But it was too late. The last seven who remained at the old camp had died in the night.

168

The cobbler, who seemed to know a little of everything, conducted a funeral service from memory and ceremoniously covered the bodies with snow, rocks, and loose earth.

On the plateau throughout the day, eager, willing hands had pitched into the task of building a crude Tabernacle in the middle of the space that had been set aside for the encampment. Although it was built of pine boughs instead of the traditional silks and material of the Tabernacle that accompanied the children of Israel in the wilderness, the sight of it worked an almost miraculous change in the spirit of the people. It lifted them up. It put reverent pride in their steps as they went about their tasks in the camp. Shoulders that had sagged through their days of trial and through months of captivity squared with a new purpose.

With the natural flair of their race for the dramatic and the poetic, the fugitives were quick to draw the parallel between the historic flight out of Egypt and their own flight from captivity to freedom. As they felt the pride of tradition and history swell in their hearts, they steeled themselves to new resolve.

Schultz, the one gentile among them, built a symbolic Ark from which all shielded their eyes as he carried it into the Tabernacle. For superstition held that to touch it meant death, as it had to Uzza of old. As Schultz came from the Tabernacle, a white-bearded ancient stepped from the crowd which had turned their backs on the profanation of the temple that was symbolized by the action of Schultz, a gentile, in touching the Ark.

He had not come forward as their rabbi before this, the ancient told the people, because he had felt no call to teach and lead them in the ways of Jehovah. But with this demonstration of their yearning and reaching for the guidance of the Almighty, it was his duty to lead them in the way of their ancient faith. And so for the first time as a congregation, the people worshipped together, although it was not the Sabbath.

169

"With no intent to be profane," Lustig observed, "Franck added that they had all certainly fasted.

"The night was given over to prayer and thanksgiving, and there was a noticeable calm that came over the people. They had returned to the God of their fathers and were prepared to endure whatever was in store, as those of their race had for five centuries.

"As though it were an omen, three stray goats—obviously from a herd, since they were tame—wandered into camp late in the night. The next morning, the thirteenth day of their flight, they feasted. The goat hides they dried and tanned over the fire and used to repair their shoes and boots.

"The fourteenth day they set out along the plateau, hauling the sick on litters that they made of pine trunks and limbs and which were dragged along by the sturdiest. For the first time in many days they sang as they marched. And this time it was a real march. There was new determination in their step and in their hearts."

The going on the level plateau was easier. They covered perhaps ten miles that day and possibly twelve the next. Franck and Schultz estimated they were well out of the U.S.S.R. and maybe as deep as a dozen miles into China, paralleling a Russian frontier which ran roughly from northeast to southwest.

Both nights when they camped they set up the primitive Tabernacle which the people had come to revere as a symbol of God's protection and of the ultimate victory and freedom. They had started out with a vague urge to escape, no matter where. Now the symbolic rites seemed to fix a goal in their minds. The goal had become as symbolic as the Tabernacle and the rough Ark. It was Zion. To each and every one of them, it was Zion.

For a week they traversed the plateau at a rate Franck judged to be ten to twelve miles a day. Excepting for the pursuing soldiers, they had seen no other humans. Yet each

170

day they had come across evidences of human habitation. Sometimes there were ashes of a recent campfire. At others, they noted that the grass had been cropped by grazing sheep, goats, and horses. Each day there were stray goats or sheep to keep them in food.

They traveled on the alert. Scouts went ahead, watched on the flanks, and brought up the rear of the column.

At the beginning of the third week, the plateau suddenly rose into sharp peaks and crags. For six more days they struggled on across even more precipitous heights than they had encountered just beyond Naryn. To facilitate progress of the column, they had regretfully left the Tabernacle behind. But the Ark which Schultz had constructed was carried by the bearded rabbi and volunteer bearers on long poles, poked through rings at each corner of the rough box. To shield it from view, the rude representation of the Ark was covered with goat skins.

One woman and three men fell to their deaths from the treacherous pinnacles. The superstitious laid this to their abandonment of the Tabernacle, the "house of God." The rabbi ridiculed this with the quite un-Orthodox opinion that "the house of God is in the hearts of men."

On the twenty-ninth day, Franck and Schultz called together the cobbler, the rabbi, the doctors, and the young lieutenants. It was unlikely, Schultz conjectured, that they had covered as much as 250 miles. No one, of course, could tell within 25 to 50 miles. In any event, if they continued southwestward, they would wind up in the Pamirs—the top of the world—from which radiated the great mountain systems of Asia, with mighty glaciers and peaks that towered four miles above sea level. That way, too, lay Afghanistan where they definitely did not want to go.

Schultz and Franck calculated that if they turned southward, they had a fair chance of coming out somewhere near the Indian border of Sinkiang, perhaps somewhere in the vicinity of Tibet. That they could have so little knowledge of geography seems incomprehensible.

It seems likely that the plateau which the fugitives had traversed was the extreme northwestern corner of the vast area known as Takla Makan. That they encountered goats and sheep of a semi-domesticated type seems to bear out this possibility. Yet the failure to meet any humans, while not unlikely, is strange. Possibly, allowing Schultz' margin of error of twenty-five to fifty miles in distance, they were within sight of the Pamirs, not far from the point where Afghanistan forms a sixty-mile buffer between Pakistan and Asiatic Russia and where all three countries adjoin Sinkiang.

The council Franck called with his lieutenants was not to ask their advice but to inform them of his decision to alter their course. To the south, it was obvious, lay another comparatively level expanse. (This was unquestionably the northern extremity of the Khotan region.)

Those who had been stricken and had survived struggled valiantly to keep up with those who suffered only from exposure and undernourishment. All were footsore with stone bruises, frostbite, open sores, and painfully swollen ankles and legs. Progress of the march was cut down to four or five miles a day at most.

On the thirty-third day of the march, the fourth after the change of course to the south, they limped painfully onto the plain they had seen from the peaks. Here, Franck decreed two days of rest.

A new Tabernacle was improvised out of scrawny fir trunks and boughs. The makeshift representation of the Ark was ensconced in its traditional place. And again the people gathered to worship and give thanks.

Franck and Schultz now had little fear of pursuit. Their concern was with what lay ahead. It was imperative that they avoid, if possible, any contact that would lead so large a party into the hands of police or the officials of any state. Should

172

they encounter officials, it would only mean that they would be turned over to Soviet representatives and set back, probably to their deaths, certainly to slavery. If they were to succeed in entering India it could not be in a group. Further, they realized, this could not be accomplished without help, but from what source it might come, they had no idea.

The cobbler alone seemed to have any conception of where they were, apparently because he had traveled the world and seemed to have some sort of instinct for orientation.

The thirty-fourth day, leaving Schultz in charge of the camp, Franck took the cobbler and the rabbi southward, in an attempt to locate themselves geographically. Franck and his two companions traveled southward for a day and a half. Near noon of the thirty-fifth day, they came upon a river and along its bank a caravan trail that led to the south. Warily they watched and, toward evening, spotted a caravan coming in their direction. But it followed the course of the river that turned in a northeasterly direction, which somewhat relieved their fears of discovery.

The cobbler reasoned, and correctly, that if there were caravans, there must be a town or city nearby. (The river, Lustig assumed, was the Khotan in Sinkiang, leading to the city of the same name which was an ancient center of Buddhism, noted for trading in agricultural products and manufactured articles, including silk, cotton, linen, rugs, felt, and articles of jade and metal.)

If there were a city, perhaps he could find help. The kind of help they needed would have to be bought, and they had nothing of value. God, the rabbi reminded them, would provide, a sentiment to which Franck could hardly subscribe— at the time. Sending the rabbi and the cobbler on to find whatever civilization might be near, Franck turned back to the camp. He arrived early the next morning. What he saw, he certainly was not prepared for.

The place had been transformed. There were horses staked out all around the perimeter. In a makeshift pen at the eastern

173

extremity, a herd of no less than two hundred goats were corralled. About a hundred feet away, a herd of sheep grazed under the watchful and obviously inexperienced eyes of seven or eight uncertain shepherds.

Schultz met him with a grin, asking how soon the rabbi would be there. Now was really the time for prayer and thanksgiving. The Lord certainly had looked out for them. And he explained to the completely baffled Franck what had happened: At noon of the day before, mounted scouts of a nomad band had ridden out of the southwest. Armed and warlike, they had ridden close enough to survey the docile tatter-demalions. When the Jews had offered no resistance, the scouts had fired a few shots and ridden away in the direction from which they'd come.

Alarmed, Schultz had posted armed-guard detachments in strategic positions with orders to hold fire unless attacked, and then only when he had given the signal.

Within an hour, twenty-five wild horsemen returned, riding in a breakneck race to reach the encamped party. With their mad shrieks and howls, firing their rifles into the air, they apparently expected to panic their victims. They rode with a strangely crazed frenzy and abandon—right into ambush. The affray lasted no more than ten or fifteen minutes, Schultz related. The attackers tried to ride down the defenders, their horses rearing and plunging. When the tide of battle turned against them, those who were still alive and mounted turned to retreat.

Schultz and a dozen of his best men caught horses of those who had been killed or wounded and started off in pursuit of the ten or so who had escaped. They followed for about three miles when they saw the herds. The surviving attackers, now in panic, were trying to move their livestock to safety while digging in for a stand against their vengeful pursuers.

His men fought with abandoned and murderous fury, Schultz told Franck. They were demons, merciless, and raging. It wasn't pretty to see. The Jews used semi-automatics; the foe,

174

rifles. The enemy hadn't a chance. It was all over in a few minutes.

All through the night, the people had been bringing in the spoils of battle. Yes, there were casualties. Six of Schultz's men, twenty-two of the nomads. The latter were Kirghiz tribesmen. Wandering where their herds take them in search of grazing, they have no respect for political boundaries. One of the Kirghiz who spoke Russian told Schultz that his kinsmen were taking their herds to Khotan for trading.

Seeing what they assumed were defenseless men and women, the nomads had concluded that they had discovered a gold mine. For they could take the captives to Afghanistan and sell them into slavery. Schultz was concerned that several of the band had escaped and had fled to the west on horseback. For the Kirghiz tribesmen were Moslems who could unquestionably recruit a quite formidable force of their kinsmen or fellow tribesmen, motivated by acquisitive self-interest in recovering the herds and capturing slaves, as well as by considerations of religious revenge.

In addition to the loss of their livestock, there was a likely possibility that the nomads would learn of the mass escape from Issyq Kul and of the reward for recapture of the fugitives which the escapees knew had been offered. In such an event, they might well return with Russian troops who would have no more respect for political frontiers than the nomads had.

The encounter between the Jewish fugitives and the Kirghiz herdsmen had very definitely and unexpectedly improved the economic situation for Franck's people. But it also had doubled their danger. For they were now hemmed in on three sides: To the northwest, by insurpassable mountains and unfriendly Afghanistan. To the west, by mountains, the vengeful Kirghiz tribe and, probably, Moslem Pakistan beyond. To the north and northeast, the direction from which they'd come, by mountains and danger of pursuit. Only to the south did there seem hope of finding haven.

While the people celebrated victory, mourned their dead,

175

and counted the spoils of battle, Franck and Schultz fretfully awaited the return of the cobbler and the rabbi with news of what lay to the south. Franck took stock of their tactical position and found it not untenable. He posted scouts in the hills on all flanks. All through that night and up until noon of the next, the thirty-seventh day, the two leaders worked feverishly, mining the hills at the strategic points on the three dangerous sides.

The rabbi and the cobbler did not return that day, nor all the next. With the danger threatening his people, Franck would not leave them to go in search of his missing lieutenants. Schultz refused to go, on the grounds that if there were trouble, he wanted to be with his friend.

On the thirty-ninth day, just after dawn, a sentry on the southern flank came in to report a group of seven men approaching. None of them wore a Russian guard uniform, so he assumed the rabbi and the cobbler were not among them. Franck and Schultz went out to meet the mounted group that was riding straight for the camp. That was a mistake that was to cost the captain the dearest price he was to pay for the liberation of his people.

As Franck and Schultz approached, two of the riders galloped up to meet them. They were the cobbler and the rabbi. Their five companions, the returning lieutenants explained, were from Khotan, a town that lay two days' journey to the south. They were Buddhist with no militant religious prejudice and even less political interest. They had come to arrange safe passage into India—provided suitable payment could be arranged through certain Jewish agencies in Kashmir, which lay 200 miles south of Khotan over good caravan trails.

The five Chinese rode slowly forward, their eyes shrewdly taking in the sight of the herds that grazed on the plain. The rabbi, more surprised than they were, sat his horse, looking speechlessly at Franck. The cobbler, who had a knack for swift mental adjustment, seized the opportunity to start bar-

176

gaining with the apparent spokesman of the Chinese who understood Russian.

The people would need clothing, the cobbler started out, for their masquerade as Indians or Chinese on the caravan trail. Now, roughly a hundred cheap outfits of cotton, with silks for the leaders—and boots for all, of course. Let's see. How about half the sheep? *All* of the sheep! Robber! Pickpocket!

In the midst of the haggling, which was vastly amusing to Franck and Schultz, one of the sentries from the west galloped into the group, frantically shouting that the Kirghiz tribesmen were approaching. Fifty or sixty of them, all mounted and armed, were bearing down on the camp from the west.

Franck and Schultz went into action. They shouted for the sentry and the rabbi to dismount. They sprang onto the horses and raced for the western outpost. Arriving at a point where he had set up the batteries and detonator contact, Franck surveyed the situation. The attackers, possibly three-quarters of a mile distant and out of rifle range, had halted. He could see the flankers riding forward cautiously to reconnoiter.

There was a defile, about fifty feet wide, through which they would have to ride to reach that part of the plateau where the fugitives were encamped. Sharp cliffs rose on either side. These two rocky walls were mined with enough dynamite to fill the narrow pass with rock and seal it off. This would delay the attack until the avenging tribesmen had scaled it on foot, a tactic they would not be likely to attempt, knowing that Franck's band was armed with automatic weapons which could deliver a devastating crossfire. On the plain, mounted, the tribesmen had the odds all in their favor, but not afoot in the hills.

Franck and Schultz decided to close the pass with a blast without trying to claim any more casualties among the nomads. Franck ran to the contact switch. He threw it. Nothing happened. No blast, not even the spluttering buzz of a short circuit.

"Franck knew that their batteries were gone. They had

177

tested them the day before," Lustig took up the narrative. "There just wasn't enough current to carry.

"Neither Franck nor Schultz had to go into any huddle to know what to do. Each grabbed a length of fuse. Franck dashed for the wall at the left, Schultz for the right wall. They scrambled and stumbled and clawed their way to the charges they had planted. The flankers were closing in. The main body of the enemy was moving slowly forward.

"They worked like madmen lengthening the tail of live fuse they had left for just such an emergency when they had packed the dynamite. From the opposite sides of the rock walls above the defile, they could see each other. Franck waited tensely, for a moment after he had finished, for Schultz to give him the 'ready' signal.

"They waved to each other, lit their fuses, and started sliding and scuttling down the rocky sides to safety.

"Franck took a last look as the mounted men as they rode at a walk for the defile, little suspecting what they were in for. He slipped and fell, got up and ran to where he knew he was beyond range of the explosion.

"Franck turned to watch the explosion, leaning against a small pine to recover his breath. What he saw left him limp and sick. There in the middle of the defile, crawling along on his hands and one knee, the other leg dragging behind him, grotesquely twisted, Schultz was trying to reach safety.

"Schultz had fallen from the cliff face. His leg was apparently broken. Blood streamed from his forehead and into his eyes.

"Franck hesitated only a moment. He started to go to his friend's aid. The horsemen had stepped up their pace from the walk; the leader was less than fifty yards from the injured Schultz. There might still be time to save him. Franck began to run. Schultz waved at him frantically, shouting 'go back, go back,' in German.

"The explosion came with a sickening impact that knocked Franck to the ground. He said that he covered his head with

178

his arms instinctively, screaming curses at God, at all Russians, all Moslems, all Jews, at the world. A falling stone knocked him unconscious.

"When Franck came to, it was hours later. Worn out with physical exhaustion, he had courted the sleep of unconsciousness, rather than face the reality of his awful sorrow at the loss of Schultz, which he subconsciously knew he had suffered.

"Franck told me," Lustig continued, "that he had known no more than two or three friends in his hectic life. He honored me by including me among them. But there was only one comrade, one brother, as he phrased it.

"The rabbi and the people prayed in the Tabernacle that housed the Ark which Schultz had built them as a symbol of their faith.

"The cobbler delivered a eulogy from the pile of rocks beneath which lay the body of a man who had helped to make his brothers free.

"And when they all had gone and left him alone with the memory of a comrade, Moses Franck quietly knelt and planted a Cross amid the rocks.

"Franck's most vivid memories were always of action. Plans, routine, details interested him only when there was no one else to look after them. And even then, he was likely to count them of little importance," Lustig explained, as he concluded the story of the liberation and the flight.

"I suspect that he rather lost interest after Schultz, with whom he had shared so much, was gone. Franck outlined the final chapter of the escape in a few brief sentences. I can do no more than tell you what I noted down.

"As the people gathered on the plain after the explosion that brought down half a mountain, the cobbler took up his bargaining with the Chinese. In return for the herds of goats, sheep and horses, the Chinese were to supply suitable clothing for the party. Also, to avoid the suspicion that would be aroused by 100 people traveling together, the fugitives were to be split

179

into five groups. Each of these was to be guided by one of the Chinese to Khotan.

"From Khotan, the escapees were to travel the caravan routes to India. Not all were to go to the same destinations. As caravan hands and guards, as Hindu pilgrims, it would be a comparatively easy matter to cross the borders or to travel inside India, only recently become an independent nation and not yet too well organized politically.

"Once beyond the frontier, they were strictly on their own. The Moslems would not treat them kindly, should any be stopped for questioning. The Indian government would most assuredly turn anyone known to be a fugitive over to the proper Soviet authorities. It would, therefore, be wisest to travel in groups of no more than two or three, to stay well away from all officials and, above all, to avoid involvement with Moslems. For the latter were bitter about the situation in Palestine which the Pan-Mohammedan world felt was holy war."

From the points to which they would be delivered in Kashmir, it was at least 1,200 miles to Bombay, which was impossible to reach without crossing Pakistan at some point. The narrowest would be the neck, about 50 miles wide, at Kangra between Kashmir and the Punjab.

Unless the people were in some physical danger, it seems apparent that Franck felt little responsibility for them. On the forty-first day, when the last group got under way with its Chinese merchant-guide, Franck felt that his real work was over. There were others, he believed, who could better organize the detailed sort of job that remained.

There was the rabbi to handle negotiations with Jewish aid organizations that might be difficult to contact in India. There was the young medical student who had the patience to counsel the people wisely and whose advice they would accept. There was the cobbler who could play a fine game of intrigue with politicians, should the need arise for a bit of bribery or blackmail.

180

There were others who had not been worth the space they took on the trail when it came to a fight or an emergency, but who had good family and financial connections. A sort of executive group, they rose by some strange process of social osmosis the moment they were called upon to contribute no more than words and an impressive presence. Now that there was no longer the need for real leadership, for decisive thinking and action, for individual capability, these men somehow surged to the front. They, not Franck, wore the silks. They, not Franck, represented the people, by self-acclamation, and assumed command of their destinies, as third-rate men must when they have no further need of the first-rate, whom they so vastly outnumber. Yet, in spite of them, the fugitives made progress along the road to Zion.

It was the middle of July when Franck left Khotan in the last contingent. His shoulder, badly crippled in the boat explosion at Issyq Kul, had been severely fractured and had knit without having been properly set. By now it was giving him more pain than even he could endure, and he finally allowed the old doctor to fix it up as best he could.

Franck made the journey to Srinagar, a distance of nearly 300 miles from Khotan, in about three weeks. He found that twenty to thirty of his people had already made it safely to Bombay, that money and credentials—where or how papers were obtained has never been explained—were available for another ten persons. Within three more months, the newly risen politician-leaders estimated, all would be out of India, some by plane, some by ship, all with one goal in view. Either immediately or eventually, all hoped to reach Israel.

"For Franck," Lustig added as a sort of postscript, "the waiting was a bore. But he insisted on being the last to leave the lovely city in Kashmir, which was the most beautiful and peaceful place he had ever known.

"In November of 1948, he reached Bombay and later that month, Madrid. But peace and quiet had come too late to

181

Moses Franck. He could not enjoy it while he felt that other men were still fighting for his right to dignity and freedom.

"He turned up in Tel Aviv early in 1949. I met him in the army, as I have said. We fought side by side in the Holy Land, on the border of Jordan, in the desert, and in the streets of Jerusalem.

"Not all of the details of the flight from Issyq Kul came from Franck, himself. The rabbi who came with them, and to whom I have talked, supplied some. The young doctor, now one of the leading physicians in Tel Aviv, after distinguished service in the Israeli Army, filled me in on others.

"Moses Franck died in a skirmish near Lydda. I loaded his body onto a jeep and drove it to Tel Aviv.

"I wish I could say I heard his last words. I didn't. I don't think he suffered very much at the last. No death in battle is merciful, but it can be sudden. His was.

"Franck had called to me only a moment before I found his body. He'd pulled a grenade pin and was about to hurl it into a roofless house where Arab snipers were holed up. A bullet caught him as he took aim. The grenade fell to ground and he sprawled on top of it, just as it went off.

"They buried Moses Franck that night on a hill overlooking the sea."

13.

Communication Lines

THERE HAVE BEEN, frankly, many friendly critics and helpful aides in the preparation of this book who have vigorously objected to the inclusion of the chapters on Moses Franck. Their grounds are generally the same as those upon which the objections to the stories of Abdul and Shirshoff are based.

Abdul was—or is—a murderous old cutthroat with personal motives for looting and freebooting that were stronger than any consideration of furthering the cause of God and religion.

Shirshoff is unquestionably a forger, counterfeiter, and blackmailer, motivated at best by considerations of personal vengeance, if not by those of material gain.

Moses Franck, the most severe critics contend, was no better than a footpad and "mugger," in his earlier escapades in Germany. Whether he had killed fifty or sixty men, he could not remember, probably having lost count.

By including Franck, I am accused by some of sacrilege, of contradicting the purpose of the secret army. Why, it is demanded, am I allying saints and martyrs in a holy cause with criminals and murderers? I can only answer, as Father Reed and others have, that Christ was crucified between two thieves—that God moves in ways that are not always apparent to the minds of men.

Criticism of the Franck story has also come on another score. Why, it is asked, have I gone into greater detail in the chapters of his career than I have on those of others who acted purely out of religious and spiritual conviction? I must reply that such detail was available on Franck while it was not available about others.

Since this book is nonfiction, I can supply only those facts which are reasonably well established and verifiable. Lustig and others were able to relate more details that could not possibly harm anyone, largely because Franck is dead and there is little likelihood that any of his people will ever return to the Soviet Union.

The necessity to disguise persons and places for security reasons is the foremost consideration in every published line about the secret army or any of its activities. In many instances, the slightest unguarded detail might well furnish a clue to the identity of some secret soldier—with tragic result. In no case does this apply more stringently than to the lines and channels of communication which reach from outside the Soviet empire to those who carry on the organization and the fight of the secret army.

It is obvious that Abdul the Persian first operated quite independently of any other unit of the Moslem column of the secret army. It is a safe assumption that his was the original force and that from it sprang other units, chiefly under leadership of his numerous sons and nephews. As their operations widened in scope and in geographical extent, channels of communication and contact had to be established. Since Abdul's area of activity began on the border of Iran—he had never been certain whether he had been born in Persian or in Russian territory—it was a natural precaution to set up his command and communication center on Iranian soil. When his sons attended schools at Istanbul, Ankara, and Baghdad, they came into contact with active anti-Communist elements of the Mohammedan world.

That fairly close and regular contact is maintained from

outside the U.S.S.R. with Moslem forces inside is not open to question. My interview with Hamid in Tangier definitely established that. It is extremely unlikely, however, that the Moslem intelligence maintains any contact with that of any other column, probably not with Christians and certainly not with Jews. That the Moslems who escaped with Franck from Iyssq Kul had some sort of knowledge of the Moslem underground is evident. They apparently knew where to go, how to get there and were confident that they would find shelter.

Certain of the Christian contingent of Franck's fugitives also had contact—enough, at any rate, to know there was possible sanctuary and probable help at Talass.

Franck, himself, knew nothing of any organized Jewish underground. Indeed, the proportion of Jewish population in the Soviet Union is so small, the influence of anti-Semitism so great, that it would be difficult for the Jews to maintain any effective organization outside prison walls. Strength of the resistance of the column of Judah was, however, amply demonstrated, once the fugitives got safely outside the Communist orbit. They experienced no difficulty in contacting agencies with the money and influence to send them to their ultimate destination. The Jewish column in the Soviet domain is unique in that its membership is almost wholly among those who have been imprisoned or are under sharp surveillance. For there are few free Jews in Russia.

Certainly in his earliest days, Rabbi Levitzky had aid and collaboration from some sources within revolutionary Russia. In the later years, he carried on, isolated and alone, excepting for his sons and the members of his *sub rosa* congregation. It has been pretty well established that since World War II, the Jews have rebuilt an effective system of contact and communication that reaches from West Berlin into Poland and the Soviet Union. Far from flagging in the face of fantastic odds, they have intensified their efforts to send in help and to bring out information.

Christian communication lines have been comparatively

free and open since the first days of the revolution. They began with refugee Orthodox priests. They were strengthened with the reports of the Jesuit Fathers Walsh and Gallagher and others in the early and mid-twenties.

Today, there are channels reaching from the United States to Berlin, into Warsaw and Moscow and throughout the Soviet empire; from our Pacific Coast and from Hawaii into Shanghai, Peking, and throughout China and Korea. (On the score of Christianity in China, it should be remembered that the Chinese priesthood and hierarchy of the Roman Catholic Church alone was more numerous than in any other country, excepting Italy, while communicants numbered in the millions. Anti-Communist activity of the religious resistance in China cannot now be revealed. Neither can it be fully investigated, for reasons which are obvious.)

It is fantastic with what apparent ease and frequency leaders and members of the secret army are able to make their way out of the Soviet by well-organized underground routes. They turn up in Athens, Tangier, Teheran, Ankara, Istanbul; in Finland, West Germany, France, Spain, and Italy. They bring messages and reports, pleas for aid—almost never financial—and requests for cooperation and collaboration.

An American organization financed by public but unofficial contributions, the Crusade for Freedom, whose radio beam pierces the curtain of censorship, largely in the satellites, is the most comforting medium of communication to the embattled forces of the secret army. This is not even to intimate that the Crusade is allied in any way with the activities of the religious resisters. But its Radio Free Europe is, electronically at least, the most powerful voice of hope to be heard in the prison-world of Communism.

"Radio Free Europe," an Orthodox priest, who had come from Leningrad underground in 1950 and who returned in 1951, told me, "is, perhaps unintentionally, a powerful ally to the secret army. Because it does a work of morale building that is unequalled. The layman, the fighter in the ranks, has

186

no chance to take part in communicating with the outside world, as many of us leaders do. They hear the RFE Crusaders, all right. Hundreds of them, indeed, hundreds of thousands, have taken courage from the realization that they are not fighting alone, that not only God but also men of the free world are on their side."

No organization can exist without a well-organized and functioning communication. Since none could long exist if centered in the Soviet, it had, of necessity, to be set up outside.

"Doctor Nicias" is a quiet little man. Little in the way of personal adventure has ever befallen him. Nothing exciting, he insists, ever happens to him.

"I am a scholar and a scientist," the Doctor explained to me in Monaco, "and I am old. As a scholar, I abhor regimentation of thought and opinion. As a scientist, I distrust the final and the positive. As an old man, I can indulge my one definite belief: In the Almighty Power which keeps in orderly balance all the opposing disruptive natural forces and without Whose governing laws those forces would erupt into universal chaos.

"I am also," he added as an afterthought, "a Greek. And as a Greek, I champion freedom wherever it has been lost— or has never been found."

So the white-haired man explained his connection with the secret army. "Do not say," he warned, "that I have ever been in the Soviet Union. I have been no closer, since the revolution, than Athens. Nor have I been in the captive Communist countries, which border Greece, since they have fallen. Please, do not say that I ever intend to go to them. I am not a man of action as are our Fathers Zurikov and Janicek and Mueller. No, I am no more than an observer, a listener if you prefer."

A listener Dr. Nicias assuredly is. He has constructed radio receivers that are sensitive enough to pick up broadcasts from the remotest points in Asiatic Russia from the least powerful transmitters. His receiving centers dot the map of western Europe from Mount Athos in his native Greece, across Free Ger-

187

many, France, Italy, Portugal, Britain, and Ireland. They are located in the United States, Canada, and Japan.

"There are at the moment," Dr. Nicias stated in Monte Carlo where he was interviewed in 1950, "twenty-two receiving centers in all. Most of these have two or more separate monitoring panels. It is possible, for instance, in one center to monitor stations in a particular belt of wave lengths on one receiver, while the other receiver picks up messages in a completely different stratum—let us say Budapest and Moscow, or Shanghai and Vladivostok."

The twenty-two centers are so constructed and located that they pretty well blanket all possible bands of transmission. The headphones are on listeners, somewhere, practically around the clock. Unless the air is hopelessly jammed by static, not an official broadcast from the U.S.S.R. or the satellites goes unrecorded. The listening monitor repeats the words of the broadcast into a tape recorder. Some of the more recent sets have been constructed so that they can be recorded direct from headsets. In Greece, broadcasts from the Soviet Union are often clear enough to be recorded from a loud-speaker. The same is sometimes true in Italy, France, and Germany with broadcasts from the satellites.

All recordings are transcribed and copies of each sent to the other centers in the chain. Thus is a fairly complete record kept of what the people are being told in the Communist world. Such reports, incidentally, have provided documentation for some of the material in these pages.

"During the war, with the rapid shifts in population, the migration of multitudes of people, and the swift movements of military units, we were able to put quite a bit of our own short wave transmitting equipment inside the Soviet Union," Dr. Nicias explains. "Most of it went in as army equipment. We even managed to get some of it through with your country's military aid materiel.

"Certainly it was costly. A great deal of it was set up in various military sectors without the Russians even knowing

188

what it was for. In some instances, I have learned, transmitters which I designed were taken to remote dumps, where outmoded military equipment was stored, and left there. Operators would return and put it to use for one or two sending sessions. Then, before there was a chance to follow the wave length to the sending point, they'd close down and move on to the next spot where equipment was at hand. In other words, the stations did not move, only the operating personnel.

"Since, apparently, Soviet radio engineers are none too well-equipped scientifically, it has been possible for a single operator of ours to use bona fide Red Army transmitters of truck-portable design to send brief messages, say of sixty to ninety seconds duration, without detection. If you are monitoring carefully, that is enough.

"Since the messages go into the ether and are lost instantly, it is difficult to prove what has been sent unless it has been recorded. More messages get through from the secret army than might be imagined. Hundreds of radio operators and engineers of the Red Army are also in the secret army. Nevertheless, losses in personnel in this communications branch of our service are greater than in any other activity of the religious resistance movement.

"How many secret transmitters got into the Soviet Union? I cannot say. Neither have I any idea how many are active today. I can say that a weekly average of ten to twelve minutes of messages from *sub rosa* transmission are picked up from Russia. Yes, I suppose the Communications Ministry in Moscow does record them too. It stands to reason that it would. The question is whether they can make a 'fix' on the wave length and follow it to the location in time to apprehend the senders."

Dr. Nicias arranged for me to inspect such a receiving center as he had described. It was in Canada. There were four monitors busy when I arrived. They were all religious.

"Can you understand Polish?" asked the director.

189

When I admitted that I could not, he started the tape play-back and a stream of Polish and static poured out.

"How about German? Are you able to understand that?" my host quizzed.

"No," I admitted.

The German recording was played. Followed two more in Russian and in Hungarian. I could not understand them. Were there no translations? None, the director informed me.

After luncheon at the best hotel which could be found in the town, the bearded priest took me back to the center. It was in a seven- or eight-story office building, atop which was an antenna of imposing proportions. There were antennae of equal size on practically all the surrounding buildings.

"Don't you do the translations here?" I asked the director.

"Yes," he answered. "But they are all rendered into French. I cannot permit you to take a copy with you, but I will allow you to look at anything you wish. You should not make notes. I cannot prevent your doing so, but I would prefer that you didn't."

I read sheaves of translations of Russian, Hungarian, and German broadcasts.

"Nothing," I asked him in disappointment, "from any underground channels in the Soviet Union?"

He laughed at my apparent lack of knowledge of the intricacies and scientific mysteries of radio. "Even though we could pick up the proper wave length," he explained, "the impulses would be too faint. No, that's largely intercepted in Greece and, sometimes, in Japan."

"Isn't it illegal to operate without a license?" he was asked, and he smiled again at my confusion.

"Only to transmit, not to receive."

Dr. Nicias was in Boston a few months before publication of this book.

"You saw what goes on in our centers," he said. "Now you should be convinced that there is no adventure and excitement
190

in my job with the secret army. It's such a prosaic life I lead, you probably won't even mention it in your book."

Two weeks later, I learned that the doctor's son, a Greek Orthodox priest who had disappeared in the border clashes between Greeks and the Bulgarian Communists, had been condemned in Sofia by the People's Court as a spy.

14.

Columns of the Cross

"FATHER JANICEK" is the pseudonym of a Polish priest who has made his way underground into Russia and out since 1939 to contact and lend leadership to the secret forces of the religious resistance within the Soviet Empire.

He is a stocky, muscular man with wide shoulders and huge hands, possibly in his middle forties though he appears ten years younger. Father Janicek is of extremely conservative tendencies and, like many men of action, glosses over the drama of his own exploits, taking them as a matter of course.

"Getting into Russia," he insists, "isn't really too difficult. But getting out is something else again.

"You see," he adds seriously and with no intent to be humorous, "no Russian border guards can imagine that anyone could possibly be insane enough to want to get into the Soviet Union. Their entire thinking, indeed their whole training is based upon the quite logical assumption that anyone, given half a chance, would want to escape. So, except at rail and ship points of entry, Soviet guards are alert only to keeping the people prisoners behind the border.

"Even the guards are assigned to duty in groups. They never work alone. Should one follow the natural urge to make a break, he would run the risk that one of his comrades would follow instructions and shoot to kill."

When Father Janicek went into Russia his method was as

daring as it was ingenious. Late in the fall of 1939, shortly after Stalin and Hitler signed a treaty that gave the death blow to Poland, which for more than a millennium had been a strong-hold of Christianity, Father Janicek let it be known to certain members of his parish near Grodno that he wanted to go into Russia. He needed the uniform and identity papers of a Soviet soldier. It wasn't, he recalls, as easy as it sounds. For just any soldier wouldn't do. It had to be one whose physique and appearance were very near to his own. Then, too, the soldier had to be a member of a unit which was soon to be returning to Russia.

Father Janicek couldn't run the risk of meeting the real sol-dier's comrades in the ranks. So he planned to present himself to Soviet military authorities after the soldier's company had been shipped home. His story would simply be that he had been captured by guerrillas and had just escaped. A desperate risk, but Father Janicek was certain it would work. What made it doubly difficult for those faced with the job of bring-ing in the soldier was that the priest absolutely forbade any killing—first, because he was, as he says, "a man of peace," and second, because he wanted to question the soldier.

The Roman Catholic priest's reason for wanting to enter the Soviet Union in the disguise of a soldier was his own, con-cerned with what he believed was the welfare of his parish-ioners. He had been seized on the highway, as he had come from hearing confessions, one day in early December, by a Red Army squad. Excuse for taking him into custody was that he had no Soviet identity papers which had been issued to most of the people of his village that morning. They brought Father Janicek before a young military police officer who took him severely to task for ignoring the orders of the Red Army's district commander. As the bawling-out progressed the priest sensed that the officer was trying to convey informa-tion and a hidden warning to him. The gist of the monologue went like this:

"You can bring punishment upon the whole village by violating the simple rules that we, who have come to free you from capitalist oppression, have set up to help preserve order and security. I am not even sure," he went on with an outward display of insolent superiority, "that your entire village will not be relocated, transferred to some area where their work will be more productive for the welfare of all the people.

"You probably know, too, that priests of a foreign church are not tolerated in the People's Republics. Therefore, I warn you against any further violations of regulations.

"Should your people be relocated, it is unlikely that you will go with them. They will have no need of you. In the church which is recognized by the Kremlin they will find no foolish fear and superstition which enslaves the minds of men. I warn you, one more such violation and the time you have to remain with your people will be even shorter.

"We will not tolerate any breach of order or discipline by any filthy Pole, much less a priest. We have come here to protect you from your rulers but you Poles will have to prove your fitness to be our brothers. That will demand respect and work—and you will work *where* we Russians need you . . . That is all. Dismissed."

As the military issued him his identity card, Father Janicek went over the lecture delivered by the young officer. One thing was certain. His people were to be deported. The priest was sure the lieutenant was trying to emphasize that. Sooner or later he would be separated from his people. His one chance to continue serving them was, somehow, to get into Russia before his parishioners were transferred. There would then be a chance to learn where they had been sent and of his joining them later. How he did not know, excepting with God's help.

"The idea of entering Russia disguised as a soldier was not mine. It did not develop step by step as the result of puzzling it out in the mind. It came as a revelation from On High, after hours of praying for guidance," Father Janicek had said, looking back over the years. "Dangerous, you ask? How so,

194

my son? There is no danger, only duty to your people and to your God."

It was that simple for Father Janicek, a man of faith.

For two weeks, his guerrilla friends prowled the banks of the canals by night, taking keen mental measurements, at a distance, of the Red Army soldiers who were assigned to guard duty on bridges, barges, and towpaths. When a soldier did not fit the general physical characteristics of their priest and contrary to his exhortations against violence, the prowlers were likely to steal up in the darkness, whip a short length of bailing wire around a Russian throat and silently ease the unwanted guest into the water where he'd be found floating face down by his comrades in the morning.

On the night of December 15th, their search was rewarded. The sturdy soldier, guarding a bridge, didn't even put up a struggle. He went quietly with only a single guard to the sacristry of the parish church from which the priest led him into the woods where the guerrillas had adjourned. The civilian fighters, who hated all Russians and not without cause, wanted to kill the young soldier as soon as Father Janicek had finished questioning him. The best way to get the uniform from any Russian was from a dead Russian. But their priest, a man of peace, would permit no violence, not even a slight maiming which the guerrilla leader begged to be allowed to inflict— with his fists, just his bare fists and a few assorted wrestling holds.

Father Janicek recalls that the soldier gave up his uniform without a struggle. He confided to the priest that he had no desire to go home to Russia, particularly in the army. He welcomed freedom if only for a few days. Maybe, the soldier hoped wistfully, he might get to America. The Polish priest was all for letting the young man go on the spot. The guerrillas, with the tragedy of a race implanted in their beings, counseled him never to trust a Russian. They'd keep him under guard until they knew Father Janicek was safe. Then, they promised on the Crucifix, they'd let the boy go unharmed.

195

The guerrillas had picked well for their priest. Questioning the soldier, whose identity as Private Petrovitch he was to assume, Father Janicek learned that his unit was to be shipped back to Leningrad within two days. The guerrillas, who maintained an efficient spy system in the local barrooms, verified the accuracy of the information. They took the real Private Petrovitch to a coal barge and put an armed guard over him —an act which, Father Janicek insists, was not at all necessary.

Next morning, the citizens of the town were routed out of their homes before seven o'clock while squads of Red Army men went through each house, barn, building, and woodshed in search of contraband. This consisted chiefly of arms and ammunition. Although only a small number of Soviet soldiers had disappeared during the "friendly occupation," the Russians were angry enough to retaliate with ten lives for every one. This was what they threatened. The mayor of the village suggested that maybe the missing might not have been killed at all. Maybe they had just deserted. This earned the old man a private interview with the civilian political chief, a Party member and NKVD agent, who was attached to the commander's staff. But it served to take the emphasis off the search and nothing incriminating was turned up.

The young military police officer visited the priest with a detail of soldiers where he loudly repeated the threats and warnings of two weeks before.

On Christmas Eve, Father Janicek in the uniform and with the papers of Private Petrovitch appeared at military headquarters.

"No, I was not afraid," he has said. "I was in God's hands. I had prayed for a sign that I was doing the right thing and it had come to me from the young lieutenant whom I had seen two or three times after that with his thumbs hooked in his belt, his index fingers overlapping in the sign of the Cross."

God was surely with the disguised Father Janicek when he presented himself at district headquarters that bitterly cold Christmas Eve of 1939. His young lieutenant was on duty.

196

"Private Petrovitch's" story was that he had been captured by Polish guerrillas two nights before his unit had been recalled to Leningrad for active service in the "incident" then taking place in Finland. He had only just managed to get away.

"The way I told it, every word was true. If I lied," the priest has told the author, quite seriously and earnestly, "I am sure that God has forgiven me."

Hardly looking up from his papers, the young lieutenant heard the story, started the wheels of army routine in motion to process Private Petrovitch back into the ranks. His identity papers were cursorily inspected and stamped. That Christmas Eve he spent in Red Army quarters. On New Year's morning of 1940, he was inside Russia, one of a carload of ill, slightly wounded, and stray soldiers who, like himself, had become separated from their outfits.

Two weeks after his arrival in Leningrad, Private Petrovitch was re-assigned—to Headquarters Company of the 112th Infantry, stationed at the Baltic seaport of Riga in Latvia, where the Soviet had established naval and military bases, as they had in Estonia and Lithuania.

Foreseeing the fate of the three independent nations—within a matter of months to be swallowed by the U.S.S.R.—Private Petrovitch had himself assigned to conducting an inventory of religious property and treasures. He proposed the idea and created the job with wholehearted approval and support of his superiors.

In this capacity—and now as a noncommissioned officer, recommended for schooling for a commission—Petrovitch began contacting religious leaders in first, Latvia and, later, Estonia and Lithuania. Since the populations of Estonia and Latvia are largely Lutheran, his work there was chiefly with ministers. Quietly, he warned them of the impending annexation, advised them to go underground and instructed them how to do it. He was instrumental in having new identity papers issued to hundreds of ministers, priests, and rabbis, having them relocated as tradesmen or professional men so that they

197

could carry on the work of religious resistance in comparative safety.

Before he had finished the work he had set out to do, the three countries were annexed by the U.S.S.R. and the program of repression and persecution of the religious was under way. Petrovitch seized this as an opportunity to continue his job "before the priests had a chance to get away with fortunes that rightly belong to the state," he told his superiors.

That Father Janicek as Petrovitch could continue without suspicion and detection for nearly fifteen months is testimony to the intelligence and care with which he worked. Spies and secret agents were everywhere in the Red Army as well as in the civilian population.

In May, 1941, in the Estonian textile city of Narva, as he knelt before the Crucifix in an underground chapel, came the betrayal of Petrovitch.

The circumstances leading up to the betrayal of Father Janicek, masquerading as Petrovitch, are utterly incomprehensible to anyone who had not had close contact with Communist-indoctrinated youth. Given a peculiar type of mentality and a border-line psychotic personality in an impressionable adolescent, the Marxist can accomplish frightening things. Generally, he is able completely to erase the capacity to differentiate morally between right and wrong. The skilled manipulator of such youthful minds is often able to eradicate all sense of personal morality and to construct a mentally robotized being which is no more human than it is individual. The aim, indeed, of Communist education is to subordinate, to eliminate the individual, and to mold the mass mind into an obedient instrument.

It was in April, a few weeks before his betrayal and arrest, that the first link was forged in the chain of events that was to bring to an end the fifteen months of secret work which Father Janicek had pursued in the Baltic states. On his "official rounds" of the churches, ostensibly making an inventory of property so that the People's Government should not be "cheated" of its just dues by the priests, rabbis, and ministers, Petrovitch encountered a Lutheran pastor whom he hoped to help. It was at Narva in Estonia.

Perhaps as a test of the Russian soldier's sincerity, the pastor asked Petrovitch if he were prepared to administer the Sacrament of Extreme Unction. A neighboring Catholic woman was dying. No Roman priest was available or could be asked to take the risk with all the agitation against the religious that was prevalent. Young converts to the new local chapters of the Godless and the Atheists were rising in power and in their own swaggering esteem. Petrovitch was not suspect. Indeed, by the pro-Russian element, he would be hailed as a delivering hero in the uniform of the Red Army. In this disguise, he could go about freely. Would he not, then, go to the dying woman and put her soul at ease?

Petrovitch went. In a tenement near the railroad track, he found the woman, her son, and two daughters gathered around her bedside. At the arrival of a Russian soldier, the two girls went white with fright. Yet an idolatrous gleam lighted the youth's eyes as he stepped forward to embrace his "comrade."

"Yes, I knew the boy might mean trouble for me. But I had taken my vows to administer to God's people. This woman was dying. It was in my poor powers to set her soul at rest. There could be no consideration of personal security. God has ways of putting men to the test. Fear? Perhaps for a moment. But only for a moment. Fear is but an indication of lack of faith. If I had fear, faith conquered it."

Petrovitch—Father Janicek—performed the last rites for the dying woman. The two fearful girls pressed forward for his blessings, kissing his hands. As he turned to make the sign of the Cross over the boy, a look of burning hatred blazed in fanatic blue eyes. The youth turned away. Father Janicek left.

"I remained in Narva for a few days after," Father Janicek recalls. "The Lutheran minister wanted me to escape after I had told him of the boy. He would help arrange it, he told me. Narva was on a direct rail line from Leningrad, less than a hundred miles away, and was a port on the Gulf of Finland. It had been one of the original Soviet military bases. It was filled with military and naval personnel, although the campaign against Finland had ended a full year earlier. Possibly because of the confusion that accompanies any concentration of troops, I had heard nothing that led me to believe the boy had accused me.

"My application for travel papers back to Riga was granted. I returned to answer certain questions concerning the records I had left with my military superiors. Since I had left Riga, a few weeks before, things had taken a bad turn for the religious. Those who had managed to go underground were following my instructions and those of others to remain hidden. Although it had been nine months since the absorption into the U.S.S.R. of the Baltic countries, the anti-religious activity was just then getting into full swing. In the meanwhile, a strong *sub rosa* religious movement was already on the rise."

Every priest considers it a supreme spiritual experience to officiate at the Mass, just as every Protestant minister approaches the ritual of the Holy Communion with humility and supplication. If man ever approaches a state of grace, it is at the moment of this most impressive of Sacraments.

"It was two weeks to the day after the administration of the last rites of our Church to the dying woman in Narva. I had gone with a priest who, with God's help, was able to continue to confirm his people in their religious faith," Father Janicek takes up the story. "We arrived at an abandoned freighter in the harbor. It was early morning long before dawn. We rowed out to the old hulk which had been grounded and climbed over its dry-rotting rail.

"In the dirty hold, there was a makeshift chapel set up. On a table at one end of a cargo section stood the Crucifix, chalices, the Book. The altar cloth was snow white in the candlelight. It was still and hushed. I could feel God's presence there, comforting me. I borrowed vestments from my friend and robed myself. A few men and a woman or two tiptoed quietly in and knelt on the bare floor before the altar.

"I had a premonition. With my fellow priest, I blessed them, then asked him to take them away to safety. He begged me to go with them. I would, after I had made my devotions and had celebrated the Mass in adoration, I promised. There was no point in their staying. They left me there before the altar."

Father Janicek's premonition had been well founded. As he was repeating the last Gospel from the first chapter of *John,* he heard the thump of hobnails on the deck above. With a prayer he turned to the Host, genuflected, and made the sign of the Cross. The soldiers burst in on him, a tall sergeant in command, an officer on deck directing them from the hatch overhead.

"Two of them grabbed me. They ripped the vestments that covered my Red Army uniform. I offered no resistance. The sergeant swung a rifle stock for my head. It caught me in the shoulder. The pain of it sent me reeling blindly against the table that held the chalices and the Crucifix. I remember trying not to upset them.

"The spiritual humility of the celebration of the Mass left me for a moment when one of the guards kicked at the table and it went over. I kicked at him as the Crucifix toppled to the floor. The sergeant closed on me and his hobnails scuffed the sacred pages of the Book.

"For the first time that I could remember, I cursed. I screamed horrifying words at them in Polish, Russian, German. I struck out at them, sobbing in blind fury. I wanted to kill them!

"How many times, my son, I have prayed for forgiveness! The awful words, taking the Lord's name! The terrible fury! The unforgiveable thoughts of violence and killing that flooded over me!

"Looking back, I often wonder whether I am worthy of my

201

office," Father Janicek ponders humbly. "I have spent many an hour in prayer for atonement."

In the melee with the guards, the lighted candles were knocked over. The old hulk was rotten and dried out above the water line where it tilted crazily with the tides that were never high enough to float it off the rocky ledge on which it had grounded. Debris and papers caught fire. The flames spread crazily.

"The officer who peered down through the hatch screeched orders," as Father Janicek tells it. "They were to get me out of there fast and never mind the flames. They weren't firemen. They were soldiers and not very good ones if five of them couldn't subdue one sniveling—as he called me, among other things I wouldn't repeat and you couldn't print if I did—stinking little priest.

"As suddenly as it had come over me, the fury died. I gave in. They pushed and shoved me up a ladder onto the deck. The flames were roaring in the hold below. Smoke was pouring out the hatch and rising like a pillar into the dawn. The officer beat me on the head with his pistol butt. Two persons dragged me to the rail—the officer and the boy of Narva. Both of them punched at me with blasphemous oaths. I fell to the deck. Before I lost consciousness, I looked up at the boy. He was kicking me. But I could not feel it. He was crying."

Father Janicek was on shore when he regained consciousness. He had no sense of pain. Vaguely, he looked in the direction of the Gulf. The hulk which had been a chapel was smoldering with occasional spurts of flame and sparks puffing, apparently, from the open hatch.

"It was like a volcano that threatens to blow off at any moment. I gave a prayer of thanks that our secret chapel had been destroyed. So had God protected those of His Own who might have returned and been caught."

It is difficult to characterize a man like Father Janicek. He is far from a simple man as his words are likely to lead one to assume. His *faith* is simple, to be sure. But he is essentially a man of action. He decided or, as he puts it, he was guided, to leave Poland. He acted without hesitation. He was guided to warn the religious of the Baltic states to go underground. He conceived a plan and acted upon it. The outburst of fury, which he felt was so sinful, was the reaction of a man of deeds. In the application of his creed, the Polish priest is completely undeviating. It is sinful to be proud. It is sinful to be profane, or violent. It is sinful to lie, even to the enemy, the Russians.

On their return to Riga, the arresting guards locked the soldier, who had been unmasked as a priest, in the military jail. There he awaited the arrival of a civilian police agent to question him. If the OGPU man expected to exercise his peculiar brand of "persuasion" on a prisoner who was reluctant to "confess," he must have been disappointed. Without pressure, bullying, threats, or physical torture, Father Janicek wrote in his own hand a full confession of his acts from the moment of leaving Poland to his betrayal and capture. This so upset the civilian secret police, sent from Moscow to spy and inform against the army, that they did not set the trial date for six weeks. During that time, they attempted to persuade him to implicate others. Frankly, Father Janicek couldn't have implicated anyone had he chosen to. For he had never learned a single name of those with whom he had dealt.

"The agents who questioned me suggested names. I did not know any of them. They suggested certain pastors and priests of churches that were mentioned in my military reports. I could not remember a single one. They framed leading questions by which I might implicate certain of my superior officers in the army. None of them had had even the slightest suspicion of my work. Finally, the date of my trial was set for June 20th.

"My appearance before the court was a mere formality. I had freely confessed my guilt, of which I had a worldly pride that I tried to put aside. For I knew it was the work of God.

"The so-called 'trial' lasted less than two hours. The following day, the 21st, I went back to have sentence pronounced. I was condemned to death. It was to be the next morning, be-

fore a military firing squad. All night long I spent setting myself right with God. I confessed to Him. I asked forgiveness and
for strength to meet the greatest earthly trial of all. I prayed
for faith to drive out fear.

"They did not come for me at dawn," Father Janicek con-
tinues his chronicle. "They had not come at ten o'clock. There
were three others with me in the cell who were to share my
fate before the firing squad. Although none was a Roman
Catholic, they all begged me to pray with them and for them.
A barrel-chested Jewish soldier who had murdered his captain
with his bare hands in a fit of rage asked me if I could pray
to his great Jehovah. I said that we both could. What he asked,
I cannot say, for his prayer was silent. I saw great tears gush
down his face. Not tears of craven fear, but tears of relief that,
as his life was about to end, he could communicate with his
God at last."

At noon, an agitated officer appeared before the bars and
called the four by name. He read an official military order in
a nervous rushing voice. It said that Stalin, as Minister of War,
had commuted the sentence of all the condemned to life imprisonment at hard labor. He ended with an unwritten postscript.

"The Nazis invaded Soviet soil this morning. We are at war
with Germany." Looking at the priest, the young officer who
seemed vaguely familiar to Father Janicek added, "And may
God have mercy on us all, Father."

Within two days, Father Janicek, still known as Petrovitch,
was sent in chains with a labor company to build roads ahead
of the Russian retreat. He turned up missing one day in September after a Nazi bombing and was written off as killed in
action.

It is almost unfair to Father Janicek to cut off his narration
with a summary. But he himself will go little farther. When it
was told to the author, the priest briefed the remainder of his
career in the secret army in a few swift sentences. Were this fiction, it might be elaborated. As it is not, there is only one thing

204

left to do. That is to tell it as the one who lived the story tells it.

In the winter of 1942-1943, a doctor turned up in the Stalingrad Military Hospital who possessed what his colleagues called "miraculous surgical skill." It was openly known that he talked of God, made the Sign of the Cross, heard confessions, blessed his patients, and administered the Sacraments. But his professional skill was more important during the months of the grim siege than was his ideology. So he was tolerated as an eccentric.

When the people of Stalingrad in 1943 petitioned Stalin to permit public prayer for the dead of the city which was named for him, the suspect but celebrated surgeon known as "Doctor Janicek" was among the committee which presented the formal document. It was signed by seventy thousand citizens of Stalingrad and hundreds of thousands of others throughout Russia. Stalin gave reluctant consent.

But, furious at having been outmaneuvered, Stalin ordered the arrest of the religious committee from Stalingrad. Not one was ever apprehended and their leader, Dr. Janicek, seemed to have been swallowed up by the earth.

Father Janicek, who uses this pseudonym for purposes of this story to protect relatives now in the part of the U.S.S.R. which was once Poland, says, "I went into the lake and forest region of Karelia, the badlands of Russia. There, among the political outlaws and escaped convicts who inhabit that country which borders Finland, I found the staunchest members of God's secret army. I worked among them, happily and quite openly, until my escape in February a year ago.

"Oh, yes, I am qualified to practice as a physician and surgeon. You see, I once taught in a medical school in Germany."

When he was interviewed, less than seven months before publication of this book, Father Janicek was trying to locate the people of the parish near Grodno which he left in 1939.

"I have fairly substantial evidence that the entire village was relocated, as a group, in an experimental farming development in Siberia," he told me. "If I can verify it, there is only one thing for me to do. That is to try to get back in and through to them."

When these chapters had been transcribed from notes made in Montreal, where I had traced Father Janicek from Berlin, the Polish priest read them carefully and thanked me. Two weeks later, he was to keep an appointment with me in New York. He did not show up. All efforts to locate him have since failed. The portions of his history concerned with his confession and the death sentence in Riga have been documented in Soviet newspapers of the time. So has the incident of the petitions of the people of Stalingrad which he took to Stalin in 1943. The University at Munich verifies his statement that he taught anatomy there in the middle 1930's.

There is no intent to make any great mystery of where Father Janicek may be today. It is the author's opinion that he was able to locate the place of exile of his parishioners. If he has, there can be no question that such a man as Father Janicek has gone to join them, to bring them into the ranks of God's secret army.

15.

Far–Flung Legions

JUST HOW DEEPLY the secret army of religious resistance penetrates the life of Soviet Russia is demonstrated by the career of a priest whom we shall call "Father Zurikov."

When Russian troops seized Lithuania in 1940, Father Zurikov was a diocesan parish priest in the city of Kovno. For some years, ever since Pope Pius XI had issued the original call for the Russian work, he had been engaged in certain phases of the secret army's activity. That he had often aided the flight of fugitives from the Soviet Union in the years when Lithuania had been an independent nation was no great secret among his parishioners. As a matter of fact, aiding escapees from what was recognized as the oppression of Communism was considered a service to the cause of freedom. It was a violation of international relations which the Lithuanian people and even their officials were inclined to applaud.

Once a part of Poland, Lithuania is strongly Roman Catholic. Immediately, therefore, after the Communist regime was established in 1940, commissars, imported from Russia to rule the newly annexed state, went to work to remove priests and ministers from positions of influence among the people. It was proclaimed illegal to deal in silver or to keep silver coins out of circulation. It was a simple matter to turn this ukase against the priests. The police had only to wait until the collection was taken at a church service or to seize the poorbox with its coins and the priest could be charged with hoarding or speculating in silver. This was a crime punishable by imprisonment.

Among the first Lithuanian religious to be arrested on this pretext was Father Zurikov. It is likely that because of his well-known activities on behalf of fugitives from Communism he was so early singled out for an infraction of the law. The new masters of Lithuania were surely eager to get rid of a leader who exerted so strong an influence over many people, particularly since he was actively and outspokenly a critic of Communism. Father Zurikov was, therefore, given a swift, "closed" trial and sentenced to three years in a slave labor gang. He was assigned to a project of the Fisheries Trust, near Okhotsk on the extreme eastern seaboard of Asiatic Russia just north of the Japanese islands.

Because of his prior communication with the secret army, as well as his publicly known enmity for Communism, the priest was able to find a friend within a few months of his arrival at Okhotsk.

"Perhaps it seems like one of those unbelievable coincidences of fiction," Father Zurikov told me in Quebec, "but it is true.

"The wife of the director of the cannery where I was assigned to work was a Lithuanian. As a young girl, she had often attended Mass at my parish church in Kovno. Her father had been a comrade of mine in several instances where we aided escapees from Russia in the days before the annexation. She had come out to the maritime province from Latvia as a bride only a few weeks before my arrival at the cannery, her husband having been stationed at Lepaya in Latvia with the Russian navy during the Finnish campaign. Since their marriage, he had been assigned as commandant of the Okhotsk area and as director of the cannery.

"In such a place as a prison camp, there are always those prisoners who receive favored treatment by the officials. My countrywoman volunteered to have my job transferred from

208

the cannery to her home. For the time being, I preferred to remain with my fellow-prisoners who needed whatever Faith I might help them to, God knows. They hadn't much else. Their hours in the awful stench of the fish cannery began before dawn. Long after night had fallen they were still on the packing line.

"It was stupefying, back-breaking work with the sickening smell of fish always in the pit of your stomach."

A man of humor, in spite of the ordeals he has endured, Father Zurikov added, "Ever since those months in the cannery, Friday has been my day of complete fasting. I just can't bring myself to inhale another fish."

Unlike Father Janicek who believed that God guided him in every step, Father Zurikov felt "that I ought to take some action to get out of a bad situation and just pray that God was with me."

Father Zurikov went on with his narration. "No sooner was I in the Okhotsk area than I started figuring out ways to get free. I was sure there were better ways of serving God than staring into the unblinking eyes of a lot of dead fish.

"Once every couple of weeks for about four months I had seen my young friend pass, sometimes in the cannery, sometimes on the road as we marched in manacles to or from the job. But I had spoken to her only once. Each time she saw me, the tips of her index fingers had been crossed in front of her in what was the sign of the secret army. I had known the sign for years while I had helped Russian refugees before the fall of my country.

"About five months after my arrival at the camp, I was summoned to the office of the director. His wife was there, going through a huge stack of books. She did not look up as I entered. The director was very businesslike in his questioning:

" 'I see by your commitment papers that you are Lithuanian. My wife's people have sent her a number of scientific treatises on fishery. They are in Lithuanian and Estonian. Can you translate them into Russian?'

209

" 'I am adept at both tongues which differ more in the spoken than in the written versions, since they are both Baltic-European languages. I can translate them easily,' I answered. The director was silent for a moment. I could almost read the thoughts which were racing ahead on his ambitious path to recognition and power. If I could translate these works there was nothing to prevent the director from publishing them under his own name. He would be accounted a scholar, a scientist, and one of the foremost authorities on fisheries in the U.S.S.R. He might win the Stalin Medal or even the more coveted Lenin Medal. The director looked up at me.

" 'With stenographic help,' he inquired, 'how long do you think it would take you to translate this volume?' The director picked one off the stack at random and handed it to me. I leafed through it before answering.

" 'In quiet surroundings, with freedom to work when I choose, with no interruptions and decent food,' I replied, 'I might do it in two months, ten weeks at the longest.'

"The director thought for a moment. Again I believed I could read what he would have called his mind. If I translated the work where his subordinates could learn what I was doing, it might someday be brought out that he had not done the job with his own talents, which were questionable if even existent."

Father Zurikov, a master of many languages, has a way with English. He is completely adept at expressing himself in it and has an ear for colloquialism and slang. There is hardly a trace of an accent even though he has had little time to perfect his use of our language. It was impossible to listen to him without amusement even when he was discussing a subject that meant life or death.

"The director had a name," Father Zurikov continued the story of his Siberian adventure, "that would sound like double-talk in English. He never was any saint to me but his wife was. So let us skip his name. Use of it might bring harm to her.

"I don't know whether it was telepathy exerted by me, or

210

gentle wifely persuasion. But I walked out of that office with a new job. It was to be done in his quarters on a hill overlooking a garden and the sea. A prison office worker came in once each week to type up the manuscript which I had written in longhand.

"Each day I had opportunity to talk with the director's wife. She was unhappy in this forlorn spot at the end of nowhere. On the 60th parallel of latitude, Okhotsk was frozen solid in winter. The summer lasted no more than eight weeks. The garden which semed so desirable to me after the squalor of the barracks and the cannery was no more than a collection of rocks fringed with moss.

"The nearest railhead was a thousand miles south by sea. She said she was just as much a prisoner as I was. The problem of escaping from there was simple in only one respect. There was no choice of routes. To the west lay a vast track of uncharted wilds. True, no one would be likely to follow a fugitive into it. But neither would a fugitive be able to stay alive very long. There was only one way out. That was by sea. The only ships that came or went were the trawlers that brought the cargoes of fish from the North Pacific and the Bering Sea.

"Fortunately, Okhotsk had been proving an unsatisfactory base, not from the standpoint of its location for the trawlers but because of the shipping situation. More even than most governments, the Soviet bureaucracy was bound up in red tape—no play on words intended. It could move with the most deliberate pace. It could also move swiftly. When the Nazis turned on Stalin, things fairly flew. Our guards were recalled to Europe for active duty in the war. The director was summoned back to naval service. Orders were that the whole base was to be abandoned within forty-eight hours. The prisoners were to be transferred to the Fisheries camp at Olga, just north of Vladivostok.

"Only hours before we were to sail, a banged-up automobile came in from the north. Its driver was the only passenger. He

211

was a big, bluff, florid man with a week's growth of beard. But he wore a fine otter-lined broadcloth coat and otter cap to match, although it was nearly the first of July. His papers identified as Dr. I. P. Bulganin of the Mining Trust. His surname, an uncommon one, was much in the spotlight in those days. For N. A. Bulganin was a member of the Council of People's Commissars. The befurred newcomer let it be assumed that he was a brother of the great man. He had been on a technical expedition into the mining country to the north. He had to get back to Moscow immediately and would like to join us."

It would take nearly a month on the slow fishing trawlers to sail the thousand miles of the Okhotsk Sea, through the Tartarskie Strait that separates the mainland from Sakhalin Island, to Vladivostok. Since he wished to make rail connections as soon as possible, Bulganin ordered the director to put in at Sovietskaya, five hundred miles to the north of Vladivostok. There he would be able to take a branch line of the Trans-Siberian and save days.

Father Zurikov had been assigned to the same boat with the director and his wife and the mining expert. Night and day the priest worked on the translations which the director was spurring him to complete before they reached Vladivostok. The midnight before they were to put in at Sovietskaya, one of the sailors summoned the priest from his work and took him into the smelly compartment in the bow. There he pointed to a huge shapeless mass sewed in canvas.

"You just died and will be buried at sea with the crew as witnesses. Somebody stuck a knife in you," he explained to the uncomprehending Father Zurikov. Then he crossed his index fingers in the sign. Stealthily, he led the priest to the stern where a dinghy trailed in the boat's wake. He pulled on the rope, and hauled the skiff close. "Get in and change your clothes," he ordered. There were a good suit of clothes and an otter-lined overcoat.

The boat arrived at Sovietskaya an hour before dawn, ahead

212

of schedule for the first time on the trip. The director was not up to bid his guest goodbye.

"But as the small boat pulled away from the trawler, for the dark pier, I saw the director's wife silhouetted in the light of the open cabin door," Father Zurikov finishes this first chapter of his story. "There was a light wrap on her shoulders and she held it closely about her with her arms crossed over her breast."

Father Zurikov had plenty of time on the trip over the entire length of the Trans-Siberian Railway to take stock of his situation. The railroad was clogged with shipments of iron, coal, and vital war metals.

Concerning his identity papers, there were two possibilities. Either their former owner had really been Dr. Bulganin or he had been an impostor. Whichever it was there was danger. If Bulganin had indeed been the brother of the Vice Commissar, the papers were just too hot to keep much longer. If he had been an impostor, it was even worse. In either event, Father Zurikov knew he couldn't get much farther with them. He had thirty-seven days of the trip to Chelyabinsk to lay a plan.

First he had to get rid of those papers. Although the true situation was not being revealed to the Russian people who were removed from the immediate invasion front, Father Zurikov heard enough of telegraphed bulletins and radio broadcasts to surmise that there was chaos in the Red Army facing the Germans. He recalled the campaign in which little Finland had chased the Soviet soldiers across the frozen map of the north with a handful of ski troops, and a heartful of courage. He had little respect for the Russian army that was on the losing end of a fight. He had little respect for the Russians anyhow. If he could just become a refugee, there was an excuse for losing his papers. New ones would then have to be issued. The Germans, he knew, had invaded Lithuania. That was home ground.

It was mid-September when Father Zurikov arrived at Smo-

213

lensk. Day and night, civilian refugees streamed into the city. It was an easy matter for the priest to skirt westward in the night, destroy his dangerous papers, and join the river of humanity that flowed into the city. The otter-lined coat which he had carried since late in July now served him in double capacity. It kept him warm and it also gained the respect of the military guards who courteously took the priest to the office of the military commander of the city.

Since wearing a fur coat of such quality in European Russia is obviously of, or close to, the elite hierarchy, the commandant eyed him with almost abject deference. For all the soldier knew, this proletarian plutocrat might report him to the political higher-ups if he did not watch his step.

The colonel-general in command of the sector issued orders fast. The civil government was to lose no time issuing "Professor Zurikov" identity and travel papers so that he would not be delayed on the vitally secret mission which was taking him to Kharkov. Such was the substance of the story the self-appointed "professor" had told.

"My conscience didn't really bother me. After all I had been a professor once in a theological college in Vilna," Father Zurikov added in explanation. "And my business in Kharkov certainly was secret."

Boldly, now, Professor Zurikov went his way. To Kharkov via Moscow was certainly a roundabout way. The otter coat and cap carried him through. In Moscow he went to the Ministry of Education, right to the top and talked to the brass, V. P. Potemkin himself. The priest was taking long chances but they paid off. He must, he told Potemkin, go to Kharkov on important personal business. He realized that in wartime no one could put his personal affairs above those of the state. In Lithuania, then invaded by the German Wehrmacht, he had taught languages in an advanced school. Was there not some way in which he could get to Kharkov and at the same time serve the nation in its moment of tribulation? Potemkin assigned him to the State Institute in Kharkov, under J. L.

214

Baranoff. He would teach "ideological rehabilitation and indoctrination, so important," as Potemkin put it, "in these times of danger to the Motherland from the forces of Fascism."

The day "Professor Zurikov" started his course in "ideological indoctrination," there were young spies planted in his classes by Baranoff. He was expected to teach the state-endorsed doctrines of atheism and scientific materialism, the idolatry of Lenin and Stalin.

"They were mostly children whose parents had been sent away to imprisonment or labor camps," says the priest who is today in Barcelona. "The state had taken over their education and support in exchange for the services they would render later in the army, in labor, the trades, or—in cases where they won the favor of Party members—the professions.

"Here's how I managed to confirm these youngsters in the religion of their fathers, whether Orthodox, Roman Catholic, Protestant or Jewish. I would retell the story of the creation, for instance, according to the Book of Genesis. When confronted with my perfidy later by Baranoff, I would assure the director that this was merely to point out the error of such ideas and that I would demolish the story the next day with the case for the scientific origin of species.

"Somehow, I managed to present a weak case for the doctrines of atheism and yet to satisfy, at least partially, the objections of Baranoff for more than seven months. One evening in August of 1943, however, one of my students came to me secretly and asked that I perform a marriage ceremony for his sister and a soldier who was returning to the front the next day.

"The student was one whom I had pulled from the wreckage of the school barracks, which had been hit by a German bomb dropped by air raiders from occupied Rumania. His arm had been pinned down and badly mangled. I had applied a tourniquet and nursed the child through the night, since the hospitals were too full and the doctors too busy. He expressed his

215

gratitude and affection for me in many little thoughtful ways and I had grown to know him well.

"As I finished the rites of the marriage Sacrament, in the kitchen of a bomb-blasted tenement near the railroad yards, Baranoff and three NKVD police (now the MVD) stepped in from an outside stairway. The whole business had been a frame-up. The poor child, who had been the unwilling instrument of Baranoff, sobbed in my arms until I was led away.

"The big black limousine, into which the gloating Baranoff and the police agents forced me, careened through the rutted streets. Suddenly the warning sirens wailed, the drone of bombers pierced the silence of the night. The lights of mills and factories blacked out, to be replaced by the searching anti-aircraft beams. The driver of the limousine pulled to the side, dived for cover, followed by Baranoff. The guard on my right hesitated a moment, pulled at my arm, then jumped out and ran for the cellar of a nearby house which had almost been demolished in an earlier raid. The second guard gave me a mighty shove that sent me sprawling out of the car.

"I got up and ran—ran for my life and freedom in the darkness and amid bursting bombs. I cannot say how far I ran, nor how fast. It may have been for two minutes or five or ten. A red flash of fire, a stabbing pain in my legs and a scream that died in my throat were the last things I remember of that ghastly night.

"It was two days later when I regained consciousness. I was in a civilian hospital ward with no sign of guards or of Baranoff. My legs ached beneath the bandages and the aged doctor who came to take my history told me I'd be lucky not to lose them both.

"I had been picked up with no identity papers. (I had turned them over to the OGPU men, fortunately.) I feigned loss of memory—no recollection of who I was, where I was, or how I came there. Across the face of the huge chart, the doctor tiredly wrote: 'Shock, amnesia.'

"After the amputation of my left leg, I was sent, still a vic-

216

tim of amnesia it was assumed, to a convalescent center near Sevastopol on the Black Sea. There, for nearly six years, I was tolerated as a sort of old madman who liked to play priest, marrying people, teaching children their catechism, preaching at funerals, hearing confessions.

"I was pointed out by official guides in the resort country as a harmless old fellow, a bit dotty but pleasant. Yet, I established a strong following of Catholics, Orthodoxists, and Jews who knew I wasn't so crazy, and carried on God's work as He revealed it to me."

Father Zurikov's leaving Sevastopol was not of his own planning or even of his own volition. In 1949, although just past sixty, he was in failing health, no doubt due to his prison privations and the later loss of his leg.

For a year, his secret parishioners and friends, among them a young doctor, had tried to convince the white-bearded man who stumped about on a wooden peg leg to escape from Russia. Every day he lived in danger of arrest. There was always the possibility that the tolerant attitude of individual police officers might change. In addition, he was in almost constant pain and was unable to obtain proper medical attention. His situation demanded hospitalization. And even though he was looked upon as a kindly old crackpot by the officials, it was certainly dangerous if not suicidal to risk going to a hospital without proper papers.

But Father Zurikov apparently had a stubborn streak, insistently refusing to abandon "not my work but God's work before my time was done." Finally, on a night in July of 1949, the young doctor and some friends took the situation in their own hands.

Administering a sedative to relieve the pain of the amputated leg, the doctor put Father Zurikov quietly and tenderly to sleep. In the darkness, strong and willing hands rowed the unconscious priest to a Greek vessel that lay off shore and smuggled him aboard. At Istanbul, he was transferred to an Italian ship bound for Genoa.

217

Today, Father Zurikov is in Paris where he sometimes writes American friends for help for the secret army. To him, help doesn't mean money. It means the furnishing of Bibles and prayer books in the Lithuanian language which he manages to get beyond the iron curtain and into the hands of those who find in the Word the strength to hope for God's return to the Soviet domain.

16.

They Too Were Carpenters

"PASTOR MIKOYAN" may still be alive today somewhere in Russia. He may even be free.

The history of the Baptist minister has been supplied by a Roman Catholic priest and verified by two ministers, a fellow Baptist and a Lutheran. Pastor Mikoyan was known to all three during their activity in the religious resistance movement in the U.S.S.R. in the years just after the Second World War. Documentation of salient points concerning his case is contained in Soviet newspaper accounts of his trial.

Since his story has come from third parties, the background information on Pastor Mikoyan is necessarily sketchy. That he had two brothers, who were builders or possibly carpenters, is known from the brief reports of their sentence to hard labor in 1949. A mimeographed hand bulletin which was circulated by *sub rosa* religious organizations in East Germany in 1950 identifies all three as "artisans." The pastor apparently worked at the building trades with his two brothers. His field of activity in the leadership of the secret army was the most dangerous sector of all, the Moscow area.

In the biographies of all religious resisters great stress is put upon identity papers, job assignments, and travel permits. In a police state such documents are a vital part of daily life. Without them on his person, a citizen may be arrested at any time. Any police officer may demand to be shown them even

219

though a citizen may be doing nothing more suspicious than walking down the street. But possession of identity documents, ration cards, job papers, and a variety of permits is by no means protection against police interference. Particularly is this true in Moscow.

The capital city swarms with secret agents, officious bureaucrats, Party political brass of varying degrees of tarnish, and just plain busybodies. Any of these may call an armed guard or policeman and demand that a perfect stranger present his credentials.

Like the rest of the world's capitals, Moscow harbors a vast multitude of mediocre men. There are the ambitious with little else to recommend them. There are the Party hacks and hangers-on. There are the socially acceptable but intellectually inept. There are, of course, the heavy thinkers, the deep-domed planners, the puppet pundits of the Party press, and the lions of literary and artistic circles. In contrast to the abysmally low standard of living of the rest of Russia, this comparative handful live on a scale that would have been envied by their counterparts of the old Imperial Court. The wealth of Moscow living, naturally, is like a magnet that attracts thieves and criminals. For most of them, ration cards and identity papers are worth a man's life which few of them would hesitate to take. Consequently, it is not enough just to have the proper credentials. It is imperative to hold on to them.

There is not alone the danger of having one's papers hijacked by some thief on a dark night. A favored method of official discipline is to rescind ration cards and issue new ones entitling the holder to less food, less clothing, less fuel in winter. It was because of disciplinary ration cuts that Pastor Mikoyan was apprehended as a leader of the secret army.

The circumstances surrounding the minister's own papers are fairly typical of those of many younger leaders in the secret army. Like all school children in the Soviet, Ivan Mikoyan had begun his military training when he was twelve.

At sixteen, he had started his compulsory service. When Ian was nineteen, he was assigned to service at a Red Army base in Latvia. That was in 1938. When the Germans invaded Russia, he was on reserve status and was called to active duty. He served with distinction in the siege of Leningrad and when the Red Army advance opened in January of 1944, Mikoyan's infantry unit was thrown into the vanguard of the forces driving the Nazis out of Estonia which they had occupied for two years. Young Mikoyan was badly wounded in the lower leg and spent the duration in a hospital.

Just how Mikoyan became a religious is not known for certain. Father Janicek, who had known the young minister slightly, says that it probably came about through contacts with civilian nurses and doctors. Many of the secret army were extremely active in the hospitals, for reasons that are quite obvious.

It was the summer of 1946 before Mikoyan, a noncommissioned officer by that time, was transferred home to Moscow and discharged from the service. As a disabled veteran with certain prerogatives, the twenty-seven-year-old Ivan applied to the Construction Ministry, headed by S. Z. Ginsburg, for assignment in the building trades. His request was granted and he joined his older brothers, both of whom had also seen active war service. Because of his disability, however, the youngest Mikoyan soon found that he was unable to do the heavy work, and he was transferred to teaching the trade in the Industrial School in Moscow.

Each year, the Soviet Union drafts a million youths between the ages of twelve and sixteen for industrial training. Upon completion of their courses, these draftees are obliged to work for five years for the government.

Among the two hundred youngsters who attended the courses in carpentry which Pastor Mikoyan gave there were children of many races. Their parents were of a number of religious sects and creeds.

With the success of the secret army in 1942 in forcing

Stalin to permit public prayers for the dead of Stalingrad, the demand had spread to other war-ravaged cities and towns. Novograd, Leningrad, Zhmerika, Smolensk, and Vitebsk, all of which had endured long siege or bombing, were notable among the communities where open prayer had been sanctioned. In the confusion of war, pressure against the religious and the secret army had been relaxed. The common danger was the uppermost concern. When it was over, however, the Atheists and the Godless became concerned once more with finding a menace to attack. As Soviet imperialism spread to the countries of Middle Europe and took on buffer satellites, the old Bolshevist hue and cry against the religious were once more raised. It was re-broadcast throughout the Soviet Union proper.

The Baltic states and east Poland as well as the satellites, having been occupied by the Nazis, were, the Godless and the Atheists proclaimed, hotbeds of Fascism and religion. Things had been too lax in Russia, too. They must crack down, renew the war on the Church and God, stamp out religion. The old laws were revived and strengthened. The old campaign was renewed with greater vigor than ever as the Union of Atheists and the Association of the Godless opened new membership drives.

As has been stressed before, the religious had been more or less openly active in the hospitals during the war. Almost every wounded soldier had come into contact with some leader or member of the secret army. They had learned to respect and admire the people who had brought them solace and comfort in trying times. It would be difficult to find a Soviet soldier who had not prayed to some God as he faced death or as he tried to endure the pain and fear that were in him. Probably in no class of the Russian populace had the secret army enlisted more followers than in the Red Army. That ex-servicemen were resentful of the activity of the politicians against the valiant religious is evident from the reaction of the brothers of young Pastor Mikoyan in taking risks on behalf

222

of the religious and giving aid and encouragement to Ivan's work in the secret army.

In giving new impetus to the old hysteria, the politicians of the anti-religious movements were well aware of the increased strength of the resistance through its following among war veterans. A large segment of private opinion was on the side of the religious. This represented a great potential force of opposition to the aims of substituting the religion of politics for the religion of the Church.

The Godless needed a horrible example. They needed it preferably in Moscow where it would attract national attention. The best way to bring a secret opponent out into the open was to give him something to fight about. And so it happened that Pastor Mikoyan was the victim who was snared in the propaganda scheme to stir up sentiment once more against the religious.

The young trade school teacher had gained wide popularity with the youngsters whom he had as pupils. Often, after school hours, he was invited to their shabby homes for a glass of tea or for the bitter coffee that only Russians seem have a taste for. It was on such visits that he learned whether to trust the elders with the secret of his real calling. His brothers, too, got the word about among those who could be trusted that Ivan would confirm the people in their faith.

Soon, the short calls grew into larger meetings at which all would quietly sing hymns and bow their heads in prayer, led by Pastor Mikoyan. Although his services were conducted for congregations which seldom exceeded five or six, the young minister managed to get about quite a bit, in the fashion of the old-time American circuit-riding parson. At first, his rounds included no more than two or three homes. As the months went on, however, they grew to a dozen, to twenty.

Whether all the members of his expanding congregation were Protestants or even Christians was never known. Probably Pastor Mikoyan never bothered to ask. If they needed

223

him to help them to God, that was enough. That he observed no exclusive sectarianism—as indeed few leaders of the secret army do—is evident in the events that led up to his discovery and arrest. They occurred during and after the season of the Passover.

An old law that had not been particularly well observed or enforced during the war years was revived just before the Christmas season of 1948. It forbade the observance of certain religious holidays, excepting in the state-controlled church. No serious violations occurred at Christmas. At least none that the anti-religious felt they could prosecute. The anti-Semitic campaign they had also sponsored was gaining in strength. The Jewish holidays offered them a better chance. To augment the law forbidding religious observances, new ukases were issued by Stalin. They were definite and applied to the Jews. They ordered full attendance at all schools by children of Jewish parentage or extraction. They further prescribed the dates during which the regulation applied. These dates covered the traditional period of fasting and feasting, the Passover. The new laws also provided that enforcement and punishment for violations were to be in the hands of local authorities.

On the morning of the traditional feasting which inaugurates the eight days of the Passover's observance, several of Pastor Mikoyan's students failed to report to class. It was an omission the teacher-minister might well have overlooked, excepting that he had no choice. As each of his scheduled classes met, a member of the Union of Atheists was officiously on hand to check attendance. Day after day, the list of absentees grew.

In an effort to confound and confuse the Atheists, the Pastor went to his Christian friends with a plea that they keep their children out of school too. But in the revolutionary land which broadcasts the fiction that it does not practice discrimination, this failed to work. For while the identity cards of non-Jews noted no religious designation, the papers of all

224

Jews carried the information of their religious affiliation in the space allotted to the place of birth: As an example, "Georgia-Jew."

Non-Jewish children, therefore, who remained away from school during the days of celebration of the Passover, were not punished—"disciplined" is the word the People's Court used. This discipline was the seizure of food ration cards of every member of a Jewish family whose children stayed away from school. Absenteeism was, in itself, evidence not only that the elders had observed the forbidden religious holiday, but also that they had taught the children from the religious books which were proscribed by the state. Therefore, everyone in such a household was guilty of violating the law and must be "disciplined." Ration cards of all offenders were, consequently, taken up by the police, to be restored after an unspecified period at the discretion of the authorities in charge of rationing, many of them Atheists.

It was difficult to get food enough in Russia even with ration cards. Without cards, it was impossible.

For days after the harsh measures went into effect, Pastor Mikoyan sat in the classroom with a heavy heart as he looked into the hungry eyes of starving boys and girls. His efforts to persuade their classmates to share meager luncheons met with some success. But there was not nearly enough to go around. The good man went hungry, himself, giving up his none too plentiful meals to those who seemed to suffer the most. A week after the punishment had gone into effect, with no signs that the authorities would soon relent, the Pastor began asking for contributions of food from his growing circle of secret parishioners. Knowing the cause, they gladly gave.

The Pastor's brothers helped collect food, too. They begged for a crust of bread or a head of cabbage here, a few leaves of tea, or a ration stamp there. They went hungry so that they might contribute almost their entire rations to the hungry children.

Distribution of the contraband food to those who were being "disciplined" was managed under a most ingenious plan. Its conception leaves only admiration for Pastor Mikoyan. He used the very officials who had rescinded the ration cards to cover his distribution plan. By his scheme extra fuel and a stove were also obtained.

Like politicians everywhere in the world, those of the Soviet Food Ministry had their pet projects, were particularly partial to the least sensible and most costly projects, and were determined to prove their little schemes would work, no matter what the cost.

A certain Comrade Zotov was carried away by the idea of cooperative or communized food preparation. Since the comrade was the People's Commissar for Food Supply, his whole department was infected with the same enthusiasm. Now, there was nothing new about cooperative kitchens; they had first been tried out in the days of the famine. But they had proved successful only in the farming districts and in small communities. Even those that had been successful had died out during the war. Zotov and his minions, however, firmly believed in them and were eager to promote cooperative kitchens wherever they could, especially in Moscow and the larger cities. The reason is obvious enough to anyone who has had experience with the sort of genius peculiar to politicos. To establish cooperative kitchens on a national scale would add to the number of employees in the department and allow greater meddling in the affairs of more citizens. In other words, it would increase the power of the Food Supply Ministry.

To the Ministry office went Pastor Mikoyan. He proposed that a kitchen cooperative be set up in the Industrial School to feed not only the children at luncheon but also their parents at supper. The idea of using the schools as a feeding center had apparently never occurred to the great official minds. Perhaps this was the solution to centralized food preparation in the larger population centers. Not only would the

226

Food Ministry sanction the plan, it would even send experts to instruct the members in mass-production cooking.

A stove arrived next morning with a supply of fuel to operate it. The "experts" appeared on the scene with a side of beef and quantities of vegetables. Tass, the official news agency, was persuaded to send reporters and photographers to "cover" the event. The Food Ministry was determined to give the experiment a big public send-off.

Details of the first big feast, thrown by the government agency, are included in the reports of the testimony at the trial of Pastor Mikoyan some months later. According to the government version, the Food Ministry was just playing along to trap the violators of rationing regulations "who were stealing food from the mouths of their fellow citizens." This is an unlikely story, for it seems the cooperative kitchen project existed far longer than would have been necessary if the only purpose had been to expose rationing violations.

It is probable that few school children in Russia were better fed than those in the Industrial School in Moscow. The project became the experimental model for others which the Food Ministry proposed to set up in industrial communities throughout Russia. It received wide publicity.

Pastor Mikoyan was made the honorary director of the kitchen. It was he who inspected the credentials of the parents who came for the evening meal. It is a certainty that no one was turned away hungry. The Jewish children and their parents never missed the withheld rations after the kitchen opened.

What the three brothers feared most was the day when their food project would fall under the scrutiny of the security police. It was inevitable. That hurdle came up and was taken without breaking stride. Comrade Zotov, a power with Stalin and a member of the Politburo, proudly conducted Comrade Rovotsky, of the MVD, on his first official inspection.

That there were no suspicions aroused for ten to twelve weeks seems evident from the fact that the "Zotov project," as the press called it, was a source of national news and propaganda. However, it dropped out of headlines and radio bulletins as quickly as it had cropped up. How discovery of Pastor Mikoyan's real objective in establishing the cooperative came about is not known. The reports of the trial do not give that information. Neither do they mention the details of the weeks of imprisonment endured by the three Mikoyans before they were brought to trial.

A double charge was brought against them: Conspiring to violate food rationing regulations and plotting to subvert justice meted out by officials of the Union of Socialist Soviet Republics.

Testimony presented by the People's Prosecutor brought out that Ivan Mikoyan was a "foreign religious." There were "affidavits" from four separate individuals testifying that the religious rites of marriage had been performed by Ivan Mikoyan. There were others that upheld the prosecutor's contention that he christened children "lawfully registered in the security police records." Still others bore out accusations that Ivan had baptized children "by dangerous immersion in the river" and not in accord with the regulations laid down by the Education Ministry governing "legal church activities."

There were sixty-seven written accusations against the three brothers of collecting food and ration stamps to subvert "the punishment of those who had violated the law" laid down by one man in the Kremlin. It seems that the act of starving young school children was a perfectly "justifiable disciplinary measure to teach respect for law"—according to the dictates of those who make war on God.

Unquestionably because he had made Zotov and other highly placed Party members and government figures look bad in the eyes of the people and because the Atheists and the Godless wanted a propaganda cause of celebrated proportions, Pastor Mikoyan's sentence was unusually harsh, even for Russia. His brothers received twelve years apiece at hard

228

labor, the Pastor twenty years—for feeding the hungry as his Master had done twenty centuries ago.

Where Pastor Mikoyan or his brothers are cannot yet be told. But certain leaders of the secret army know and have vowed to deliver them.

17.

The Lice Tank

"MUCH HAS BEEN WRITTEN about the NKVD methods of torture and torment to extract confessions," the priest who endured it all and lived to tell about it has said. "Outside sources tell and speculate about truth serums and will-breaking drugs. I cannot deny their use, but I can say that tuberculosis, scurvy, and exhaustion are the greatest allies of the police in Russia—and their greatest weapon to break a man's will, self-respect, and moral resistance is the louse—the common, filthy louse and his companion, the bedbug."

The alleged crime with which "Father Maguire" was charged, on the February night in 1946 when the secret police rapped on his door in Leningrad and dragged him off to the "house of temporary dentention" in the Shapalernaya, was never put in writing on any document until the day of his "trial" weeks later.

As the black van in which he was transported turned along the waterfront street that traces the coast of the Baltic, Father Maguire could make out the hulks of ships and feel the cold wind that screamed in from the sea. Since they had brought him away without his overcoat, the priest was chilled through when they arrived at the iron gates of the prison.

"I couldn't help shivering but I knew I had to stop—for I couldn't let them think I was frightened," he told me when I interviewed him in Florence. "My guards noisily and with

230

much cursing propelled me up the stairs to the clerk's office on the second floor. It was dimly lit, dirty like all official places in Russia, and cold.

"A sleepy young officer in a warm uniform, his overcoat open at the collar and his cap on the back of his head, started barking questions at me, between yawns, as he filled out the official forms:

" 'Name? Mee-wire? Spell it!'

"He learned from his questioning that my father was Irish, that my mother was Polish, and that I had been born in eastern Poland in what had become part of the Soviet Union and I was therefore considered a Russian citizen. No, I had no identity papers other than the working papers issued by the Ministry of Labor.

" 'Did you have permission to emigrate to Leningrad?' the officer asked.

"I smiled at that one. I not only had permission but had been thoughtfully provided with guards in 1941 just before the Germans declared war on the Soviet and when the Labor Ministry was recruiting workers for the happy family of mill hands for the Motherland, in which I had worked for five years.

" 'Do you know a Father Propkin, an Orthodox Priest who served in the army of the Czar?'

" 'I do not know him by that name, perhaps by some other. I know a great many religious.'

" 'You know a great many who served in the army of the Czar?'

" 'I do not ask people their personal history. I cannot answer.'

"He wrote 'refuses to answer,' and looked up at me severely.

" 'You will recall and you will answer before you're through. Then we will probably shoot you.'

"The questioning continued for more than an hour: the routine things like whether I was married, why not, where I hid my money—I had none and told him I had taken vows of poverty which he neither believed nor understood.

231

" 'Then,' he said slowly and with triumph, 'You admit you are a Jesuit.'

" 'If a humble man of no pride may boast, I proudly proclaim I am a priest of God.' The young officer took up a pen with red ink and printed in large letters across the front of the questionnaire, 'Jesuit'—then he ordered the guards to take me away."

The "tank" into which they thrust Father Maguire, with a great show of brutality and force, had been built originally to accommodate perhaps twenty persons. There were more than eighty in it the night he was arrested. The only ventilation was through the grating in the iron door. It was sweltering from the heat of the bodies and from the steam pipes which hissed and clanked overhead.

As his eyes became accustomed to the dim light, Father Maguire squeezed into a space near the door where he could sit up, provided he drew his legs up to his chin and propped his back against the door. There was a single toilet in the corner—it did not work and the reek of it mingled with the sickening odor of unwashed clothing and bodies, most of which were not only dirty but diseased.

Some of the men slept on mattresses filled with straw. Father Maguire saw swarms of vermin crawling over the mattresses and over the arms and faces of the sleepers who scratched and slapped and cursed in unconscious torment. The priest began to scratch within fifteen minutes and knew that "the treatment" was already under way.

In the morning, Father Maguire recognized four of his fellow tank mates. One was an Orthodox priest, another was an aged rabbi, the third, a layman who had once served on the altar when he'd celebrated a *sub rosa* Mass. The fourth he'd known in his factory and suspected of being an informer.

Father Maguire waited to be recognized but only the young worker spoke to him. The priest surmised there were spies among them and he was correct as he learned later.

For eleven days, during which he left the tank only for a

232

daily half-hour airing, there was no call for Maguire, though most of the others took turns being "interrogated." On the twelfth morning, the guards came for Maguire. They took him to the fourth floor where they shoved him into a cubicle presided over by a cigar-smoking Madame Efimova.

"The questions I was asked are irrelevant today, as indeed, they were then. It was the method of asking them—as if she had rehearsed before a mirror. She was calm and polite at the start. She became tense and stared with what I am sure she believed to be a hypnotic gaze. She stood up and paced. She turned quickly and bent over me closely, menacingly. She blew cigar smoke in my face, she pounded on the table and ranted.

"On the question of loyalty to the state, Efimova became tender. Her eyes filled with tears as she expounded on the benefits to the people, on the 'saintliness'—she actually used that word—of Comrades Lenin and Stalin. What book of the Bible, she wanted to know, compared for sheer literary beauty and poetry to the Communist Manifesto? If there was such a thing as divine inspiration—and, mind you, she wasn't admitting anything—would I not confess that Marx and Engels were more greatly inspired than Luke and James?

"I was a foreign agent who had stolen into their Motherland to plot the assassination of Comrades Stalin, Vishinsky, Molotov, Beria—the great, the gentle, the forgiving Beria. I denied it. I was an Irishman, wasn't I? No, I was a Pole, now a Russian. Lies, all lies, she insisted.

"At lunch time, Efimova, exhausted with her exhibition, was relieved by Lieutenant Smirnoff. His approach was vicious. It included raps on the hands with a pistol butt, face slapping, choking, the hand held over the mouth and nose—shutting off the breath while guards held me. The first day's session lasted from eight in the morning until ten at night—fourteen hours with nothing to eat and no time out, with a third interrogator relieving Smirnoff. I would sign nothing. Then back to the 'lice tank' and another night of verminous torment."

Every other day for seven weeks, Father Maguire was inter-

233

rogated, bullied, beaten, tormented, starved, tortured by the lice and bedbugs and the heat of the cell. He saw strong men break down and cry as their blood and health and self-respect were drained away by the voracious vermin. Others who had endured imprisonment for months were toothless and hairless, wan and gaunt from scurvy, all resistance, all will and self-reliance gone, staring, empty hulks of what once were men.

Late in April, Father Maguire, who had signed no confession but who had been implicated in the untrue confessions of others, went on trial with seventeen religious of many faiths.

"We were charged with 'ideological sabotage' on evidence that we had taught from the Bible and books of the Jewish faith and advocated resistance and revolt against the state.

"The details of the three-day trial are too ludicrous and dimly defined to go into. The very fact that I had signed no 'confession' was used against me. It was used as proof that I was a 'resister,' a Jesuit!

"All were found guilty as was charged and expected. Four were condemned to death—I, to twenty-two years at Solovetski concentration camp, called 'the prison of no hope on earth.' "

Solovetski Island, "the prison of no hope on earth," lies in the White Sea, an arm of the Barents Sea, which thrusts inland between Archangel and the northernmost peninsula of European Russia jutting down below Murmansk.

Late in April, when Father Maguire arrived with a trainload of prisoners, it was still covered with dirty snow, the boggy roads a half-frozen river of mud lined with high, rickety sentinel posts and barbed wire.

The guards who met them when they detrained from the railroad line that runs north from Leningrad to Kem were actually prisoners like those they cursed and prodded along with bayonets. They were mostly thieves and criminals who had served in the Red Army, a cutthroat crew under the command of non-convict officers. They were to be not only the keepers, but the teachers and examples of proletarian culture

234

for the political prisoners who were mainly teachers, religious, professional men, workers, and intellectuals.

Lumbering is the single industry at Solovetski. It is conducted by the Lumber Trust, which has an economic arrangement for the purchase of labor from the MVD—literally a traffic in slave labor. The camp officials, therefore, waste little time on the formalities of entry, quarantine, orientation—except for the regular "cultural and educational" lectures conducted by certain favored prisoners.

After such a lecture session, his third night at Solovetski, Father Maguire was surprised to see a tall, white-haired man rise, move to the center of the frigid barrack room, and bow his head in prayer. Hurriedly, a number of prisoners rose and scurried away. The two prisoner-guards who had been at the door turned and ran out into the night.

The voices of men who had sung the "Internationale" to wind up the lecture proceedings a few minutes before were now lifted joyously in a Protestant hymn. As they finished, the leader again bowed his head and the words of the "Lord's Prayer" came in a chorus of mixed tongues and dialects from the throats and from the hearts of emaciated, bent, and broken men. Some of the voices quavered, tears stood in their words, but the tone of the proud old man was loud and calm and clear.

Not until they had finished was there an interruption. Then a civilian guard commander, red-faced and blustering, burst into the room, followed by the two convict-guards who had run away earlier.

"Schweitzer," he bellowed, "you can't do this to me. If this gets back to Moscow . . . Please, Schweitzer, in the name of mercy, stop it. Please," he pleaded, "don't make me break you. Don't make me kill you . . ."

The old man looked at him with calm compassion. "There is no death. You cannot kill me. Only God can take me away —in His own time and in His own way."

"I can take you away to solitary confinement. And this time for sixty days," the commander threatened.

235

Pastor Schweitzer looked at him for a moment. "There I can pray," he intoned solemnly, "for forgiveness of your sins and blasphemies as well as my own. In solitary, there is peace, but I shall not be alone for God is there, too."

"Take him away," slobbered the guard. "If they ever hear of this in Moscow—they'll never forgive me."

"But Jesus will! He will," said the old man as they led him away.

It was "Father Mueller," who told Father Maguire the story of Pastor Schweitzer. A Lutheran minister who had gone to Latvia from Germany as a youth, Pastor Schweitzer had been among the first imprisoned when Latvia had been annexed, largely because he was of German birth. Later he had been convicted as a foreign spy, and he had been at Solovetski since 1941.

The guards, both convict and civilian, had a mortal fear of the old pastor whose spirit no amount of "corrective" discipline, hardship, starvation, or torture could break. Well over sixty, Pastor Schweitzer was assigned to the back-breaking task of pulling a sleigh into the woods and out again when it was loaded. He went at his work with a hymn on his lips. When the guards beat him with whips or rifle butts, the saintly old man would look up at them and mutter, "God forgive you."

At the fifteen-minute break for the usual meal of thin barley soup, hot water, and a crust of bread, Pastor Schweitzer would set up a rough timber cross and lead his fellow sufferers in prayer and singing. Often, no one dared to join him and the old man would go through his religious service alone.

It was many months after they had taken Pastor Schweitzer away to solitary before Father Maguire and Father Mueller saw the old man again. But day and night while he was away they could hear his voice from the solitary cell, a hundred yards removed from the barrack, raised in songs of praise to the Lord.

It was a blistering cold night in January, 1947, when Lublinski, the new commandant, released him with warning to cease his "infernal singing." He came in quietly in the middle of the night. In the dark of the frigid barracks, Pastor Schweitzer sat on his cot.

"Brothers," he said, more faintly than he had ever spoken before, between racking, tubercular coughs, "will you join me in singing 'Ave Maria'? I could not be with you on Christmas."

From all corners of the black barrack, voices joined in the sacred song, Pastor Schweitzer's above them all, leading their spirits and their thoughts back to the days when they were men.

Lublinski stormed into the room. The singing continued. He grabbed the old man, hysterically beating him with the butt of his pistol about the mouth, nose, and eyes. Not a scream nor a whimper did he wring from Pastor Schweitzer.

"I'll teach you. I'll break you. I'll show you corrective measures you've never dreamed of," screamed Lublinski. Four convict-guards dragged the old man away.

"For a few minutes we could hear him singing. Then his voice was stilled. In the morning when we turned out we could see in the middle of the company formation a block of ice on the ground. Lublinski had played the hose on Pastor Schweitzer in the Arctic night.

Frozen into a human statue, the body of Pastor Schweitzer lay in the attitude of martyrdom—his arms outstretched, forming a cross. So said Father Maguire of the holy man, known as the Saint of Solovetski, who fought in the ranks of the secret army—in "the prison of no hope on earth."

It was more than a year after the martyrdom of Pastor Schweitzer, his true name, when the Orthodox Father Mueller came to Father Maguire, the Jesuit, with a plan to escape from Solovetski.

It was a dangerous undertaking. For it depended on help from outside the camp, as well as upon that of a civilian guard. The latter might easily betray them. In such an event, the two priests would be allowed to make their break and then would

237

be shot down for attempted escape. But even death is preferable to life on Solovetski Island.

The escape of Father Maguire and Father Mueller from the "prison of no hope on earth" took months of planning, the cooperation of a Norwegian ship captain, the bribing of a civilian guard, and the self-sacrifice of a heroic elderly rabbi who gave up his own freedom and, without doubt, his life for his friends.

Neither priest ever knew the rabbi's name. The old man's job was in the central work assignment office. Maguire and Mueller worked in the forests, felling trees, dragging out logs, pulling sledges from sunup until after dark.

Popoff Island, or Solovetski Island, a name it takes from the prison, boasts a small harbor, accommodating timber ships. Because of the shortage of "free labor" in the unpleasant region of the White Sea, prison labor often was pressed into loading the ships.

The rabbi-clerk would assign the two priests to loading details at every opportunity over a period of several months. One night he met them in the barracks and whispered his escape plan. Father Maguire and Father Mueller were ready for anything. The odds were greatly against them. No more than a dozen men had escaped in thirty years.

The day of their break they had less than two hours' notice. All day they had pushed huge sleds of timber onto a Norwegian freighter, stowing the cargo in the hold and lashing it onto the deck. The guards worked the loading gangs without mercy. At 10 P.M. the rabbi came aboard to check the crews. The rabbi whispered to the priests: "The last loads should be in place by midnight. In the chief engineer's cabin are workmen's clothing for us all. You, Maguire, will go in at 11:45, change, and go astern. Mueller will follow in five minutes. I will come last."

After he had stolen into the engineer's cabin and changed from prison garb, Father Mueller met Father Maguire on the afterdeck. They waited nervously for the rabbi. At midnight, they heard a commotion, the rattle of guns, loud cursing from

238

the engineer's cabin. They saw guards swarming up the gang-plank and in the excitement they scrambled down and back onto the pier, mingling with the Norwegian crew which was being herded off while the Russian guards searched the ship.

"How many were with you?" they heard the guard commander ask the old rabbi as they hustled him off the ship.

"Look at the assignment records," answered the bearded patriarch.

"Give them to me. Where are they?" demanded the chief guard, while his subordinates sadistically jabbed their prisoner in the neck and back with their bayonets.

"Go find them. Find them," screamed the rabbi. "I'll tell you where the records are—at the bottom of the sea."

The priests had to stand and watch while their brother was dragged by the heels, kicked at every step, to what undoubtedly was his doom.

Knowing the ship would never be allowed to sail until it was thoroughly searched, Father Mueller decided they should try to make it by land. Kem, the nearest rail-head to Solovetski, is reached by an isthmus that is submerged excepting at low tides. Then it is a stretch of half-frozen bogland. Their one hope was that the prison authorities would search the other two ships in the harbor, never dreaming that the fugitives would risk escape by any other route than by sea—that they would take the desperate chance of going back into the interior of Russia. This is exactly what the prison guards did, affording the escapees precious time.

Through a morass of mud, up to their waists in the salty marshes, the fugitives struggled through the numbing night along the half-submerged isthmus that leads toward Kem. Carefully they skirted Kem in the Karelo-Finnish state of the U.S.S.R. and headed for the dense forested land of lakes where the doughty Finns had held the might of the Red Army at bay in 1940. Boldly they traveled by day, westward from Kem toward the Finnish border.

Karelia, with its twenty-five hundred lakes, is inhabited

239

largely by fiercely independent Finns who resent the Russians sent by the government as settlers in the wild country which supports its inhabitants largely through fishing, hunting, fur trapping and lumbering. Its pine and fir forests afford protection for escaped political convicts and outlaws, refugee farmers from the collectivization program of the Soviet, and highly independent tribes of nomads who roam the country with their reindeer herds.

So unfriendly are these elements to the Russians that Soviet soldiers seldom leave the main vehicular arteries—which parallel the Murmansk Railroad—and then only in large numbers. The Russians who inhabit Karelia are bribed by the Soviet government with extra food and rations to remain there.

The third day of their escape, weak with hunger and fatigue, the fugitive priests encountered a small band of nomads who gave them food, recognized them as escaped prisoners, and took them to "Father Markovsky." The latter is a fictitious name, used to protect a priest who went underground during the Russo-Finnish war.

A remarkable man, according to Father Maguire's description, the leader of the most feared underground group in all of the Soviet domain is short, stocky, blue-eyed, with fair hair and beard—typically Scandinavian. The religious activity of Father Markovsky is quite open, but his other activities are strictly *sub rosa*.

It is his organization—a tight-knit body of fierce and fearless men of Roman and Orthodox Catholic, Protestant, and Jewish faiths—that knows the unguarded points where a man or two may slip across the forested border into Finland in the dead of night. They maintain contact between leaders of the secret army within and outside the Soviet. They know how to obtain documents that will take a man to safety in northern and western Europe.

Many are armed. All are devoutly religious according to their own faiths, and intensely loyal to Father Markovsky who metes out justice to them according to God's law, holding their innate violence and lawlessness in check. He is, until God's moment comes, priest, minister, rabbi to his people, beloved by them and feared by the Kremlin which has put a higher price on his head than on that of any proscribed outlaw of the U.S.S.R.

After five months of living among Father Markovsky's people, the fugitive Father Maguire and Father Mueller were spirited across the border one stormy autumn night.

Father Mueller is now in West Germany, preparing to return as an aide to the priest of Karelia. Father Maguire is presently in Spain, where he may be teaching and training others for leadership in the secret army.

18.

Silence in the Satellites

THAT THERE HAS BEEN no mention, other than in passing, of the activities of the secret army in the enslaved satellites is the result of deliberate design. There are a number of reasons for such omission. The chief one, already stated, bears repetition. It is simply that the slightest reference to religious resistance in Poland and the Balkans would unquestionably bring new repression against the clergy of all denominations, as well as against suspected laymen.

All that is needed to bring new official waves of terror and persecution in the satellites is an excuse. Whether the evidence linking the religious be true or false, the slightest pretext will be seized upon as a basis for propaganda against the churches and their leaders. This was amply proved in the uprisings of workers in East Germany, Poland, and Czechoslovakia in June of 1953, and again in January and February of 1954, when new demonstrations threatened.

Official government "news" broadcasts in Warsaw, East Berlin, Budapest, and Prague at those periods were unanimous in trying to pin the blame on the Roman Catholic Church. On June 10, 1953, Radio Budapest, according to monitors in Frankfort announced:

It has definitely been established that the demonstrations of disloyalty that have marred the unity of the People's Republic of

242

Czechoslovakia had been fomented by agents and provocateurs of the Church.

The disgraceful exhibitions in the Eastern Zone of Germany, where the Red Amy of the Soviet Socialist Republics is selflessly protecting the rights of the People's Provisional Republic to exist against the threats of the imperialistic Fascists of the United States, have been traced to the door of the reactionary Church. The banners and placards (posters) carried by the demonstrators were professionally printed. The slogans have been heard before from the West. They were produced in Paris and in West Berlin. They were smuggled into the Soviet Zone by agencies that would sabotage the industrial, economic, and social progress that as been made in the Provisional People's Republic, in such revealing contrast to the static situation under the puppet Bonn regime.

The printing of posters in France and West Berlin, the smuggling of them into the People's Zone, the obvious military organization of the marchers' units, all point to a conspiracy between the political and religious reactionaries of the West to disrupt and discredit the governments of the People's Republics.

The Church cannot deny that many in the processions carried crucifixes.

If, as apologists for controlled propaganda have been known to insist, the government agencies do no intentionally color the news, then the numerous errors in fact can only be laid to bad reporting. The quoted "news report" stressed only the facts it chose to reveal. There were the obvious political reasons for not telling all the facts.

To begin with, the statement that posters were printed in Paris and West Berlin was quite true. However, it was not the *whole* truth. The fact has been amply verified by intelligence agencies that unquestionably the majority of the tens of thousands of printed posters, handbills, and pamphlets were produced in East Germany—in the underground, by underground agencies. It simply did not serve the government to have its controlled press mention this. For that would be open admission of the existence of resistance in spite of the security police.

In the second place, hundreds of demonstrators did carry crucifixes. Many more hundreds carried replicas of the Cross. There were also banners proclaiming, "Restore God to Germany." The reasons for omitting such information are fairly obvious, in view of the Magyar Republic's official position as persecutor and prosecutor, judge and jailer of Cardinal Mindzenty.

As a matter of fact, Lutherans outnumber Catholics in Germany by an average of about six to four, while other Protestant denominations reduce the ratio of the Catholic population even further, to about 34 per cent. It is, therefore, reasonable to assume that the protestors represented substantially the same proportions, religiously. But it was apparently not politic in Hungary to mention this probability.

The Budapest broadcast on this item in the news concluded:

The influence of the Roman Catholic clergy was openly evident in the revolt of the reactionaries in Czechoslovakia, because the security police efficiently and conclusively fixed responsibility on Rome for literature that was distributed and for leadership of this intolerable revolt against the People's Governments.

Practically any fancied offense by a religious is attributed to "Rome" in satellite propaganda. Opposition to Godless Communism is an honor which the Roman Catholic Church neither deserves nor desires to claim unto itself. That it cannot was abundantly demonstrated in the rioting of June 1953.

Within forty-eight hours of the outbreak of the strikes, reprisal measures were well under way. One in every ten of the 50,000 taken into custody in the hectic week in East Germany was a religious. Five thousand clericals were jailed, an estimated three thousand of them non-Catholics. If none was rounded up in the wave of arrests that accompanied the Soviet-inspired unrest in the following January and February, it was possibly because few of the religious had been released.

In the Czech and Polish disturbances that occurred practically simultaneously with the June uprising in the Soviet Zone of Germany, retaliation followed a similar pattern. It was swifter, however. And in Warsaw there was an added overtone of anti-Semitism which was heard in the hateful vehemence with which the controlled press and radio attacked "the Jew agitators and conspirators."

There is every evidence to support the belief that the religious resistance is far less active in the satellites than within the Soviet Union. Religious leaders who supply aid and assistance, organization and direction to the secret army from outside the U.S.S.R. insist that this is true. Whatever activity they are supporting in the satellites is largely in the direction of helping their clericals to escape the danger zones, rather than to send new leaders in.

In Czechoslovakia, Hungary, Poland, Rumania, and Bulgaria—as well as in Tito's Yugoslavia, despite all protestations and propaganda to the contrary—one of two conditions prevails for every member of the clergy. Either he is under police surveillance or he is imprisoned.

Being under surveillance means for the religious that his every move is closely watched by the police. His comings and goings are strictly and severely regulated. Papers and permits are issued to him on a temporary basis. If the cleric is not under actual house arrest, he must report regularly to the security police, like a criminal on parole.

Imprisonment has been experienced by well over half of the religious of whatever denomination in the satellites since they have become Sovietized. In other words, some 50,000 priests, ministers, rabbis, mullahs, and spiritual leaders and teachers had been jailed in the nine years from 1945 to 1954. The charges were largely trumped up on some political pretext or other, usually summed up in the heinous crime of "obstructionism." The 50,000, it is to be noted, by no means represents the total of religious objectors who have served or are serving prison sentences for their opposition to the anti-religious tenets of Soviet socialism in the satellites. It accounts only for the clerics. It does not include hundreds upon hundreds of laymen. There is no way of making any check upon the latter.

(The figure of 50,000 is a conservative estimate. It was arrived at by reference to assignment rosters and roles, reports and records of eight religious organizations which maintain contact with their people in the satellites. These are located in Athens, Rome, West Berlin and Frankfurt, Copenhagen, and New York. In addition to Roman Catholic and Orthodox, Lutheran, and Jewish agencies, three less centralized and more general Protestant sources have supplied information.)

Not a single known religious has escaped rigid police questioning and investigation since Communism was impressed upon the European satellites, an area comprising over half a million square miles and more than 100,000,000 population. This takes in Yugoslavia, as any realist must. Clerics have been given a freedom of choice—collaboration or persecution. To the everlasting glory of the clergy of all denominations, the vast majority chose the thorny path of conscience. The comparative few who did not have been put to effective propaganda use.

In 1950, several hundred of the conformist clergy were shipped to the Kremlin-sponsored "peace congress" in Warsaw. A few well meaning fellow-clerics from the West accepted invitations to attend. No purpose could be served by calling the roll at this late date. Surely their faces, if not their principles, were red when the most publicized event on the agenda was the presentation of a religious album in praise of Stalin and entitled "God Is With Us."

It is, incidentally, utterly ridiculous and unrealistic to assume that the clergy in this country or any other country is completely lily-white on the score of Communism within its ranks.

"Find one single card-carrying Party member among the American clergy before you 'smear' their noble calling,"

246

scream those with the "three monkey" philosophy of "see no Communism, hear no Communism, speak no Communism."

Nonsense. It would be quite as difficult to produce a "card-carrying Party member" among the clergy in any of the satellites. In all of Poland and the Balkans, there are fewer than three million Party members. Among the two hundred million people of the entire Soviet Union, no more than one in thirty belongs to the Party. It is most unlikely that a clergyman, even a collaborator, could aspire to so lofty an eminence as Communist Party membership. This is for the elite. And certainly no man of God, even a left-handed one, is on so elevated a political and social plane as the Union of Atheists or the Association of the Godless. The Party doesn't expect the clergy to join it, suffice that the clergy serves it.

Dr. Hewlett Johnson, Dean of the Cathedral Church of Christ at Canterbury, is a notable, if nonillustrious example of how the clergy can serve in the cause of those who have declared war on God. President of the British-Soviet Association, the white-haired Red Dean is on the editorial staff of the Communist *Daily Worker* in London. He has been the guest several times of Stalin, through the Russian Patriarch Alexei. At the behest of Moscow, he has visited all the satellites. Dr. Johnson's junket through Poland, Czechoslovakia, Hungary, Bulgaria, and Russia was a triumphal procession where his way actually was strewn with flowers.

In Warsaw, center of the secret army's stiffest resistance in the satellites, he parroted the only phrase he had learned in the Polish tongue. It was written for him by some unsung genius of the Information Ministry, and it read: "I am a Communist. Jesus was a Communist, too."

On his arrival back in London after the junket—all expenses paid by the British-Soviet Association—the Dean stated that everywhere in the Soviet Union and the satellites he had found nothing but "freedom and happiness."

Apropos of the freedom and happiness, an American newsman inquired whether Dr. Johnson had visited Lutheran

247

Bishop Lajos Ordass, Orthodox Metropolitan Barnabas Voislav Nastich, or Catholic Cardinal Mindszenty. The Dean of Canterbury Cathedral turned sharply and, in anger more befitting a tough policeman than a ranking prelate of the Church of England, castigated the reporter as "a red-baiting tool of the Fascist capitalist press."

Nowhere was the Dean's service to Communist Russia more clearly evident than in a sermon he preached from the pulpit of Canterbury on July 17, 1953. For forty minutes, he harangued his congregation with "proof that Americans had dropped germ-laden bombs on China and North Korea."

Fortunately the American clergy does not have to apologize for any such member as the small-bored Dean Johnson. Yet it has been heard from many a pulpit in this country that Bishop Ordass, Metropolitan Nastich, and Cardinal Mindszenty got no more than their just rewards from those who have openly avowed enmity for religion. Such words, of course, are circulated behind the Iron Curtain as justification for the seizure of church property, for further accusations against the religious, and for new persecutions of those who would resist in the name of God.

In the Balkans, there was almost no opportunity for the clergy to go underground. Little of the confusion and chaos that covered the escape of thousands of religious into new identities at the time of the Russian revolution existed in the satellites.

The Nazi occupation forces of wartime had clamped tight police state control onto the peoples of the Balkans. Every citizen was well catalogued and ticketed as to age, racial extraction, religious affiliation, and employment status. The Communist cell leaders conducted as efficient a system of espionage against the civil population as they did against the Germans. When the Nazis retreated, they left behind a working model of the spy state which the new Moscow-trained masters not only understood but took under control without shifting gears. Consequently, the religious, as well as their people, were caught in the prison of the slave state.

For the satellite population of 100,000,000 there is little more than five per cent of the land area of the Soviet Union. Flight or concealment is, therefore, ten times more difficult than it is for those in the secret army in Russia.

Vigilance of the security police, contrary to popular belief outside the Soviet domain, is exercised far more efficiently in the satellites than in the U.S.S.R. itself. This is true, to mention only one reason, because the bureaucrats are most officious when they are closest to the capital. In the Soviet Union, this limits the most dangerous zone to Moscow and its environs. In the Balkans, Budapest, Belgrade, Bucharest, Sofia, and Prague all lie within a distance no greater than that from New York to Chicago.

Czechoslovakia's northern border is Sovietized Poland; its western margin borders Russian-occupied Germany. Hungary faces occupied Austria on the west and is surrounded by Communist Yugoslavia, Rumania, and the U.S.S.R. Bulgaria and Rumania jointly present less than 350 miles of coastline, rather densely settled and well patrolled, along the Black Sea facing the Soviet Union. Only along the southern frontier of Bulgaria is there real access to free territory—to Greece and, for about 50 miles, Turkey. The 200 miles that faces Greece is highly militarized on both sides of the border, a deterrent to escape or to penetration.

If Yugoslavia and Albania are included, the situation is largely the same, excepting that both have access to the Adriatic. Unquestionably the most isolated of all the satellite peoples are the Albanians, not only geographically but also spiritually. An island of Mohammedanism amid a sea of Christianity, Albania could expect assistance from religious sources only from Turkey or North Africa. Yet in three years of research, Hamid, without the pledge of secrecy, made the one reference to organized resistance in the satellites. He mentioned that one or more of the sons of Abdul the Persian went to Albania. He further provided information—which it has been impossible to verify or to corroborate—that Moslem agencies in Turkey maintain regular contact with operatives in Albania.

It has been fairly definitely established from a number of sources that the Albanians openly defy Communism. Western intelligence agencies are in the large part convinced that Albania is the weakest Communist link in the satellites.

19.

The Jesuit Command

IN THE OLD Imperial Russia, the Church of Rome played an exceedingly minor role in the spiritual life of the people. The number of its parishioners was a comparatively insignificant minority—no more than 20,000 in the city of Moscow. During much of the time from the tenth century until the revolution, Roman Catholics were proscribed, if not actually by law or edict, at least by the actions of several political, religious and racial groups, chiefly the Cossacks.

From the time of the schism between the Catholic churches of the East and of Rome, roughly the tenth and eleventh centuries, Orthodoxy was the religion of the people of Russia. When, in the fourteenth century, the Metropolitan See was moved from Kiev to Moscow, the Orthodox Church became, in reality, the state church. Peter the Great, by effecting certain changes in the administration, became the actual constitutional head of the Russian Church in the eighteenth century. By the time of the revolution, it had grown in wealth, power, and numbers to the greatest single Orthodox Church; its communicants and clergy often were extremely and openly hostile toward Roman Catholicism.

When the Vatican, then, sent its Famine Relief Mission to Russia in 1921, the action was prompted by motives of pure Christian charity. It was not to care for Roman Catholics, since so few communicants of the Church were then, or ever had been, in Russia. Yet, in the following year, the Church of Rome quite definitely took the lead in encouraging the forces of religious resistance. It set up an active program to combat the atheistic doctrines of Communism wherever they were to appear. Reverend John J. Furnis, S.J., explains the attitude of the Church of Rome toward Communism.

The objectives of the Vatican have never been political in the slightest degree. Whatever opposition the Church has displayed has been neither toward the Russian people nor their rulers. It has been against the tenets of Godlessness and the deprivation of the individual's rights to freedom of conscience and freedom of worship.

Let us assume that the government of the Soviet Union were to restore religion to its former place in the life of Russia. The Church of Rome would undeniably be relegated to a minor position. The Orthodox Church would gain immeasurably in spiritual influence and power.

Only in the annexed east of Poland and in parts of the Baltic states would the Roman Catholic Church be even mildly strengthened. This, of course, is excluding the present satellites where Catholicism embraced a majority of the people in Czechoslovakia, parts of Hungary and Yugoslavia, and Poland.

But it must be stressed that the Church began its fight on the side of God against those who had outlawed and declared war on Him back in 1925 and 1926, twenty years before any strongly Roman Catholic areas came under the influence of atheistic Communism. The battle of the Church has been against the openly or covertly avowed enemies of God.

There may be some difficulty on the part of the non-Catholic —indeed even on the part of some Catholic laymen—in understanding the antagonism of the Church to the tenets of the Red religion of Moscow. Why, one might ask, should the Pontiff require that all Low Masses be concluded with prayers for the conversion of Russia to Christianity?

One explanation lies in the acceptance by a large segment of

Catholic communicants and clergy of belief in the "divine revelations" at Fatima in the mountains of Portugal.

According to the spiritual belief shared by most Roman Catholics, a vision of the Mother of Jesus first appeared to three peasant children in the remote village on May 13, 1918, and on two subsequent occasions. The vision, it is believed by many, predicted the eventual supremacy in Russia of the Bolshevists, the abolition of religion by the Soviet state, certain events leading up to the Second World War, and the threat which a Godless Russia would present to the world after the war.

(It was the extreme accuracy of the predictions in 1918 of events that were to occur twenty years later that figured in the acceptance, finally, of the divinity of the revelations. Although they are believed in by the majority of the Catholics, acceptance has not yet become part of Church dogma.)

The vision further is believed to have warned that when the predicted threat of Godless Russia had become a reality, as it is today, there could be neither hope nor assurance of peace until Russia is reconverted to religion. But the Virgin promised the world, through the children, that when God should be returned to Russia, there would be lasting peace.

Knowing and having studied every document and affidavit relating to the visitation at Fatima and believing firmly that it was in reality a twentieth century miracle, Pius XI acted according to his faith. His successor, Pius XII, continued what he believed was a divine commandment.

In such light did the Pontiff send out the call in 1926 for the Russian work. Those who answered then, and those who have answered since, responded as they would have to any mission. For conversion of nonbelievers, whether in the wilds of Patagonia, or in the Red Square of Moscow, is a Christian duty that has inspired the devout since the days of St. Paul. It has, therefore, been much in the spirit of missionaries that priests have volunteered for the Russian work.

A teaching and missionary order, the Society of Jesus has

253

taken the lead in mission and conversion projects of the Church for four hundred years. It is to be expected, therefore, that the Jesuits would respond to the Vatican's call for volunteers for the Russian work. This should seem doubly logical, since the Jesuits serve the Pope, directly through the General of the Society in Rome.

In the foregoing connection, it is interesting and possibly revealing to take into account that the Jesuits were originally founded as a semi-military order. The original constitution, approved by Pope Paul III in 1540, designated the Society as *"Compania de Jesus."* Its English translation is "company (military) of Jesus."

The Company grew out of the meditations of a Spanish soldier, St. Ignatius of Loyola, who was elected its first "General," the title held by his elected successors down through the centuries to the present, Very Reverend John B. Janssens. That the Society is patterned strictly along military lines cannot be disputed. In fact, many "Jebbies" refer to their organization, the largest single order of the Church, as "the Army."

Having had some slight knowledge of the foregoing historic facts—along with a number of popular misconceptions about the Jesuits—when Father Reed first dropped his unintentioned hint, I assumed that the Society probably was the guiding spirit and genius behind any religious resistance movement in the Soviet empire. Since this report is as factual as it can possibly be under the difficult circumstances, I must set down all conflicting as well as supporting evidence and opinion.

Whatever there has been of conflict has come from the Jesuits. Earlier, I have told of the evasive politeness I met with in Rome. Later, in Barcelona, there was the interview with "Father McGrath," the Jesuit who had been behind the Iron Curtain and was then preparing to go back.

Father Gallagher, of the Vatican Relief Mission to Russia, had remarked to me and Kenneth McCaleb, my newspaper editor, that he had been for two years "a captain in the Eleventh Red Army Cavalry Regiment." His superior on that mission, Father Walsh, had written nearly twenty years later, "The Holy See, in defense of the Christian Faith, has never ceased from combatting this international and official attempt to impose atheism by force upon the individual, the family, and the state."

There was the verified story of the experience of "Father Zurikov" and that of "Father Maguire," of Polish-Irish extraction, who had escaped Solovetski.

At the time in 1953 when I was released from my pledge of silence and began the first series of newspaper articles on the secret army, two Jesuits of the New York Province were assigned to steer me from the path of editorial error. These were the Rev. James R. Barnett, S.J., and the Rev. John J. Furnis, S.J.

It must be stated that their assignment to the editorial task was purely for purposes of *keeping me from making misstatements of fact concerning the Jesuit Order,* not to censor any information I might have about individual members. That, however, did not preclude argument when it came to points they might question.

For many hours every week for better than a month, the two Jesuits were with me, hearing the information I had collected, questioning, advising, making suggestions. From the first, Father Barnett, the senior of the two, was cautious, questioning, argumentative. He gave the impression of greatest skepticism. Father Barnett cited the Rev. Vincent McCormack, American assistant to the General, as denying that there were *any* Jesuits in the Soviet underground. The assignment rosters of the Society showed that, he argued.

"Would there," I asked, searching for the facts, "be some circumstances under which certain assignments would *not* be recorded? Suppose, contrary to what you believe, Father, that there *were* Jesuits who had volunteered for such a mission? Would they be *listed* in a roster available to anyone who took the trouble to write to Rome?"

"Of course not," Father Barnett answered. "But you have

255

estimated that there are possibly a thousand Jesuits on such missions. This is a ridiculous assumption, and I cannot take any responsibility for allowing you to assume any such obviously erroneous figure."

"How many of the Jesuit Order are there who are not accounted for on assignment rosters?" I asked.

"Not more than ten per cent," the priest answered.

"Unless I have been misinformed," I said, "there are 36,000 members of the Society of Jesus."

Father Furnis, sitting alongside Father Barnett at the luncheon table in the Pen and Pencil Restaurant in New York, looked at his senior and smiled.

"And that would seem to figure out, not to one thousand," Father Furnis put in, "but to thirty-six hundred."

Throughout the weeks that the two Jesuits advised me, Father Barnett was not only cautious and conservative, he was downright discouraging. At one time, he remarked that he had heard rumors of such activities but that he had "checked with several unquestionable sources and was convinced that, so far as the Society is concerned, there is no basis to support what you are writing."

Now, in direct opposition to the stand of Father Barnett was that of his subordinate. Father Furnis, who had been in the Philippines when the Japanese occupied the islands in 1941 and who spent the nightmare remainder of the war in a concentration camp, respectfully contradicted Father Barnett.

"I have talked to many Jesuits who have been behind the Iron Curtain. I believe I have been personally closer to some of them than you have, Father," said the younger priest. "Even if I did not know, which I do, I should be very much disappointed in the Society of Jesus if I did not believe we were fighting against the enemies of God in Russia and everywhere else in the world."

Seeking sources of verification and documentation—and possible expansion—of certain material, I was referred to a group of Jesuits, now headquartered at Fordham University

256

in New York. In one building, a temporary wartime barrack on the campus, which they have remodeled with their own hands and practically no funds, eight priests maintain what has been called "the G.H.Q. of the secret army," and "the anti-Politburo." Neither of these terms, it should be added, aroused any great enthusiasm on the part of the Jesuits who staff the Russian Centre. Indeed, they warn against "romanticizing or overemphasizing the part of any individual in a work that is directed by God."

The Rev. Feodor Wilcock, S.J., in charge of the Russian Centre, has personally visited every Jesuit station in the countries under Communism within the three years between 1950 and 1953. His reaction to the Russian work in its relationship to the revelations at Fatima is typical of that of a number of priests who have been leaders of the hidden army:

"We are interested in seeing Christianity restored to its proper place in Russia. . . . This is the promise of Our Lady of Fatima, but she required that we do our part in order to bring it about. That is always God's way: when He sees us doing what is in our power, he arranges all the rest.

"Our plans are definitely long range; we do not expect to see results immediately. Human nature is impatient and finds it hard to wait for God's moment. However, it is our duty to make the normal preparations, so that when God's moment does come, He will find us ready."

As Jesuits of what is called the "Oriental or Eastern Rite" of the Catholic Church, spiritually inspired by the miracle at Fatima, Father Wilcock and his colleagues also have a very different sort of vision in view. It is of the day, not too far distant, they hope and pray, when "the moment" will have arrived, when atheism will have lost its battle against God in the Soviet empire.

The preparations to be "ready," being made at the Russian Centre must be very practical by virtue of their very farsightedness.

Chief aim of members of the group is *to train priests and*

257

others (the italics are the writer's) *for the Russian apostolate.*"
To accomplish this, they have taken a leading part in the establishment and development of Russian departments at Fordham and other Catholic universities. They sometimes lecture and teach the Russian language, history, culture, art, literature, economy, and related and integrated courses to the 150-odd students enrolled at the Russian Institute, directed by the Reverend J. Franklin Ewing, S.J., at Fordham.

Father Wilcock and his associates refuse to concur in the opinion of this writer and of other Jesuits that such education of laymen would supply obvious and qualified civilian leadership when and if Communism should fall in the Sovietized areas of the world. Their aim, they iterate, is purely religious and for the restoration of the worship of God as a reform, not for political revolution. To bring this about, their further stated objectives are: (1) "to be a Catholic center of information on the Russian apostolate," and (2) "to keep contact with the Russian Orthodox (people) and engage in any other Russian activities."

Part of their job of obtaining information consists of monitoring—on a short-wave receiving set designed and built by members of the staff—radio broadcasts from Russia. They also produce books, tracts, and pamphlets in the Russian language. It is the belief of other Jesuits that such literature somehow finds its way underground into the Soviet Union to bolster the spirit and resolve of the members of God's hidden army. The Russian Centre fathers fail to confirm or deny.

The staff of the Russian Centre is an amazingly diverse group of men. English-born Father Wilcock speaks Russian, Polish, Slavish, and Chinese. As director of the Shanghai Russian Mission of the Society of Jesus, he was interned by the Japanese, enduring privation, persecution, and hardship throughout the years of the war in the Pacific. A few years after liberation, he saw the rise of Chinese Communism, through which he remained with his people, aiding many of the thirty thousand Russians in Shanghai—largely refugees from Bol-

258

shevism or their descendants—to escape to the Philippines. This was a far from easy task, since few of them possessed any papers of citizenship and many had to be gotten out through underground channels.

With Father Wilcock throughout all these trying years were Fathers Andrew Ouroussoff, Nicolai Bock, and Fionan Brannigan. Father Ouroussoff is the last of one of Moscow's oldest princely families and is proscribed in the Soviet domain on twin grounds that he is both an aristocrat and a priest. Father Bock, born in St. Petersburg, was Imperial Russian Minister to the Vatican—he was then a layman—when the revolution broke out. Father Brannigan, an Englishman like Father Wilcock, was among the first Jesuits to volunteer for the Russian work.

There are two American-born Jesuits at the Russian Centre, Fathers Edward J. O'Kane and Maurice F. Meyers, both of the Chicago Province, and a third Englishman, Father Paul Dickinson.

Although the staff members of the Russian Centre are far from communicative about either the details or generalities of their work, they are not at all secretive. From Father Wilcock, I received several leads to Jesuits and others who had been engaged in the work of the secret army, some inside and others in directorial capacities outside the Soviet domain. Several of these were able to bolster by verification many incidents related in these pages—and others which have not been included for lack of sufficient supporting evidence.

From Father Wilcock has come the brief outline of the career of the Jesuit Father Walter Cizic (pronounced *Chizik,* his true name), high on the list of American heroes who have gone into Russia. He, too, went openly as a priest, went also as a prisoner to Siberia, volunteering to go to what he must have known was certain death to be with his people.

Short of physical stature but of rugged frame and prodigious strength, Father Cizic was of Polish descent. In his boyhood he had mined coal and worked as a puddler in Pittsburgh steel

259

mills. He hitch-hiked to New York in the early 1920's and applied for admission to the Society of Jesus at Fordham University.

The priests who knew him as classmates and as teachers during his prescribed fifteen years of study as a novice and as a scholastic recall Father Cizic as a man of great humor, kindly understanding, and simple piety. Upon his own request, Father Cizic was sent to Poland to take over the duties of a parish priest about 1937.

The young American taught his parishioners new and efficient methods of farming, managed to buy farm machinery and tractors, improved seed and fertilizers, and taught his people to increase the productivity of their labors and the fertility of their fields. By 1939, Father Cizic was beloved not only by his Roman Catholic parishioners but by the people of all faiths who made up the small farming community in eastern Poland.

When the hobnails of Communist and Nazi military boots plowed furrows of desolation and slavery over the farms of Poland, the village of Father Cizic was occupied by forces of the Soviet. The Russians seized everything, the fields, the machinery, the harvest—the people. From Moscow and the self-imposed Red rulers of Poland came a judgment, a ukase affecting the entire village. The whole farming population was to be "relocated" in Siberia, where a "Soviet Scientific Agrarian Project" was to be launched in the frozen wasteland.

As the "labor force" of men, women, and children was being registered by their new masters, Father Cizic was marked for deportation back to the United States. He had an American passport and the foreign policy of the Kremlin, at the moment, dictated that nothing be done which might antagonize the neutral United States.

Father Cizic smiled at the Red commandant who was questioning him. From his pocket, the priest took his American passport and tore it into confetti.

"God's Kingdom," he is reported to have announced calmly, "issued no papers or passports. I must go with my people."

It would have been easy for Father Cizic to have left and returned safely to America. No one, least of all his people, would have blamed him.

To Siberia went Father Cizic, physically a slave and a prisoner. But his spirit was brave and free and, until the day of his death from tuberculosis ten years later, the heroic priest baptized the children of his people, taught them their catechism, confirmed them in their faith, heard their confessions, and administered the Sacraments. He acted as spiritual guide to members of the Orthodox and Protestant churches as well as those of the Roman Catholic faith. Physical torment and torture, undernourishment and failing health could not deter him. And it is recorded that the Communist guards had a superstitious fear of Father Cizic's godliness, a typically Russian mystical fear of his spiritual strength and power. The story of Father Cizic is to be the subject of a full-length biography by Father Wilcock, who has devoted to it years of study and research of the most scholarly sort. Soon to be published, the biography of Father Cizic is an awe-inspiring drama of a "spiritual soldier of God."

In spite of his critical attitude throughout the weeks of his invaluable and helpful work with me, Father Barnett reluctantly joined Father Furnis in passing on the presentation of the material as it applied to the Jesuits. As a postscript, I should like to add one more note on Father Barnett's reactions.

After our work together, Father Barnett was given leave to take part in the inauguration by Trans-World Airlines of its route of the shrines. Coming as his trip did during preparations for the Marian Holy Year in Rome, it gave the Jesuit new opportunity to contact fellow-priests of his Order throughout Europe.

At a reunion with Father Furnis, McCaleb, and me at the Pen and Pencil, where we had spent so many hours in argument and debate, Father Barnett volunteered a statement that

261

went far toward putting certain of my former doubts and reservations to rest. "I have," said this man who had dedicated his life to the service of his Church and his God, "talked in the last months to many who have caused me to revise considerably some of my opinions about the Russian work and what you call the secret army."

20.

Until God's Moment

ORTHODOX AND PROTESTANT sources are far more cooperative about giving information, verification, and documentation, where possible, than the Jesuits are. On the other hand, the agencies through which Orthodoxists and Protestants operate and negotiate are much more cautious about revealing their identities as organizations. There are several valid reasons for this.

Starting with the Orthodoxists, their hesitance in assuming responsibility for aid and support of the secret army stems from the division of authority, from the autonomy of the various metropolitans and patriarchs in the fourteen or fifteen nationalistic branches of the Eastern Church. There are patriarchs in Alexandria, Antioch, and Constantinople. All are in Moslem countries and because of the influences of nationalism, communicants react to varying political considerations.

For example, Egypt being anti-British, the Orthodoxists who acknowledge the Patriarchy of Alexandria are likely to be pro-Russian. On the other hand, Turkey receives United States economic and military aid, is pro-American and violently anti-Soviet. The pre-revolutionary Russian Church, however, stemmed from Constantinople.

The Estonian Orthodox Church was separated from the Russian Church when the Bolshevists abolished religion during the revolution. It was pronounced reunited by edict in 1941

263

when Stalin made the pretext of restoring the church. The Finnish Orthodox Church also proclaimed autonomy from the Moscow Patriarchate in 1918. Still independent, its members are individually extremely anti-Communist. In fact, much cooperation was given by the Finnish Orthodox in the verification of material concerned with Karelia and Solovetsky.

There are Orthodox Churches in Rumania, Bulgaria, and Yugoslavia, each with its own head. To say that none of these is an exactly thriving institution is to be guilty of petty understatement. The Greek Orthodox Church is the state church. Its government is pro-American. It is the closest in geographical location to the satellite Orthodox Churches. Like factions of the church in Constantinople, which extend aid, maintain contact, and supply financial as well as spiritual support to resistance forces in Russia, the Greek Church *unofficially* has given help to individuals and groups in the satellites.

There is unquestionably amicable intercommunication between the Church of England and that of Greece, as well as the Finnish Orthodox. Any such ties, however, are largely on a parish level and I could find no evidence of hierarchical cooperation. The Church of England (Episcopal) has some interest in the Baltic states where a few congregations operated prior to the annexation of 1940. There is abundant reason to assume that an exceptionally active Episcopalian column is active in the Baltics and in Karelia.

However, any effort to link the clerical government of the Church of England with either the activities of the Orthodox or with Episcopalians in the secret army is met with evasions, flat denial, or angry suspicion in London. Angry suspicion was the reaction of Dean Johnson of Canterbury when he was confronted with a request for introductions to church officials who might have knowledge or information of the secret army.

In contrast, both lay and clerical Episcopalians in the United States are eager to assist in developing any information of resistance activity. Again, this is not on a high official level. There apparently is no central clearing house for information,

264

no top organization of communication, nor any real concerted effort to cooperate with agencies of other denominations. At the first request for permission to quote names, there is uneasiness. One Canadian cleric summed it up:

"It isn't the Communists who inspire hesitance on our part. It is the very nature of our church structure as the Church of England. There are political implications that could conceivably prove embarrassing to the Crown and detrimental to the government and the national welfare."

This would not seem to apply to the Episcopalian clergy in the United States but, nonetheless, it seems to have infected many of them. They are willing to talk about it in private but not for publication. They are willing to show letters and unofficial reports, but not for quotation. They are eager to send an investigator along to someone else who might give information but no identities.

In spite of these hurdles, it has been possible to piece together a picture of considerable outside support for the secret army, particularly by the Orthodox and—considering that their numbers behind the iron curtain must be comparatively few—by the Episcopalians.

The Lutherans are, by all odds, the most active of the Protestant denominations within the Soviet domain. Here again the fact finder is handicapped by lack of real centralization. However, there is no attempt to disguise the character of the semi-official support that has been extended to the forces of anti-Communist resistance. Particularly is this true for the Lutherans in Germany and the adamant stand they have taken against the Sovietization of the Eastern zone. Lutheran resistance is personified in the imprisoned Bishop Ordass, one among thousands of his coreligious who have defied the atheistic tenets of the Red regime in the satellites.

Reaching into the Baltic states, and through East Germany into Czechoslovakia, the Lutherans maintain a lifeline of communication with the small but growing forces of resistance in the satellites. In both the United States and in Germany, there

265

are reliable sources that have been willing to give access to documentation that is more complete than any, excepting only that which is available from Roman Catholic sources.

The Lutherans were responsible, too, for indicating the part played by private agencies of other denominations, notably, in addition to Orthodoxists, Baptists, and Methodists. Editors of the Baptist publication, *War Cry,* have come forward with a few added chapters on the activity of their own clergy in the religious underground, and have offered to try to obtain documentation of others which I have learned but have been unable to verify.

Since the publication of my original articles, based largely on the information of the Roman Catholic column of the secret army, and part of the Lutheran material which I had, at that time, been able to verify, a number of other religious groups have volunteered information on their own activities. Among these is the Church of Seventh Day Adventists which has raised a sizable fund—how much has not yet been designated—to "carry on the battle for God in the Communist world."

So far as the Moslems are concerned, it is evident that those in Russia present an almost unanimously united front against Communism. It is further apparent that the Moslem "columns of the Crescent" operate more openly in defiance of the Soviet officials than the Christians and Jews in the secret army. There is also a wealth of documentary material. But it is more difficult to obtain access to this material than that of any of the other agencies.

Most difficult of all to document or verify are the activities of the Jewish "columns of the Star." This is due to the peculiar circumstance of too *much* evidence. No more painstaking researches have ever worked on a project than those assigned to the compilation of the two works, *The Jews in the Soviet Union,* and *The Jews in the Satellites.* These volumes have been mentioned elsewhere in these pages.

The American Jewish Committee has in its library most extensive and reliable material which has not, as yet, been broken down or classified for purposes of a study of Jewish resistance. To do this would require time and funds. The latter is all I lack to do the much-needed job. The urge to get at such material exceeds all but my financial inability.

If, as Father Reed has complained, I have stressed what he calls "the romantic, the active, the cloak and dagger," I can only reply that that is the way it happened. After all, any cause in which a man daily risks his freedom, even his life, is no game of charades.

If I have not stressed "the dedication, the spiritual quality, the devotion to the cause of God" of such men as Fathers Zurikov, Maguire, and Mueller, of Rabbi Levitzky, Moses Franck, and Schultz, of the martyred Pastor Schweitzer, and the other heroes and saints of the secret army, it was from fear of overemphasis on what seems so obvious to me, the writer, and, I hope, to you, the reader.

They are symbolic, the personification of thousands who have given their freedom and their lives that God might live again in the hearts of men. They were spiritual soldiers in an army whose most powerful weapon was simple faith in the Gods of their fathers.

Not only among religious leaders and believers of many sects does the opinion prevail that the secret army offers the best way—perhaps the only way out of the struggle between Bolshevist socialism and the free world. It is a belief shared by military men as well.

In March of 1953, at a meeting of interdenominational church leaders in the White House, the President of the United States, General Dwight D. Eisenhower announced:

"It is my unshakable belief that it is only through religion that we can lick this thing called Communism . . . only through a rejuvenation of respect for moral values that the world can come through this long period of tension."

With laymen, civilians in schools and colleges throughout both North and South America and Europe being given a background of training and education necessary to lead in

267

event of a sudden religious—yes, or political—upheaval within the Soviet Empire, with more religious leaders preparing to take places in the ranks of the secret army, with pressures rising up from underground in all countries under Red Communism, the moment may be closer than conservative Jesuits and others who know and have participated in the work of the resistance are willing to admit.

The greatest hope for Western civilization, based upon the moral teachings of the Testaments, Old and New, upon the spiritual values of the Church and religion, unquestionably lies with the secret army and its ultimate victory over the forces of atheism—in God's name and in "God's moment."